American Conspiracy Theories

American Conspiracy Theories

JOSEPH E. USCINSKI

AND

JOSEPH M. PARENT

OXFORD
UNIVERSITY PRESS

UNIVERSITY PRESS

Oxford University Press is a department of the University of Oxford.
It furthers the University's objective of excellence in research, scholarship,
and education by publishing worldwide.

Oxford   New York
Auckland   Cape Town   Dar es Salaam   Hong Kong   Karachi
Kuala Lumpur   Madrid   Melbourne   Mexico City   Nairobi
New Delhi   Shanghai   Taipei   Toronto

With offices in
Argentina   Austria   Brazil   Chile   Czech Republic   France   Greece
Guatemala   Hungary   Italy   Japan   Poland   Portugal   Singapore
South Korea   Switzerland   Thailand   Turkey   Ukraine   Vietnam

Oxford is a registered trade mark of Oxford University Press
in the UK and certain other countries.

Published in the United States of America by
Oxford University Press
198 Madison Avenue, New York, NY 10016

© Oxford University Press 2014

CIP data is on file at the LOC

9780199351800 (hbk.)
9780199351817 (pbk.)

CONTENTS

LIST OF FIGURES AND TABLES

Figures

Tables

ACKNOWLEDGMENTS

You might think that we are ace conspirators. After four or so years of studying stratagems, subterfuge, and schemes—real and imagined—one could be expected to acquire a practical facility with such arts. Alas, the truth must out: we are deplorably deficient in this regard. Events have repeatedly mocked our master plans, we labor quite openly for the common good, and the present work is not remotely the product of a small group. While this may handicap our credibility as conspirators, we flatter ourselves to think it improves our objectivity as scholars. In any case, it certainly incurs a lot of debts.

There are so many extraordinary people to thank, and we are but two regular Joes. At the top of that list are our esteemed chairs, Fred Frohock and Jonathan West, who bent over backward to secure desperately needed research funding. At our home institution, many colleagues provided terrific advice and criticism, in particular Matthew Atkinson, Casey Klofstad, and Greg Koger. At other institutions, our gratitude to Adam Berinsky, Matthew Dentith, Brendan Nyhan, and Paul Herrnson for their comments and support. More than 60 research assistants endured long and grinding hours collecting data; we are forever grateful to them. Deserving special commendation are Alexander Ades, Alexander Alduncin, Marlon Baquedano, Ryden Butler, Jing Chen, Ali Jessani, Josephine Makrush, Bethany Torres, and Reid Wilcox. Dave McBride at Oxford University Press championed the project early on and was an unimprovable editor and stand-up guy throughout. We also owe debts to the Oxford staff and to our anonymous reviewers.

Uscinski needs to thank Leilany, Benny, Ruby, Mom, Dad, Kevin, Tracy, Amy, and Gram for their love and support. The last few years have been incredibly difficult, but I hope the results make up for that. Parent would like to dedicate this book to his gracious godparents: Connie and John Morse. As always, work wouldn't mean much without family and friends on the other side of the bubble. This volume was in part completed so quickly because of Abigail Becker's kindness—one could not ask for a more dignified person to go through a divorce with. For patience and friendship when the project shanghaied mind, body, or composure, thanks also to Engels Castrillo, Kennedy Gordy, Joseph Karas, Paul MacDonald, Lina Mesa, Maria Pilar Quintana, Sebastian Rosato, and Brittany Sharpton.

Finally, candor compels the authors to acknowledge their deep debts to each other. Now that we have been faithful partners for years and can finish each other's sentences (on paper anyway), we must confess this work would not have been half as good without the other, or half as good without the names above. That does not appear to add up. Perhaps this is a conspiracy after all. The final product did turn out suspiciously well. Who, then, is to blame? With all the characters above, it cannot be the work of a lone gunman.

Miami, Florida
November 22, 2013

American Conspiracy Theories

A Theory of Conspiracy

And things inside will always remain steady, if things outside are
steady, unless indeed they are disturbed by a conspiracy . . .

—Niccolò Machiavelli[1]

In the beginning was a theory, and the theory was conspiratorial. Before
the United States united, American elites were incensed that King George
III was encroaching on colonists' rights. This was no humdrum case of
conflicting political priorities; the king was secretly scheming to strip colonists of their liberty and rule over them with absolute authority. A large
literature sprang up to chronicle the king's covert plot and alert Americans
to the impending catastrophe.[2]

This ferment culminated in the Declaration of Independence, the original American conspiracy theory. To explain the causes of separation, the
authors arrive at the thrust of their reasoning by the second paragraph:

But when a long train of abuses and usurpations, pursuing invariably the same Object evinces a design to reduce them under absolute

Despotism, it is their right, it is their duty, to throw off such Government, and to provide new Guards for their future security. — Such
has been the patient sufferance of these Colonies; and such is now
the necessity which constrains them to alter their former Systems
of Government. The history of the present King of Great Britain is
a history of repeated injuries and usurpations, all having in direct
object the establishment of an absolute Tyranny over these States. To
prove this, let Facts be submitted to a candid world.

What then follows is a piling on of 27 charges against the conduct and
intentions of King George. And that was the edited version; Thomas Jef-
ferson's earlier drafts included a far more tedious train of evidence.[3]

It may not be an accident that there is a laundry list in the middle of
an otherwise stirring rhetorical document. The Founders faced a problem
that the evidence for the fiendish plot was, well, wanting. With hindsight,
we know that the British government had no designs to enslave the American people. The United Kingdom certainly committed imperial outrages,
but pre-1776 North American colonists experienced very few of them.
Compared to contemporaries like Spain's ruthless South American extrac-
tions or France's Haitian human furnace, the British Empire looks mild
mannered. Far from being highly oppressive, the British held together
a massive empire with miniscule manpower, and it would be well over
a century until they lost another colony to independence. Not long after
the American Revolution, the abolition movement gained momentum in
Britain, and for decades in the nineteenth century the country was paying
two percent of its GDP to extinguish the Atlantic slave trade, one of the
most important acts of moral statecraft in history.[4]

While that may be hindsight, even at the time the young revolution-
aries struggled to justify their actions. Contemporary observers wished
the charges against the king "had been more particularly mentioned" so
they could be better judged; others claimed the charges were stated in an
"obscure manner" lacking both "truth and sense."[5] One of the wealthiest
and most vocal rebels, John Dickinson, conceded the lack of oppression
when he wrote that the critical question was "not, what evil *has actually*

attended particular measures—but, what evil, in the nature of things, *is likely to attend* them." Edmund Burke, quite sympathetic to the colonists' grievances, also observed that where other countries complained under an "actual grievance," Americans anticipated their grievances and complained *before* they suffered.[6] This has remained standard practice for Americans, who historically have been quick to anticipate tyranny, despotism, and a full spectrum of apocalyptic scenarios, from red coats to black helicopters.

Today the American Founders are revered as demi-gods for their uncommon wisdom and heightened powers of rationality. Deservedly so; many countries do not survive long, many that do are dysfunctional, few states become great powers, fewer still hegemons, and only the United States has soared to sole superpower status so quickly. There is no need to litigate the American Revolution—it has more than legitimated itself and its results have been immense and largely happy. But it is curious and consequential that the justification for independence was a shaky conspiracy theory.

As with many things, where the Founders have led Americans have followed in droves. A steady stream of conspiracy theories has flowed in the years since the founding, imputing anti-American conspiracies to the British, French, Spanish, Bavarian Illuminati, Freemasons, Slave Power, Abolitionists, Catholics, Jews, Mormons, Muslims, communists, capitalists, and many, many more. No powerful group has escaped the attention of conspiracy theorists. Few not-so-powerful groups have either. There is no material too frail to be woven into conspiratorial yarn. Whether over small-town land-use policies, road planning, municipal recycling, or bicycle-sharing programs, conspiracy theories consistently crop up to warn of secret machinations and impending doom.[7]

Naturally, conspiracy theories flourish across space just as much as they do across time. In the ancient Roman forum or the modern Arab street, conspiracy theories are universal in their allure. In Arkansas or Sweden, birds cannot fall from the sky in any number without their deaths being attributed to UFO weaponry, Soviet-era super-weapons, or scheming oil companies.[8] Genetically engineered sharks do not exist only on the Sci-Fi

Channel's Saturday night lineup; they also attack tourists off the Egyptian coast at the behest of Israeli intelligence.[9] And while 9/11 theories have enjoyed prominence in the United States, they have been even more prominent in Europe and the Middle East.[10] Tractability forces us to study conspiracy theories in a particular time and place, but one should keep in mind the historical durability and global reach of conspiracy theories.

There are many reasons to study conspiracy theories, but the most compelling is their close relationship to politics and policy. While its net effect has yet to be fully accounted for, conspiracy theorizing is not confined to parlor games about who really shot JFK or who probed whom near Roswell, New Mexico. Conspiracy theories have been deeply entwined in revolutions, social movements, and public policy, and they have fueled political stalemate, alienation, witch-hunts, and worse.[11]

High-profile examples are legion. The most important legislative achievement of the Obama administration's first term, healthcare reform, had to address a series of conspiracy theories. One was that the bill created secret "death panels," which would determine whether individuals would receive medical treatment or be allowed to die.[12] The plot may have been imaginary, but the opposition it aroused dealt a very real blow in the 2010 midterm election. As a direct result of supporting healthcare reform, House Democrats are estimated to have lost 25 seats and control of the House.[13] The bill and its subsequent implementation had to be revised to assuage the outcry.[14]

Another conspiracy theory claimed the president was conspiring to destroy religious liberty with contraception mandates for religious institutions. The president was accused of hiding this conspiracy by orchestrating, with the supine support of liberal media, a second conspiracy: a series of diversionary tactics involving a law student, Sandra Fluke. Fox News commentator Bill O'Reilly argued that "the Sandra Fluke contraception controversy was manufactured to divert attention away from the Obama administration's disastrous decision to force Catholic non-profit organizations to provide insurance coverage for birth control and the morning-after pill. That might very well be unconstitutional." He concluded, "[i]t seems there is a powerful presence behind Sandra Fluke."[15]

Following the 9/11 terrorist attacks, conspiracy theories hindered efforts to mobilize political support for measures aimed at preventing future attacks.[16] It is difficult to accept enhanced security measures for traveling, banking, and employment if the reason for those measures, 9/11, was a hoax perpetrated to justify intrusive government policies. Similarly, it is hard to fight rogue states and terrorist groups if one believes these actors are merely scapegoats for an unmoored, insatiably invasive U.S. government.

Dismissing conspiracy theories as absurd does not change the fact that they can consume a fair amount of that most valuable political commodity: the president's time. To address the widespread belief that he was born abroad, Barack Obama had to put aside the faltering economy, two wars, and the national debt to hold a press conference for the sole purpose of releasing his long-form birth certificate. During the George W. Bush administration, the 9/11 Commission was designed partly as a response to conspiracy theories accusing Bush and Dick Cheney of staging the attacks on the Twin Towers and Pentagon. Bill Clinton consumed much of his presidency fending off allegations that he was part of a conspiracy to cover up illegal activities, including assassinating a colleague, Vince Foster. Ironically, the Clinton administration counterclaimed that it was the victim of a "vast right-wing conspiracy."

Conspiracy theorists are often caricatured as a small demographic composed primarily of middle-aged white male Internet enthusiasts who live in their mothers' basements. But polls tell a different story: conspiracy theories permeate all parts of American society and cut across gender, age, race, income, political affiliation, educational level, and occupational status.[17] About a third of Americans believe the "Birther" conspiracy theory: that Barack Obama is a foreigner who unconstitutionally usurped the presidency. A similar amount believes the "Truther" conspiracy theory: that the Bush administration either carried out or knowingly allowed the 9/11 attacks.[18] Decades after the fact, between 60 and 80 percent of Americans agree that the assassination of President Kennedy was orchestrated by a conspiracy and covered up by the government.[19] When asked about four specific conspiracy theories, a 2012 national poll found that 63 percent of respondents believed at least one.[20] Based on this, it is safe to say that almost everyone believes in at least one conspiracy theory and many of us believe more than one.[21]

The polls above are not reflecting transient or trivial responses; the beliefs appear to be strongly held and sincere.[22] Social scientists have conducted numerous experiments in which they try to get people to change their conspiratorial views in response to authoritative information, but this work is mostly in vain.[23] In fact, some individuals double-down on their belief in what is termed the "back-fire effect."[24] Like summer movie super-villains, some conspiracy theories just won't die.

Outside the laboratory, conspiratorial beliefs are just as tenacious. Informational campaigns intended to combat the conspiracy theory that vaccines cause autism have not been very successful.[25] The release of President Obama's long-form Hawaiian birth certificate stymied belief in the Birther conspiracy theory briefly, but those beliefs returned stronger than before.[26] And, though the 9/11 Commission attempted to dispel Truther conspiracy theories, those beliefs persist a decade later.[27] This has led some scholars and public officials to propose policies aimed at hindering the spread of conspiracy theories.[28] In a democratic society, it is desirable to have a citizenry that accepts overwhelming evidence so that collective preferences are based on the best available information.[29]

But to be clear, conspiratorial beliefs need not pose a problem for society or government. Nor do they necessarily lead their adherents to become obstructive or destructive. In some cases they do, but if they frequently did, then nearly everyone would be causing trouble all the time and the world would roil in conspiracy-soaked chaos. Typically, conspiracy theories are harmless, entertaining, or both. Many come and go in the night.

But in extreme cases conspiracy theories can be reckless, lethal, and violent. Belief in a conspiracy involving genetically modified (GM) food producers led several African nations to ban the importation and harvesting of GM crops. This has had dire consequences for the most malnourished populations on Earth.[30] In the same region, a conspiracy theory accusing pharmaceutical companies, doctors, and foreigners of attempting to extort profits with useless treatments drove South African leaders to block the use of HIV drugs. As a consequence, over a third of a million people are estimated to have died unnecessarily.[31] There are concerns in the United States, particularly with the African American community, that conspiratorial beliefs decrease the willingness of HIV-infected patients to seek treatment.[32] Conspiracy theories about vaccines are partially to blame for decreased rates of vaccination and an increased incidence of disease.[33]

Conspiracy-related race riots and Red Scares inflicted incalculable damage on the country. The fatal 1992 incident at Ruby Ridge, Idaho issued from antagonisms between law enforcement and conspiracy theorists.[34] Believing that the government was conspiring to violate rights, Timothy McVeigh bombed a federal building in Oklahoma City, killing 168 and wounding hundreds more.[35] Similarly, Eric Rudolph bombed Centennial Olympic Park in 1996—plus two abortion clinics and a gay bar shortly thereafter—to fight against the U.S. government's supposed advancement of abortion rights and world socialism. Sympathizers sheltered him for years and several country songs celebrate him.[36] The Fort Hood shooter, Nidal Malik Hasan, killed 13 people out of his belief that the United States was conspiring against Muslims.[37] And, the Boston Marathon bombers, Tamerlan and Dzhokhar Tsarnaev, frequently visited conspiracy theory websites and were convinced of U.S. complicity in the World Trade Center attacks.[38] As Dzhokhar remarked on his Twitter feed only months before their bombs killed three and injured 264 others: "I d[on't] k[now] why it's hard for many of you to accept that 9/11 was an inside job. I mean I guess fuck the facts y'all are some real #patriots #gethip."[39] Farther afield, Anders Behring Breivik's conspiratorial views killed scores of young Norwegians, and Interwar Germany's "stab in the back" myth killed millions.

There is a great concern that conspiracy rhetoric reverberating in America's polarized political environment could lead to further outbreaks of violence. Here is *New York Magazine* Editor-at-Large Frank Rich commenting on conspiracy theories involving a large purchase of ammunition by the government:

> This is exactly the kind of conspiracy mongering that led to Timothy McVeigh in Oklahoma, for Heaven's sakes. They had ammunition.

They're going to have concentration camps, black helicopters to come after you, to come after the Second Amendment. That's sort of playing with fire. I mean, some of these crazy right wing militia types are very much still out there, and these guys don't even see the irony—two Republican Senators from Oklahoma, where that atrocity happened—fanning these flames.[40]

Maybe conspiratorial beliefs drive violence. Or maybe conspiracy theories are only symbols exploited by actors who would commit violence anyway. Only with careful study can we begin to untangle the connections.

In short, there are persuasive reasons to study conspiracy theories. Taken together, conspiracy theories are ubiquitous, absorbing, and substantial; they reveal the darkest recesses of a nation's psyche. But despite the attention they receive, pressing questions remain unanswered. Who is most prone to believing in conspiracy theories? What explains the overall level of conspiratorial belief in the United States? Has America become more conspiratorial over time? What groups are most likely to be accused of conspiring and when? Who is most likely to do the accusing? Why do some conspiracy theories resonate better than others? What role do conspiracy theories play in social movements, political parties, and democracy? Do those holding many conspiratorial beliefs behave differently—politically, economically, or socially—than those holding few? Are the minds predisposed to conspiracy theories also predisposed to violence?

The gaps in our understanding are more than storms in an ivory tower teacup, churning up publications for professors, chores for graduate students, and opportunities for cash-strapped college kids to serve as glorified guinea pigs. These lacunae are a chance to set on firmer footing the public discourse on conspiracy theories. Social science has not been able to confirm or deny a panoply of popular explanations for conspiracy theorizing, leaving the field open for punditry to parade as wisdom. Although reporters are amply attentive to conspiracy theories, to date they have done little to advance our knowledge about the causes behind the stories.

Because journalism is driven by the need to attract audiences with salable storylines, journalists are pushed to extrapolate from unrepresentative cases or masquerade conjecture as fact.[41] For example, *Time* magazine listed the reptilian elite theory as one of the ten most popular conspiracy theories of all time.[42] While it is entertaining to contemplate a bloodline of shape-shifting reptilians ruling the planet, a cursory glance at the polls shows that nearly no one believes in it.[43] Reporters deserve more sympathy than antipathy for this—few have fared better even when not on a deadline—but methods are now available to better scrutinize what we think we know about conspiracy theories. Only with improved tools and tests do good explanations stand a chance of crowding out bad explanations.[44]

The rest of this chapter is laid out as follows. In the next section, we assess the strengths and weaknesses of previous studies on conspiracy theories. We then outline the logic of our explanation. In the final section, we telegraph the organization of the book in full, so readers can skip around according to their needs and interests (though we humbly suggest reading the whole book cover to cover or the mind control won't work).

THE PROS AND CONS OF PRIOR WORK

To avert any suspense, our overall assessment of the literature is that it is a helpful foundation, but also disjointed, often ad hoc, and overly absorbed by conspicuous conspiracy theories. The bad news is that this state of affairs stunts attempts at generalizable knowledge. The good news is that existing elements can be united into a general explanation. One of the advantages of political science is the discipline's ecumenical kleptomania, and below we gratefully catalog our copious debts to burgled fields. We hope to add value not only by rearranging familiar materials into a more useful contraption, but also by bringing politics and power more to the fore. We start with the bad news.

First, the study of conspiracy theories is disjointed. This is in some ways practical and a boon to the subject; scholars from psychology, sociology, political science, history, and philosophy have all provided valuable insights. Less luckily, the wide breadth of scholarship has created a situation in which many scholars talk past each other and have not yet adequately

integrated each other's findings. This may be because narrowing the intel-
lect frequently sharpens it, and universities tend to organize the search for
knowledge into silos.

Second, existing explanations are often ad hoc. Many conspiracy theories come in and out of fashion rapidly. Conspiracy theorists accused President Obama of blowing up the Deepwater Horizon offshore drilling rig
to push his environmental agenda. These theories disappeared as quickly
as spilled oil in the Gulf. Then Obama was accused of masterminding the
Sandy Hook shootings to justify his gun control legislation. Fast forward
a bit and that theory seems like a distant memory since Obama has more
recently been accused of masterminding gas attacks on Syria as a pretext
for war and orchestrating the shooting of a TSA agent.

And with each new conspiracy theory, scholars offer new explanations for its appearance. Some associated 9/11 conspiracy theories with
anti-American attitudes or Internet use.[45] Others argued that conspiracy
theories surrounding Barack Obama are driven by racism.[46] Still others
contend it is economic conditions.[47] Such explanations often have little explanatory power beyond the event each is meant to explain. For instance,
racism, which is correlated with belief in the Birther theory, would not
explain belief in Truther theories. Poor economic conditions might have
some relation to conspiratorial beliefs, but polls suggest that conspiracy
theories flourish during booms as well as busts.[48] And, the Internet, which
might explain the spread of conspiracy theories since the late 1990s, has
less traction on the Red Scares or Anti-Masonic movements. Simply because an explanation is ad hoc does not make it wrong, yet ad hoc explanations close minds and doors to more powerful explanations that might
speak about conspiratorial beliefs more broadly.

Third, conspicuous conspiracy theories may not be representative of
total conspiracy theorizing. Nearly everyone is familiar with Kennedy assassination theories, but far fewer have heard the theories that the polio
vaccine is really designed to spread autism to Muslims or that lesbianism
is a CIA plot. The multiplicity, mutability, and evanescence of conspiracy
theories make them hard to capture and raise the temptation to investigate only the most visible. Although familiar examples make great points

of departure, studying exclusively the marquee conspiracy theories masks the dynamics, diversity, and volume of conspiracy theorizing. Much of the literature lacks the wide-angle systematic compilations of conspiratorial beliefs necessary to complement more focused views. Without rigorous data across time and issue area, there is no way to find bigger explanations, much less accumulate them.

So much for the bad news. The good news is that portions of the literature are especially beneficial in building a more general explanation. Three strands are most promising. The first relates to emotional conditions. Studies suggest that conspiracy theories flourish when people feel anxiety, alienation, paranoia, or loss of control.[49] The implication is that stressful events promote anxiety and other uncomfortable feelings, which then leads to conspiratorial beliefs, the communication of those beliefs, and perhaps action.[50] Those who are initially prone to conspiratorial beliefs will be pushed to communicate or act on those beliefs; those who are less prone to conspiratorial beliefs will become more prone in the face of high anxiety.

In the lab, researchers have found that inducing anxiety or loss of control triggers respondents to see nonexistent patterns and evoke conspiratorial explanations.[51] In the real world, there is evidence that disasters (e.g., earthquakes) and other high-stress situations (e.g., job uncertainty) prompt people to concoct, embrace, and repeat conspiracy theories.[52] After the Fukushima nuclear power plant disaster in Japan, those closer to the disaster were more likely to tweet conspiracy theories than those less affected by it.[53] So, too, for 9/11 conspiracy theories: those in New York City were more likely to believe Truther theories than those farther away.[54]

Nonetheless, these explanations are incomplete. Lots of stimuli stress people; not all of them increase conspiracy theorizing. Conspiratorial beliefs are common and consistent; major disasters are not. We need to know more about conspiracy-specific stimuli and the factors that ripen a conspiratorial atmosphere. Also, the implications of this explanation are nebulous. People primed to see conspiracy theories could see an infinite number of them but do not. We need to know more about why specific conspiracy theories are contagious while others are noncommunicable.

The second strand involves ideology. Ideology is a set of interrelated beliefs that provide a way for people to understand the world.[55] Ideologies tell people what is important, who the good guys and bad guys are, what their goals are, and how those goals should be reached.[56] Without ideologies to help categorize and interpret information, the world would be meaningless. Some ideologies, such as left/right political ideology, address the role of government in society and how to achieve proper order.[57] Others might focus on economics, religion, race, or something else.

When people have new experiences and encounter new information, their ideologies direct how those experiences and information are understood. As public opinion scholar John Zaller puts it, "[e]very opinion is a marriage of information and predisposition: information to form a mental picture of the given issue, and predisposition to motivate some conclusion about it."[58] He continues: "[citizens] possess a variety of interests, values, and experiences that may greatly affect their willingness to accept—or alternatively, their resolve to resist—persuasive influence."[59] Because people want their views to harmonize, the same information may affect different people in different ways.[60] Therefore, for example, if a Democrat was told that powerful political actors were conspiring against him, he would be more likely to accept that information if it is made clear that the conspirators are Republicans, not fellow Democrats.[61]

The literature on ideology would suggest that conspiratorial beliefs are much like other political opinions: a marriage of predispositions and information. Ideology therefore supplies an important piece of the puzzle: what information will lead which groups of people to believe in which specific conspiracy theories.

The research on motivated biases provides the connection between ideologies and more specific conspiratorial beliefs. This work suggests that evidence and reasoning should play a secondary role in shaping conspiratorial beliefs. Rather, it is primarily people's predispositions that shape how they interpret new information and form opinions; rationalization comes after.[62] Therefore, people's political ideologies play a strong role in determining which conspiracy theories they will subscribe to so that conspiratorial beliefs will be congruent with their predispositions.[63]

American beliefs follow this pattern. Even though many people on the right and left are similarly prone to believing the country is headed for an abyss, a main difference between the two sides lies in whom they blame. As public opinion experts Herbert McClosky and Dennis Chong argue, each side is motivated to blame the other, rarely itself:[64]

> Despite the suspicions of both the left and right towards the government, their anti-system responses are usually triggered by different issues. In responding, for example, to a series of items concerning the influence of the wealthy and powerful on the courts, the nation's laws, the newspapers and the political parties, the far left was the most willing of the ideological groups to condemn these institutions as pawns of the rich. None of this is surprising, of course, since hostility to capitalist elites and the establishment has long been a dominant feature of radical-left politics. But the radical right is also disenchanted with these institutions, though for different reasons. Its anger is detonated, not by the institutions' alleged association with wealth or "business," but by their supposed susceptibility to the influence of an entrenched liberal establishment. In their view, government offices, the press, the foundations and other powerful institutions are overflowing with technocrats and academics trained at liberal colleges and universities. These universities are also the "farm system" that stocks the judiciary and various other professions.

The same goes for other ideologies as well. Stephan Lewandowsky and colleagues found that free market ideologies predicted endorsements of climate change conspiracy theories.[65] This is likely because those believing in free markets would prefer not to endorse the collectivist policies that are proposed for combatting climate change. Anna-Kaisa Newheiser and colleagues found that New Age ideologies predicted belief in "Da Vinci Code" conspiracy theories.[66] Alternative interpretations of history and religions are likely to appeal to those who concur with New Age science.

So individuals' ideologies appear to drive belief in specific conspiracy theories. But clearly conspiracy theories do not convince everyone with a particular ideology. Not everyone on the right believes that Barack Obama is a Muslim, a foreigner, or a false flag operator, and not everyone on the left believes that George W. Bush stole the election, faked a terrorist attack, and went to war for oil profits. Why?

We turn to evidence of a recently identified ideology that predicts (1) the amount of prejudice people harbor against powerful groups they find less likeable and (2) the degree to which people view events and circumstance as the product of conspiracies.[67] We call this widespread and stable belief system the *conspiracy dimension* and conceive of it along a continuum, ranging from extremely naive (those believing conspiracies cause nearly nothing) to extremely cynical (those believing that conspiracies cause nearly everything).[68] Most of us are somewhere in between.[69]

This conspiracy ideology predisposes people to see conspiracies and believe in conspiracy theories. When a person high on the conspiracy dimension receives information that an event may have been the product of a conspiracy perpetrated by a disliked party, he or she will likely concur with that conspiracy theory.[70] A person lower on the conspiracy dimension will be harder to convince.[71] Conspiratorial thinking exists on a dimension separate from other general political attitudes. It is separate from right-wing or left-wing attitudes and is spread evenly across political ideology and partisanship.[72] In addition, the conspiracy dimension is distinct from right-wing authoritarianism, which predicts prejudice against deviant groups; social dominance orientation, which predicts prejudice against powerless groups; paranormal thinking; and religious orientation.[73]

A predisposition toward conspiratorial thinking explains many facets of conspiracy theories and theorists. It explains why some people believe few conspiracy theories while others believe many.[74] It explains why people believe theories that are logically contradictory (e.g., many of the people believing Osama Bin Laden is still alive also believe he was dead long before the raid on his compound).[75] It explains why informational cues suggesting a conspiracy drive some people but not others to believe a conspiracy is afoot.[76] And it explains why conspiracy theorists might tend to fight fire with fire and perpetrate conspiracies themselves.[77] Richard

Nixon is the example par excellence. He was concerned with Jews, the intellectual elite, the media, and the anti-war movement, whom he saw as conspiring against him and the country. Nixon's response was to conspire against them.

Where might the conspiracy dimension come from? Similar to other belief systems, socialization is probably the most important influence.[78] Children typically learn the rules of the game early on, are raised to trust authority figures, and are taught that others respect established rules.[79] Thus, mainstream American thought appears to contain a strong anti-conspiracy theory bias: avowed conspiracy theorists are viewed with suspicion and derision, and the media as a whole scoff at conspiracy theories.[80] Nevertheless, an absolutely large but relatively small number of citizens are socialized to have a worldview in which conspiratorial thinking is more pronounced. This is perhaps because they were exposed to socializing forces that drove them toward conspiratorial thinking (i.e., a conspiratorial parent, a conspiratorial media environment, or experiencing an actual conspiracy) or because they grew up in communities with alternative norms.

The third strand of literature important to building our case concerns group identities.[81] Groups can include political parties, ideological orientations (e.g., the right), racial designations (e.g., blacks), age demographics (e.g., seniors), and geographical designations (e.g., Southerners), among many others. More specifically, we draw on social identity theory (SIT), which argues that people are quick to form in- and out-groups and behave in invidious ways because such categories furnish identity and self-esteem.[82] Even where there is little evidence to suggest it, group identities can push people to view their own group as upright and virtuous while opposing groups are viewed as biased and nefarious.[83]

In socializing successive generations, cultures may use conspiracy theories as part of a protective armament, shielding themselves from the tyranny of opposing groups.[84] Inculcating distrust and vigilance would be adaptive behaviors if groups have been victimized by actual conspiracies.[85] By this logic, one legacy of racism is that African Americans have an especially rich history of conspiratorial beliefs: the CIA planted crack in black neighborhoods, Ronald Reagan created AIDS to kill blacks, and Jews control the media and government to keep blacks down.[86] History and socialization likely combine. In producing a documentary about Hurricane Katrina, director Spike Lee defended his inclusion of conspiracy theories suggesting the U.S. government blew up the levies that flooded black neighborhoods:

> It's not far-fetched . . . a choice had to be made. To save one neighborhood, [you have to] flood another neighborhood. Look if we're in L.A., and there is an emergency situation, and we call from Beverly Hills or we call from Compton, which one are the cops coming to first. . . . Do you think that election in 2000 was fair? You don't think that was rigged? If they can rig an election they can do anything! With the history of this country—you ever heard of [the] Tuskegee Experiments? There are many other examples, if we go down the line, where stuff like this happened to African-American people. I don't put anything past the American Government when it comes to people of color in this country.[87]

Minorities of any stripe (racial, political, etc.) may turn to conspiracy theories as a way to cope with isolated status, explain losses, arrest defeat, and signal group allegiances in the face of perceived threat.[88] Famously, opinion on O. J. Simpson's guilt varied significantly between black and white Americans over time.[89] Group approaches help account for both the social and political context in which emotions and ideologies resonate.[90]

To sum, the present work is necessary because previous work has engaged a narrow portion of the literature, frequently been ad hoc, and been too absorbed by the most salient conspiracy theories. This is a slender evidentiary base on which to make claims and inferences in the search for general explanations. Yet prior work supplies a wealth of ideas and a foundation for broader explanations. Three elements contain great potential: emotional conditions, ideologies, and group identities. In the next section, we outline how they may fit together.

THE LOGIC OF THE ARGUMENT IN BRIEF

We argue that conspiracy theories ignite when socialized motive meets political opportunity (any similarity between the logic of our argument and the plot of *The Manchurian Candidate* is strictly coincidental). The core of our claims is that conspiracy theories are a manifestation of vulnerability, a symptom of heightened danger from powerful actors. Shifts in the distribution of power condition people to communicate and coordinate against common threats. The process unfolds in three steps.

The first step is socialization. We conjecture that socialization during formative years explains the lion's share of why some are more predisposed to conspiracy theorizing than others. Socialization comes from countless sources—parents, social groups, communities, religion, status, media. It is this early socialization that imprints political worldviews such as ideology and partisanship and places people along the conspiracy dimension. (With this said, our explanation leaves room for a varying genetic inclination toward conspiracy theorizing, though this is a matter for biologists to figure out.)

Few parents claim that they want to raise conspiracy theorists, and it is not clear that socialization into conspiratorial thinking is purposeful. Likely much of it is not, but assuming that some is, one might ask: given the strength of institutions in this country and a seemingly anti-conspiracy culture, why socialize anyone to conspiracy theorize at all? We contend that conspiracy theories are weapons of the weak and on balance an adaptive behavior. By definition, powerful groups are powerful; their tool of choice is brute strength; they have less need for, and fear of, fraud. Not so for those who perceive themselves as weak. They feel more exposed to divide-and-conquer strategies and need to be more responsive to threats. Groups lacking raw strength must compensate with better speed and sight.

Conspiracy theories are an early warning system for group security, and like all warning systems they issue false alarms. This may be a price worth paying. As the saying goes, "politics ain't beanbag," and who controls the state apparatus has massive and sometimes lethal effects. Erring on the safe side makes sense. Even in the more settled world of advanced democracies, the stakes are high and groups fight fiercely for the spoils that states generate. Conspiracy theories are prophylactic because they raise awareness, indicate vulnerabilities, imply measures to shore up defenses, and unify the group against others who do not share their values. Conveniently, conspiracy theories also explain away losses by scapegoating, which has the joint benefits of absolving people from blame and uniting the group against a recognizable foe.

There is nothing deterministic in these claims. Parents and educators are well aware that socialization is only a probabilistic thing. Children exposed to the same training can have wildly different reactions, and often the outcome is the opposite of intentions (most Marxists we know come from rich families). Nonetheless, from how to drive cars to how to pronounce words, largely we learn from those around us. Keep in mind that socialization also implies lag effects and feedback loops. Each generation has different formative experiences, which they transmit imperfectly to the next generation. Groups that have long labored at the bottom of the political hierarchy will be slower to relinquish conspiracy theories than those with more variable fortunes.

The second step is political opportunity. If socialization stacks the tinder, then political opportunity sets off the sparks. Presumably lots of people have lots of conspiracy theories that no one else cares about, and appeals to the most conspiracy theory-prone people are unlikely to reverberate widely. Therefore, conspiracy theories that involve the biggest groups, biggest gains, and biggest foes will gain the most adherents. Although seeing the world through a conspiratorial lens is an ideology unto itself, it is not necessarily the dominant or only one. Individuals try to hold specific beliefs that are in line with their various broader belief systems. For present purposes, this means that specific conspiratorial beliefs will align with other political ideologies to stoke different conspiratorial fires in different people (Fig. 1.1).

A Republican high on the conspiracy dimension is likely to believe in conspiracy theories that take issue with Democrats and other actors on the left. Roles are reversed for a Democrat high on the conspiracy dimension. Although people will direct their conspiratorial ire at those considered

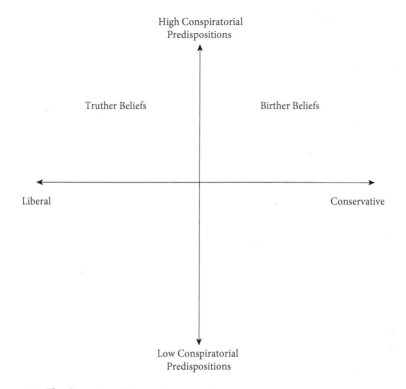

Figure 1.1 The Conspiracy Dimension.

antagonists, those most predisposed to see conspiracies will be in the vanguard. Individuals low on the conspiracy dimension will not believe in many conspiracy theories, regardless of their other opinions.

This logic leads us to expect that the level of conspiratorial beliefs will be relatively stable over time. Because power has been remarkably balanced in the United States, individuals on the left and right are equally likely to be socialized to conspiracy theorizing. Propitious circumstances will activate at best a segment on one side of the aisle or the other, and this will even out over time. Only in rare cases will a conspiracy theory appeal to a majority of the country in bipartisan fashion.

The third step is behavior. In spite of the overall stability of conspiratorial views, alternations in power will cause different conspiracy theories to resonate at different times. As groups rise and fall, conspiracy theories should follow changes in power—with those out of power playing

Cassandra. Being out of power fuels feelings of anxiety and loss of control, which fans the flames for predisposed people to talk about or otherwise act on perceived conspiracies. Although this is most visible in the country's partisan and ideological divisions, we also expect third parties, social movements, and fringe groups to disproportionately convey conspiratorial beliefs for the same reason: they are out of power.

Individual responses are by no means predestined. Reactions could range from speculation to slander to sniping. People are not unreflective objects, and adding socialization, political opportunity, and anxiety does not automatically cause a person to buy into any specific conspiracy theory—much less act on it. But it does promote central tendencies at the mass level over long periods of time. Once people articulate a conspiracy theory—who the villain is, what he or she is trying to do, what ought to be done to thwart the trick—then it is up to others to weigh its merit. Merit having something to do with advantage, theories will resonate most widely when they impugn actors in powerful positions.

To recap, we have asserted that conspiracy theories are predominantly a product of socialization and political opportunity. This happens through a three-step process where some individuals are inculcated to see the world through a conspiratorial prism, though this must mesh with other ideological commitments, which are chiefly political. Then political circumstances highlight vulnerabilities to a group's position, which prompts the conspiratorially inclined to develop and disseminate a conspiracy theory. Within these parameters, there remains a fair amount of discretion about the exact form a conspiracy theory will take and whether it will be accepted broadly. No doubt conspiracy theories are complicated, and the three-step explanation above simplifies more complex and recursive events. But as a first cut, it covers the major contours.

THE NOT-SO-SECRET PLAN OF THE BOOK

To establish our claims, Chapter 2 begins by setting down what we mean by conspiracy theories and how they differ from related concepts. Although the analytical chapters of this book make every attempt to stay

neutral and not attempt to discern truth from falsity in individual conspiracy theories, our normative commitments and research results tell us
that truth matters. So we discuss six approaches to evaluating how true a
particular conspiracy theory might be and why the line between conspiracies and conspiracy theories is present but blurry.

Since the quality of our findings rests on the quality of our evidence,
Chapter 3 discusses our methods and data collection. Conspiracy theorizing is such an intricate topic that methodological pluralism seems to be
the only sensible way to grapple with it. Previous scholarship employed
a variety of methods: cultural criticism, historical process tracing, eth-
nographic studies, experiments, surveys, and content analysis. We try to
combine these tools but make no claim to be perfectly comprehensive,
though we try to err on the inclusive side.

This book offers three unique datasets. The first is a time-series collection of more than 100,000 letters to the editor of the *New York Times*
and the *Chicago Tribune* from 1890 to 2010. These data represent the only
long-term representative sample of conspiratorial beliefs and afford an extraordinary opportunity to track the resonance of conspiracy theories in
general.[91] The second set of data is a national two-wave survey taken before
and after the 2012 election. This permits us to examine the demographic
and behavioral characteristics of individuals in relation to their level of
belief in conspiracy theories and helps us follow how those beliefs affected
their behavior during the election cycle. The third is a sample of Internet
news stories from across the Web during a yearlong period, which allows
us to snap a picture not just of conspiracy theories in new media, but of
conspiracy theories in the broader information environment as well.

Chapter 4 begins testing the arguments. Using survey data, we demonstrate that there is an underlying ideological dimension that predisposes
people to see conspiracies. Then we examine the demographic characteristics and behaviors of people who tend to see conspiracies. Do they have
fewer friends? Do they vote? Do they use their knowledge to profit from
the stock market? Are they more inclined toward violence?

Chapter 5 surveys the overall levels of conspiracy theories in the United
States from 1890 to 2010 using our letters to the editor data. Almost
every period in American history has been called the peak of conspiracy

theorizing by some author or another. Who is right? Next, we review many popular explanations of when the total level of conspiracy theorizing should be most prevalent. Unpacking the logic behind the best hypotheses, we test them against the best available data and pit them against each other to see which run the race fastest. Are conspiratorial beliefs driven by bad economic times, the size of government, unscrupulous politicians, political polarization, or racism?

Chapter 6 breaks down the letters to the editor data further and tries to understand why certain conspiracy theories resonate at certain times. In public discourse, who is most likely to be named as the villain? We argue that power drives conspiracy talk and find that domestic power asymmetries and foreign threat are the biggest determinants of when certain theories will strike a chord with the public. In this sense, conspiracy theories are for losers (descriptively speaking, not pejoratively. At least we hope not pejoratively, since all of us eventually play the loser).

Chapter 7 sums the main arguments and findings of the work and concludes with their application to, and implications for, the future of policy and politics. Should the government play a role in quelling conspiratorial beliefs? What can be done? That will be the end of the book, but not really the end. In taking stock of knowledge on the subject and our contributions to it, it seems plain to us that there remains room for better theories about conspiracy theories.

But Is It True?

[The] typical procedure of the higher paranoid scholarship is to start with such defensible assumptions and with a careful accumulation of facts, or at least of what appear to be facts, and to marshal these facts toward overwhelming "proof" of the particular conspiracy that is to be established.

—RICHARD HOFSTADTER[1]

Richard Hofstadter, the patron saint of the paranoid style in American politics, paints a timeless and tiresome scene. Inevitably, we have all debated a conspiracy theory with a true believer. These conversations start reasonably enough but then quickly crumble as the conspiracy theorist tries to make up in quantity of evidence what is lacking in quality of logic. Your attempts to gently nudge your interlocutor in a more constructive direction are unavailing. Your irritated opponent looks at you like a sucker or, worse, a collaborator. In trying to loosen the hold of a conspiracy theory, you have only succeeded in tightening its grip.

But then who are you to say you are right? Your arguments generally trace a similar blueprint of agreeable assumptions ending in a heap of evidentiary bricks. Everyone errs, and perhaps you are the dupe of a carefully constructed misinformation campaign or the pawn of a Machiavellian maestro. Unwittingly, you may be wrong and your friend right. Even when wide of the mark, conspiracy theorists have at times been correct about the big picture or unearthed information that otherwise would have remained obscure.[2] Today's conspiracy theory may be tomorrow's history.

The central question of this chapter is: but is it true? The answer matters because most of us believe in one conspiracy theory or another, and it would be helpful to know how tethered to truth those beliefs are. What should lead us to believe a conspiracy theory or not? Arguably the most important function of science is that it illuminates how we know what we know. It tells us when we are likely wrong and helps separate the inspired from the insipid. Poorly founded beliefs promote poor actions, and the preceding chapter recited a litany of damages that conspiracy theories have inflicted.[3] Over the long term, the quantity and quality of evidence supporting a conspiracy theory affect the number of people believing it. But because disconfirming evidence is baked into them, conspiracy theories are hard to prove or disprove. And because they involve danger, power, and knowledge, conspiracy theories are hard to discuss, never mind study.

While determinative tests would be preferable, the line between conspiracy theory and conspiracy is not so easy to establish. It may be impossible in some cases to know the difference. However, while reasonable people can disagree on details, no one wants to live in a world of "anything goes" theoretical nihilism. There is a consensus that the explanatory power of a conspiracy theory varies with the standards of logic and evidence it meets and that its value is relative to that of other explanations. Even if the available tests are flawed and can act only as rough rules of thumb, tests are a necessity. In this chapter, we adduce six tests—Occam's razor, falsifiability, the worst intentions test, the cui bono test, the eternal recurrence of the same test, and the impartial spectator test—and contend that running conspiracy theories through this gauntlet of six tests together can provide a relative and probabilistic estimate of how true they are.

To make our case, we first go over why conspiracy theories are hard to disprove and discuss. Then, because any serious study needs to be conceptually clear, the next section sets down definitions. We want to make manifest early and often that the vocabulary of conspiracy theories is loaded, but we do not intend the terms this way. So while we use common parlance to be accessible, this book takes no position on the truth or falsity of conspiracy theories. We do not seriously investigate the proof of conspiracy theories collectively or individually, nor do we attempt to dissuade anyone from their cherished beliefs. The third section lays out six standards for judging conspiracy theories and shows why it is so challenging to discriminate between the likely and the loopy. The final section summarizes the chapter and reflects on its themes.

THE CONSPIRACY THEORY CONTROVERSY

No one is a stranger to how quickly charges of conspiracy theorizing devolve into circular finger pointing. Pity the poor participants in these debates, none of whom wishes to play the fool or knave but all of whom suspect their adversary is stupid or crazy. The interesting thing about the DNA of conspiracy theories is that they are hardwired to elicit these responses. By their nature, conspiracy theories incorporate a lack of confirming evidence and a glut of disconfirming evidence—and this is supposed to count in their favor. Furthermore, conspiracy theories are often about the most delicate of issues: power, identity, and truth. This is a recipe for bad blood and persuasive impasse. While some theories materialize and vaporize like ghosts, others look like unkillable zombies, doomed to endlessly roam the epistemological earth in search of brains.

As if by a biological imperative, conspiracy theories beget more conspiracy theories. A few examples are illustrative. Former Treasury

Secretary Robert Reich recently commented in the *New York Times* about a supposed increase in conspiratorial accusations and polarized political rhetoric. He conveyed an episode in which he was accosted by a man who believed Reich was a communist subversive.[4] Even though he denied that conspiracy theory, he then went on to explain it with a different conspiracy theory: that the financial markets are rigged against people. It is this conspiracy, according to Reich, that drives people to believe in other conspiracy theories: "Losers of rigged games can become very angry."

Talk show host Glenn Beck routinely traffics in conspiratorial rhetoric, divining who is secretly working with whom (usually communists) and why (usually to spread communism). Beck realizes that repetitively linking actors and events to pinkish puppet masters might strike some in his audience as obsessive-compulsive conspiracy mongering. To ward off the hurtful slur of conspiracy theorist, Beck invokes yet another conspiracy theory.[5] "Why is it a concentrated effort now to label me a conspiracy theorist?" he inquired of himself on his radio show. His answer: "[Administrator of the Office of Information and Regulatory Affairs Cass Sunstein] said the government should call anyone who stands against them a conspiracy theorist. . . . This isn't a conspiracy theory. This is what he wrote about. This was his way for the government—and he said, 'Even if it turns out to be true, you have to label people a conspiracy theorist because it isolates them.'"[6]

Or consider Florida Atlantic University Professor James Tracy, who, following the shootings at Sandy Hook Elementary School, suggested that the tragedy was scripted by powerful forces, perhaps for some nefarious purpose. Responding to the strong media backlash against his theories, Tracy explained the massive resistance to his ideas by combining domino theory and false flag logic into a single accusation:

I think that there is definitely a program to sow misinformation in the stream of information in order to muddy the waters and in the process discredit the research that independent researchers and the like are putting together in alternative media. Because if you can discredit it or muddy the waters to a limited degree in one area, you can paint with a fairly broad brush, the mainstream corporate media can do that.[7]

The irony goes beyond department secretaries, talk show hosts, and professors; take a letter to the editor by a *Boston Globe* reader in response to a journalist's unbiased reporting on the conspiratorial beliefs surrounding President Obama's agenda:[8]

> I have my own conspiracy theory: Who benefits from this fear? Those who do not want us to discuss the financial industry's scamming and manipulating of the world's economy; those who support the oil and coal industry and who do not want discussion of climate change and alternative fuels; those who benefit from the weapons industry and do not want any talk of gun control; and those want to take over the democratic process by infusing huge amounts of money into it, to mention a few. These forces want us to get lost in heated discussions disputing silly fantastical accusations.[9]

For those scoring at home, the fake conspiracy theory is the one about the executive branch. The real conspiracy theory involves a consortium including, but not limited to, the financial industry, oil and coal companies, global warming skeptics, the military-industrial complex, the National Rifle Association, and wealthy Americans.

These meta-conspiracy theories make the adjudication of evidence nearly impossible. But compounding this is that conspiracy theorists do not accept that their beliefs may turn on something other than an impartial interpretation of evidence. Few people see psychological or environmental factors behind their beliefs; their ideas are simply independent and correct. Reasonable people cannot disagree. To suggest otherwise offends sensibilities, though it probably should not. Most beliefs have underlying causes.[10]

Herein lays a second problem: conspiracy theorists reject the study of their beliefs. With wearying regularity, researchers who study conspiratorial thinking are accused of being apologists for the diabolically greedy

or the flunkies of jowly Svengalis. Dartmouth political scientist Brendan
Nyhan experienced this firsthand. His work meticulously uses opinion
polls and scientific experiments to understand why people hold conspiratorial beliefs. For his troubles he has been tarred as an "establishment
toady" whose analysis of conspiratorial beliefs is "something that would
have been right at home in totalitarian regimes where those who disagreed
with the regime's leaders were declared insane."[11]

Adam Berinsky, a public opinion scholar at MIT, shared a similar fate. Just
the fact that he chose to study polls tracking Birther beliefs raised the ire of
some, who complained that he was complicit in the cover-up. One exclaimed:

> Oh gee! Look at the America-hating Marxist college professor, Ber-
> insky, carrying water for another America-hating Marxist, President
> Obama. Notice how he so cleverly couches his disdain for those who
> have only asked for the Truth about our President's past with leading
> phrases like "believe he was not born in America." The issue is no
> longer whether he was born in Hawaii, comrade Adam, the issue is
> why so many of you vermin leftist scum defend an obvious liar who
> is hiding virtually everything about his life. Now, run off for your
> updated talking points, Adam, and bang out a screed about how
> Romney is hiding something in his tax returns.[12]

The song remains the same with Truthers. On the tenth anniversary of
9/11, a draft essay from two unknown professors at the University of
Miami was singled out by the 9/11 Truth organization as the "Number
1 Hit Piece against Truth."[13] A reader of a subsequent essay argued that
studying why some people believe conspiracy theories and others do not
is a waste of time: "There are many examples of misdirection being spread
throughout the citizens. That some people are susceptible and others are
not is immaterial. The outcomes of these programmes are understood by
the people who put them into practice. Misdirection, culture war, and violence in society is a standard divide-and-rule tactic. These methods are
practiced by NATO forces against occupied peoples. They are intentional.
This is all well documented."[14]

Perhaps the most well-documented evidence of backlash involves psychology professor Stephan Lewandowsky.[15] He and several colleagues examined the link between conspiratorial thinking and the rejection of climate science.[16] Upon publication of their findings, conspiracy theorists accused the authors of a plot to smear climate change skeptics by fabricating data, misanalyzing the findings, and purposefully biasing their study so as to achieve a preordained conclusion. Some accused the corporate media and the Australian government of being in on the ruse as well. Conspiracy theorists even conjectured as to which of the co-authors was the string-puller behind the plot: "Maths Prof Kevin Judd is the mastermind behind [the study]. He is apparently a brilliant mathematician, chess and go player, and computerwizz. He is a typical reclusive mad scientist. There is no doubt he is behind [the studies]."[17]

For such inflamed responses, one might think that the scholars above had presented disconfirming evidence against a specific conspiracy theory. None had. No inquiry into conspiratorial beliefs is rigorous or dispassionate enough that it does not trigger a fusillade of defense mechanisms.[18]

Still, the conspiracy theorists have a point. Just the term *conspiracy theory* is loaded. To label a theory as a conspiracy theory or someone a conspiracy theorist may place him or her on uneven terrain. He or she may meet with greater skepticism or appear beyond the bounds of reason.[19] This could circumscribe free and fair debate. Epistemologist David Coady argues, "[b]oth [the Right and Left] assume that there is something wrong with conspiracy theories: that they are always or at least usually false, or that those who believe them or seek out evidence for them are being irrational. On the face of it, this assumption stands in need of some supporting evidence."[20]

Scholars such as Ginna Husting and Martin Orr suggest the term "conspiracy theory" and its variants are "dangerous machinery," used as tools to conceal truth and evidence.[21] Others go further and contend that the term is itself part of a plot by the CIA to silence skeptics following the Kennedy assassination.[22] To avoid any negative effects, some scholars have taken to using unfamiliar and ungainly terms, such as "state crimes against democracy" instead.[23]

Some epistemologists criticize the study of conspiracy theories as being itself part of a conspiracy, or as providing intellectual cover to conspirators. Charles Pigden writes, "Like many on the left, I think that [Karl] Popper's critique of conspiracy theories has provided right-wing conspirators (and, in some cases, their agents) with an intellectually respectable smokescreen behind which they can conceal their conspiratorial machinations."[24] Coady concurs and argues that a "great deal of contemporary political debate consists of attempts by conservatives to portray those on the Left as conspiracy theorists, and attempts by those on the Left to refute the charge."[25]

There is legitimate concern that the labels "conspiracy theory" and "conspiracy theorist" may put ideas or people at a disadvantage. But there is also a countervailing force: for some the labels are convincing and attractive terms. A recent study showed that simply using the word "conspiracy" in a description of media practices led many people to accept that a media conspiracy was afoot.[26] In popular culture, millions are drawn to shows, movies, books, and other materials that champion conspiracy theories (think of the movie *Conspiracy Theory* or the television program *Conspiracy Theory with Jesse Ventura*). Derision toward the term "conspiracy theory" and its variants is not universal; they attract some people but repel others. On balance, the terms likely have a negative connotation, but not across the board.

Wrapping up the section, because strategy and secrecy are woven into the cloth of all conspiracy theories, the standards of logic and evidence fall under a penumbra of suspicion and controversy. Confirming evidence must have been purposely obscured or destroyed so the evidentiary burden must be lighter.[27] With their explosive charges, conspiracy theories encourage people to step lightly and give conspiracy theorists a wide berth. But with such a low bar, people become promiscuous in their credulity and almost all beliefs are permitted. If conspiracy theories are an ineradicable part of life, perhaps it is a step in the right direction to define them, take some of the sting out of the terms, and be fair about how to judge them.

TRYING TO DEFUSE DEFINITIONS

It is impossible not to step on toes when studying conspiracy theories. Some approach conspiratorial beliefs as "mistruths," "misinformation," "misperceptions," "myths," and "false beliefs"[28] and wish to study them as a species of informational or mental error. Others make little distinction between conspiracy theories and conspiracies and so do not wish to study conspiracy theories at all.[29] We steer a middle course. Conspiracy theories are a pressing and delicate subject and consequently both difficult and necessary to study. For purposes of clarity, we stick to the most commonly used terms and phrases—but intend them in a neutral way. To repeat, we do not mean a pejorative connotation with our use of "conspiracy theory" or its variants, and we do not intend to injure anyone's beliefs. We have no desire to provide cover for wrongdoers or excuse crackpots. Nor is it our aim to prove or disprove any particular conspiracy theory or conspiracy theories as a class.

We define *conspiracy* as a secret arrangement between two or more actors to usurp political or economic power, violate established rights, hoard vital secrets, or unlawfully alter government institutions.[30] Our definition is most interested in systemic risks to the public and actions that menace the bedrock ground rules that minimize force and fraud. Conspiracies happen with dreary frequency, but because of the difficulties inherent in executing plans and keeping quiet, they tend to fail.[31] A key point is that conspiracies speak to actual events that have occurred or are occurring.

Notable examples include the Reagan administration's Iran-Contra scheme to trade arms to hostile nations, the FBI's attempt to cover up their actions at Ruby Ridge, and Illinois Governor Rod Blagojevitch's attempts to sell the Senate seat formerly belonging to Barack Obama. In each of these cases, the public became aware of the alleged wrongdoing through incessant media reports and the perpetrators admitted to (or were found guilty of) their activities.

At many levels, U.S. government officials have committed abhorrent conspiracies. The most infamous examples involve health research, where government scientists grossly violated ethical standards in studies of sexually transmitted diseases. In the Tuskegee experiments, rural blacks with syphilis were unknowingly left untreated for decades when a cure was available. In 2011, scholars uncovered a conspiracy where U.S. officials injected syphilis and gonorrhea into the eyes and spines of non-consenting Guatemalan citizens and then attempted to hide their crimes.[32] In both cases the president formally apologized for the government's egregious conduct.

Less well known but also relevant are the cases where American defense planners contemplated or undertook outlandish conspiracies. In 1962, Secretary of Defense Robert McNamara listened to designs to "explode bombs in U.S. cities, sink boatloads of Cuban refugees . . . blowing up John Glenn's rocket during his historic space flight . . . [and] shoot down a civilian airliner."[33] The goal of these schemes was a false flag operation to pin the blame on Fidel Castro and justify an invasion of Cuba. The plans found no reception among decision makers. Two year later, however, McNamara manifestly lied in his testimony to the Senate that "[o]ur navy played absolutely no part in, was not associated with, was not aware of, any South Vietnamese actions, if there were any. . . . I say this flatly. This is a fact."[34] The actions in question were the Gulf of Tonkin incidents, which led directly to massive American involvement in Vietnam. These examples focus on government conspiracies, but government involvement is not a definitional necessity.

For *conspiracy theory*, we use a standard definition: an explanation of historical, ongoing, or future events that cites as a main causal factor a small group of powerful persons, the conspirators, acting in secret for their own benefit against the common good.[35] The plot could be driven by foreign or domestic governments, nongovernmental actors, scientists, religious and fraternal organizations, or any other group perceived as powerful and potentially evil. Perhaps the most durable conspiracy theory throughout world history is that Jews collude to secretly control the international financial system, the news media, the FBI, the Federal Reserve, American defense policy, Hollywood, and the music industry for self-serving and iniquitous purposes. The most popular conspiracy theory of modern America may be the perception that the assassination of President Kennedy was orchestrated and covered up by a conspiracy involving one or more of the following: Vice President Lyndon Johnson, Cuban expatriates, Mafiosi, CIA operatives, defense contractors, and defrocked pedophile priests.[36]

While "conspiracy" refers to events that have occurred or are occurring, "conspiracy theory" refers to accusatory perceptions that may or may not be true. Telling the difference between the two turns on the evidentiary threshold, of which more in the following sections. But for the time being, let us employ a standard discussed by Neil Levy for distinguishing between conspiracies and conspiracy theories. His premise is that properly constituted epistemic authorities determine the existence of conspiracies. Levy defines "properly constituted epistemic authorities" as institutions in which knowledge claims are the result of a socially distributed network of inquirers trained in assessing knowledge claims, with methods and results made public and available for scrutiny.[37]

Following this standard, the Watergate conspiracy was a conspiracy theory until the epistemic authorities (in this case, journalists, analysts, Congress, and courts) gathered information, presented that information in the open, held hearings, received admissions, and handed down guilty verdicts. Authorities with known expertise in the relevant areas determined that the accusatory perception of a conspiracy by the Nixon administration was valid because there was verifiable evidence.

The conspiracies and conspiracy theories we focus on are wholesale, not retail. If companies are rigging energy markets to secure extortionate profits, it fits our definition of conspiracy. But contrast that with a woman and her lover who conspire to kill the woman's cuckolded husband. While unfortunate, especially for the husband, this case does not reach the magnitude necessary to fall within our purview. The difference depends on large-scale public harm versus isolated private harm.

This brings us to legal definitions of criminal conspiracy, which partially overlap with our definitions of conspiracy and conspiracy theory. Criminal and legal definitions do not share our emphasis on attempts to do widespread harm. Most criminal conspiracies are too minor to meet our definition (e.g., a conspiracy to rob a liquor store), and many of what we consider to be potential conspiracies are too broad to meet criminal definitions (e.g., international communism hijacking pop music to subvert capitalism.)

Conspiracy theories can explain events in the past, present, and future.[38] Case in point: some believe that the governments of the United States, Canada, and Mexico have a clandestine plan to establish a new North American currency, the Amero, as part of a supposed New World Order, which would extinguish the sovereignty of the United States. No diehard believer of this theory claims that the Amero is in common circulation yet; their concern has more to do with the future. But it would defy common sense to state that the Amero is less a conspiracy theory than, say, water fluoridation fears in the 1950s, because it has not reached the execution phase.

Some restrict conspiracy theories to explanations opposing official narratives or "cock-up" stories.[39] For them, a conspiracy theory is a conflicting response to either an official account or to an explanation that attributes events to incompetence, happenstance, and accident.[40] It is true that many conspiracy theories respond to official stories—9/11 conspiracy theories pick apart the government's investigation and Kennedy assassination theories refute the Warren Commission. But for our purposes, an official story is not essential to a conspiracy theory. It is only true that a conspiracy theory need conflict with an official account, if an official account exists. In addition, conspiracy theories can be summoned so fast, they can come out before any official (or other) explanation might even exist, and some official government accounts are conspiracy theories themselves (think of pariah dictators' justifications for staying in office).

Some scholars include benevolent conspiracies in their definition of conspiracy theories.[41] A critical feature of our definition is that the conspiracy must come at the expense of the common good, at least in the eyes of the conspiracy theorist. Believing that scientists are secretly curing cancer for the good of humanity is nice, but such a belief is uninteresting, unlikely to affect society, and sufficiently rare to be omitted for simplicity's sake.[42]

A final point is that the number of people believing a theory is inconsequential to whether it is a conspiracy theory or not. Conspiracy theories
are defined by their content, not their popularity. Polls show that about 6
percent of the population believes the lunar landings were faked, but this
is no less a conspiracy theory than alien-government cover-ups, which
some polls show have many more believers.[43] Moreover, conspiracy theories need not be well developed, have organizations or websites devoted to
them, or be the subject of public debate.

Of course, how many of these characteristics a conspiracy theory has
differs. Truther theories have organized groups, grassroots outreach movements, feature films, published books, and a significant amount of media
coverage, and upward of 30 percent of the country credits some version
of the theory. The theory that author Stephen King killed John Lennon as
part of a conspiracy orchestrated by Richard Nixon, Ronald Reagan, and
oil companies has a website and a book, but no media coverage and few
adherents.[44] And others, such as the claim that the government imbued its
coinage with demonic numerology, have no outreach, propagating materials, or news coverage.

By *conspiratorial belief* we intend a person's belief in a particular conspiracy theory or theories. Most scholarship to date focuses on such
individual beliefs. This book, however, focuses more on *conspiratorial
thought*, which we refer to as a predisposition toward seeing the world
more generally in conspiratorial terms. The core concepts of this work
are thoughts and beliefs, but these are hard to measure. One may believe
that the United Nations is attempting to subjugate the United States to
totalitarian-communist rule, but if that belief were not expressed, it would
be socially sterile.

As researchers, we can solicit these opinions by asking respondents if
they believe in particular conspiracy theories or by asking questions that
tap into conspiratorial worldviews. We might ask such questions as part
of a poll or experiment. Another way to assess conspiratorial thought and
or beliefs is through conspiracy talk. *Conspiracy talk* is recorded public
discourse, spoken or written, that seeks to expose conspiracies or spread
conspiracy theories.

Once again, for some this discussion calls to mind images of tinfoil hats, mothers' basements, and friendless seclusion. Such a stereotype refers only to a tiny fringe of the population and the mental picture should be banished at this point. Our definition of a *conspiracy theorist* is one who believes in conspiracy theories, not necessarily someone who originates, circulates, or improves such theories.[45] Because polls show that the majority of people believe in one conspiracy theory or another, most Americans fit our definition, though degrees vary.[46]

JUDGING STANDARDS

Many scientific theories turn out to be false or, put more charitably, not very useful. Scientists have famously gotten wrong the age of the Earth, the center of the universe, germs, physiognomy, phrenology, and whatever phlogiston is. Scientific theories are inherently provisional; so are conspiracy theories. This makes them comparable, but not equivalent. The strength of a theory depends on how demanding the tests it can weather relative to the best alternative.

All events have a positive probability of occurring. Every conspiracy theory *could* be true. Sometimes people secretly plan to snatch power and subvert the common good. In open democratic societies, the public is called upon to be wary of potential abuses and does a tolerable job doing so.[47] But for some conspiracy theories, when their predictions fail to materialize and corroborating evidence does not appear, they deserve withering neglect. Declaring immunity as a conspiracy theory should not confer life eternal. Conspiracy theories should be forced to make good with positive proof in a reasonable amount of time or be pitilessly abandoned.[48] There are too many pressing problems in the world to squander brainpower on an unprovable dead end.

So how is one to know when a conspiracy theory should be believed? Some epistemologists suggest discarding more conspiracy theories, others suggest discarding less.[49] As Pete Mandik asks, "There's little doubt that least *some* conspiracy theories deserve dismissal on the grounds of their kookiness. But are *all* conspiracy theories dismissible?"[50] It depends on how one defines "kooky." Further, the grounds upon which epistemologists base accepting or rejecting conspiracy theories are not universal.[51] Someone insistent on believing in a conspiracy theory can stretch any standard of evidence to accommodate that belief. And, someone hell-bent on demolishing a conspiracy theory can strangle, shoot, and stab it redundantly with narrow interpretations of standards. One person's smoking gun is another's reasonable doubt.

This is not to say that we should simply throw up our hands and, paraphrasing Edward Gibbon, accept all conspiracy theories as equally true, equally false, or equally useful. Below, we provide a series of guidelines one could apply to conspiracy theories. If pushed hard, all standards break. Yet standards are a necessity, and overlapping standards may correct for each other's deficiencies. We collect what we believe to be the best available guides, but make no claim to be exhaustive.

Occam's Razor

Occam's razor, sometimes known as the parsimony principle, asserts that when it comes to explanations, the simpler the better. Applied to conspiracy theories, this suggests that we search among competing theories for the most parsimonious—that is, the one that explains the most of the outcome with the fewest explanatory factors. An alleged scheme may become so complicated that even the most nimble conspirators could not pull it off.

By way of an example, one variation of the 9/11 conspiracy theme is that the U.S. government blew up the twin towers in Manhattan. The key contention is that carefully set charges, rather than the airplanes, took down World Trade Center buildings 1, 2, and 7. This would require several things to be true.[52] Dozens of actors would have to set charges in a number of busy buildings without detection. The charges would have to be set in such a way as to blow up the buildings in the exact locations that the planes crashed, which implies ace pilots. And the fuel-laden planes could not impair the charges or else the charges could not detonate more than an hour after impact. Following the feat, Bush, Cheney, the 9/11 Commission, FBI, CIA, NYPD, major news outlets, and *Popular Mechanics* magazine all would have had to collude to conceal explosives, destroy evidence, and deceive the public. Comparing this story to the official version, one could see how it is fairly complicated and might be rejected on these grounds.

One common explanation for conspiratorial beliefs is that conspiracy theories are attempts to cope with big complex events with simple causes. It is well established that people employ mental shortcuts to deal with information overload and complexity,[53] and conspiracy theories do draw clear arrows between cause and effect, reduce randomness, and shoehorn reality into a parsimonious, albeit cartoonish, form. However, it is not clear that people scan the competing explanations and then pick the most parsimonious one.[54] But more importantly, conspiracy theories are often far more complicated than the official accounts they toil to refute. To be fair, parsimony is often in the eye of the beholder, but simplicity is not a trademark of many conspiracy theories.[55]

The parsimony principle has an attractive corollary in conspiratorial settings: large groups are lousy conspirators.[56] Collusion and silence are extremely hard. As the number of people involved in carrying out the conspiracy increases, the secret gets harder to keep. Again, the more valuable the information, the more likely it is to get out. Many a covert workplace romance has swiftly foundered on this rock, and that only involves two people and low stakes.

As conspiracy theories fail to gain traction, conspiracy theorists must explain why. This widens the circle of silence because the media and the government must be in on it. Philosopher Brian Keeley points this out about the 1994 bombing of the Oklahoma City Federal Building conspiracy theory: "What began as a small conspiracy on the part of a few members of a paramilitary U.S. federal agency invariably swells into a conspiracy of huge proportions, as positive evidence for the alleged conspiracy fails to obtain. And, as more people must be brought into the conspiracy to explain the complicity of more and more public institutions, the less believable the theory should become."[57]

Yet there is no great rule determining the cut point between a plausible and an implausible number of conspirators. Parsimony may be a liability in some cases; too many conspirators undermine secrecy but too few make a conspiracy harder to pull off. We find it intuitively believable that groups as high as a few dozen might collude successfully for years (as Major League franchise owners did to keep out blacks and maintain their antitrust exemption, but that is anecdotal and well known). Then there is the methodological issue that we have no robust studies of conspiracies that fail versus succeed because the ones that succeed go unnoticed and are hard to estimate.

Parsimony adds a healthy dose of skepticism, but it has its flaws. After all, parsimony is subjective. One might judge that carefully placed explosives provide a simple enough explanation for the twin towers' destruction. Or one might frame the issue as a small group of very powerful governmental actors fooled the world rather than a larger group of less capable actors pulled off an improbable stunt.[58] One cannot dispense with a theory simply because it is more complicated than competing theories. Garbage can and kitchen sink models can never be eliminated because their complexity occasionally illuminates more than simpler explanations.

Occam's razor is only probabilistic: the more complicated an explanation, the less likely it is to be true. It leaves space for the Rube Goldberg machines of the world. But there is logical parsimony and emotional parsimony, and many individuals prefer the latter to the former in spite of the costs to logical consistency. The bottom line is that there is something to Occam's razor, but it is not as sharp as many would like.

Falsifiability

One of the hallmarks of scientific theory is that it can be falsified. There must be some evidence that could show that the theory is wrong. Ideas that rest entirely on faith and cannot be feasibly falsified are religion. One of the hallmarks of conspiracy theory is that a dearth of positive proof and an abundance of falsifying evidence seem to count in their favor. If powerful actors are trying to hide something, it only stands to reason that confirming evidence will be hidden and red herrings will abound. As Keeley explains, "unfalsifiability is only a reasonable criterion in cases where we do not have reason to believe that there are powerful agents seeking to steer our investigation away from the truth of the matter."[59]

So two routes to probe a conspiracy theory are to ask: "what evidence would falsify it?" and "what else would be true if I applied this level of falsifiability to other beliefs?" If there is no evidence that would falsify a conspiracy theory, or if every theory would be true if the same standards are applied, then it is no longer theory; it is theology. Falsifiability should always be a concern when debating conspiracy theories, but this concern may sometimes be overdrawn. Many canonical scientific theories are hard to falsify—relativity and evolution come to mind. And it is hard to prove the negative that secret machinations do *not* exist.

The problem may not necessarily lie in the falsifiability of any one theory, but rather that dogmatic conspiracy theorists find post hoc ways to avoid refutation. Maarten Boudry and Johan Braeckman note two ways that conspiracy theorists fend off falsifiability: through immunizing strategies and through epistemic defense mechanisms.[60] We like to think about these as hedging and doubling down. An example of hedging is the evolution of 9/11 Truther theories. Initially, many conspiracy theorists claimed that the U.S. government was the sole perpetrator of the attacks. Now that a decade has passed and little corroborating evidence has surfaced, many have changed their working theory to say that either the U.S. government had "some role" in the attacks or hid "some" information from the official accounting of the attacks. This strategy makes the theory less bold and interesting but more likely to be true. It also lowers the bar for proof and raises the bar for disconfirming evidence.

As for doubling down, the Birther theory provides a textbook example. At the beginning of his term, many accused President Obama of being born in a foreign country and of hiding that fact. To support their claims, conspiracy theorists argued that Obama had never released a birth certificate. In 2011, Obama released his birth certificate, so the theory then morphed from Obama never having released a birth certificate to allegedly releasing a forged birth certificate. Conspiracy theorists can always move the goalpost to protect their theories from refutation.

On the whole, falsifiability is one of the most reliable guides to assessing theories. It is a practical check that probes the plausibility of claims and asks people to be clear about what evidence it would take for them to revise their views. Perhaps most constructively, it entails some sort of universalizability and comparison. If the same standards of evidence were applied across the board, what would also be true? All theories have anomalies, but theories with more disconfirming evidence are less likely to be true. The explanatory power of theories is always relative, and this allows conspiracy theories to fight official accounts on a largely level playing field. The major drawback of falsifiability is that powerful agents may be able to manipulate evidence, though this is improbable in modern democracies for extended periods of time (see also the careers of Bradley Manning and Edward Snowden).

The Worst Intentions

In all conspiracy theories, the villains are often assumed to be terribly conniving and devilish. But oddly, many of these supposed offenders are otherwise considered to be the good (e.g., the President), the benign (e.g., the Secretary of Commerce), and the boring (e.g., the International Monetary Fund). Hence, we might choose to reject a conspiracy theory if it attributes a depravity that is unlikely given one's track record and institutional incentives.[61]

A couple of examples should suffice. One instance is the conspiracy theory that the Fantasy Soda Pop Company was in league with the Ku Klux Klan to put chemicals in the soda to sterilize black men.[62] There is little doubt that the Klan does not wish blacks well. But beverage companies are not known for sterilization schemes, and for good reason. Such a scheme would be traceable and incredibly illegal and would have dev-astating consequences for any organization involved. Another instance is that Proctor & Gamble (P&G) was accused of surreptitious Satanism.[63] This is in spite of the fact that there has never been evidence of mul-tinational corporations taking part in occult activity. In fact, business-people are notorious for their anodyne personalities. Mammon maybe, but Lucifer worship would be inconsistent with corporate culture and incentives.

Under normal circumstances people and institutions have normal (meaning mixed) motives. It is one thing to assume a few evildoers here and there, but another to assume there are hordes of them working in concert for long stretches of time. No doubt there are rotten people, and no doubt horrible people have carried out, and will continue to carry out, horrible plans. But big bastions of wickedness are hard to come by, and the truth is typically more bland. In addition, the notion that a malevolent group can work together in protracted secrecy should give one pause. As Popper cautions, "the conspiracy theorist will believe that institutions can be understood completely as the result of conscious design; and as collec-tive, he usually ascribes to them a kind of group-personality, treating them as conspiring agents, just as if they were individual men."[64]

Then there is the abiding problem of assessing intentions. How do con-spiracy theorists, at great distance, claim privileged access to others' inten-tions and motives? Since at least Freud, we have known that people are only dimly aware of their own motives and the explanations they give of their own behaviors are often shoddy. We are likely even worse at explaining and predicting other people's motives and intentions, which are alloyed, opaque, and shifting. Multiply conspirators, and those dynamics and dif-ficulties worsen. Draw out the time horizon, and they multiply again. But groups seldom work together harmoniously over long periods (insert the Beatles, Van Halen, Oasis, or your favorite group here). Therefore, con-spiracy theories might be rejected if they posit a group working too well together for too long.

However, conspiracy theorists have several retorts. Perhaps the con-spirator is skilled in deception; that is how he or she rose to prominence in the first place. Perhaps at the pinnacle of power there are fewer disincentives for bad behavior; power corrupts. Perhaps the atrocious act is just a one-off. Perhaps average people's motives are, on average, savage. This culminates in a banality of evil argument: circumstances can make people act abominably with little thought. And the unknowability of motives rebounds back on itself: how do non-conspiracy theorists know that motives are *not* monstrous?

On balance, the worst intentions test can act as a thought experiment to cast doubt on brazenly silly accusations, but it is a permeable membrane. We all have to assess intentions; one must either do a better or worse job of it. As Oliver Wendell Holmes pithily put it: "even a dog knows the difference between being stumbled over and being kicked."[65] There are holes in this standard that plenty of probably false conspiracy theories can pass through untouched. Yet on the margin it may force some people to reexamine their beliefs, and this is all to the good.

The Cui Bono Test

A third test is to pose the old Roman question: "who benefits?" Conspiracy theorists ask it, and this leads them to the supposed conspirators.[66] Often this makes sense. When detectives investigate a grandmother's murder, they would be derelict if they did not read her will. But simply because someone benefited from an outcome does not mean he or she caused it, or there would be an exponential growth in explanations (and incarcerations.) But insofar as the cui bono test is useful, it ought to be applied thoroughly. This involves examining the amount of intentionality and rationality assumed in the conspirators' motives, as well as the risks and benefits associated with carrying out the alleged plot.

Certainly intended outcomes must swamp unintended outcomes or no one would ever try to do anything. Yet something is always lost between potential and actual, between invention and execution. Sometimes the best way to ensure peace is to prepare for war and the biggest encouragement to war is peaceful intentions. As Popper observes: "nothing ever comes off exactly as intended. Things always turn out a little bit differently."[67] If the conspiracy theory attaches intentions directly to outcomes, it should be dubious because plans rarely turn out as designed. And considering the scope and uncertainty of many of the supposed plots, this should be especially true.

Reality has friction that can easily foul up the many moving parts of even the simplest plans. When such friction is absent in an explanation, there is solid ground for disbelief. When the United States sent its best special forces with the best equipment and best training to kill Osama bin Laden, the mission was jeopardized when one of the helicopters crashed. The soldiers had been practicing the mission in a mock-up compound surrounded by chain-link fences. The actual compound had concrete walls, which created unanticipated vortices for the landing helicopters. This sort of expensive surprise in a high-stakes mission is not uncommon.[68]

Steve Clarke is also skeptical of the intentionality imbedded in conspiracy theories and ties it to the fundamental attribution error, where people are overly apt to ascribe dispositional explanations over situational explanations.[69] Focusing on Elvis's death in isolation, a conspiracy theory could easily connect innumerable dots in innumerable ways to suggest that Elvis faked his death. But such reasoning is post hoc. As Clarke argues, "If you examine the circumstances of Elvis Presley's natural death closely enough you will be able to relate it to other natural events, and with sufficient persistence you will be able to relate all of these within the scope of physics, thereby furnishing yourself with an explanation with more unificatory power than any dispositional explanation can provide."[70] On this wider view, it is common sense that sedentary, morbidly obese drug abusers have an elevated risk of early mortality.

Conspiracy theorists could stretch the ideas of intentionality above to fit any conspiracy theory and claim that intentional actions often do bring about intended results. And just because intentions are not directly observable does not mean they do not exist. People have intentions and sometimes these intentions are no good. Richard Nixon and the Plumbers did not slip on a banana peel, accidentally violate the Constitution, and attempt to cover it up by happenstance. People often work in tandem, sometimes plans do turn out close to intentions, and there is no reason why they should not at least some of the time.[71] Even if we grant that most people, most of the time, mean well, that still means that sometimes they do not, and they may also err in their understanding of the general good.

This brings us to the idea of rationality. Unquestionably people are sometimes rational, but conspiracy theorists assume that the actors in their theories are always rational. Conspiracy theorists posit that the conspirators have a prize worth cheating for and the will and ability to stop at nothing to get it. Yet such tenacious reason and intellectual agility are not consistent with the potential costs, risks, and benefits of the alleged plot.

There is rationality and then there is hyper-rationality. Conspiracy theorists often assume that the conspirators have the foresight to know in advance how their plans will unfold under volatile circumstances. There are several grounds on which we might object to this, beginning with the fact that probably no one has such a deft touch. As Keeley puts it: "Too strong a belief in the rationality of people in general, or of the world, will lead us to seek purposive explanations where none exists."[72] Conspirators are often assumed to act in accordance with their plan at all times. But the reason we come to know about conspiracies is because life and people are unpredictable; the conspirators deviate from their plans, make mistakes, and have to improvise fixes on the fly.

Intrinsically, conspiracies are high-risk activities, and this is seldom rational. Addressing Truther theories, Noam Chomsky addresses this in his dismissal of 9/11 conspiracy theories implicating the Bush administration: "Did they plan it in any way or know anything about it? This seems to be extremely unlikely. They would have been insane to try anything like that. If they had, it is almost certain that it would have leaked. It's a very porous system, secrets are hard to keep. So, something would have leaked out, very likely. And if it had, they'd all be before firing squads. It'd be the end of the Republican Party forever."[73]

And for these exorbitant risks, the utility they will supposedly receive is often trivial. American involvement in the Middle East doubtless has something to do with oil, but that is separate from arguing that an oil scheme was the main cause of the Gulf and Iraq Wars. Going into the Gulf War, oil was already cheap and Iraqi production had almost no impact on the world price of oil. The outcome of the war—victory and major reimbursements from allies—was much rosier than expected, and still the war did not help the American economy. Before the Iraq War, the Bush Administration's optimism was wildly misplaced and widely condemned, but even in the face of sheer financial loss and rising oil prices, American oil companies were not given preferential access to Iraqi oil, and indeed none signed contracts for it.[74] Despite the prohibitive risks and costs and trivial benefits, many people are still convinced that both George Bushes went to war for oil.

In short, listeners should tap the brakes on their belief when they hear a conspiracy theory where the plot's costs and risks exceed its expected benefits. Applied evenly, the cui bono test forces us to reason through the incentives of various actors and consider friction in how potential plans turn into observed events. But on its own, the cui bono test is not a sufficient reason to come to a complete stop. While there is much merit in the cui bono test, it too has its limits. People do act intentionally to achieve goals; sometimes goals are achieved more or less directly; and there is not necessarily a clash between rationality and risk acceptance. Someone's risk profile is often distinct from his or her powers of reason. Some intelligent people ride motorcycles helmetless and BASE jump.

Eternal Recurrence of the Same

Another test of conspiracy theories is whether similar events have happened before. There may be nothing new under the sun, and if that is true then wacky or unprecedented conspiracies ought to raise more than an eyebrow. Were someone to claim that communists were conspiring to brainwash the American public, this might be rejected out of hand because it is not clear that brainwashing exists and mass brainwashing has never occurred before.[75] Life normally features more continuity than change, and that is a screening mechanism for conspiracy theories.

Yet it is not a fine mesh and a conspiracy theorist might frustrate this screen in several ways. One is to point out that new things are discovered all the time. Dismissing unique conspiracy theories is bound to blind people to the occasional novelty. And there are strong incentives for innovation. If at least some conspirators are as wily as conspiracy theories suggest they are, there is a strategic logic to design a plan no one is looking for. If conspirators want to succeed in committing the oldest sins, they will commit them in the newest ways.

Altogether, the eternal recurrence of the same does not exclude much. Across time, an infinite number of conspirators have sprung an infinite number of conspiracies, each of which varied in some way. Almost nothing is unprecedented. Nevertheless, the test has some positive value. People generally tread on paths worn by others and significant innovations are rare. As with anything new, true, and non-trivial, people should take conspiracy theories that claim all three traits with a pinch of salt.

The Impartial Spectator Test

Borrowing from Adam Smith, one good measure of the truth in a conspiracy theory is to see how an impartial spectator would view it. Independent experts without a stake in a controversy are invaluable assets. Paraphrasing C. S. Peirce, "how do I know there are tigers in India? I have never been there." Life cannot function without taking people's word on a great many things; we cannot check everything for ourselves. We must trust that experts are much more likely to be knowledgeable than we are, that the better-informed judges are less likely to err, and that the better-positioned umpires are more likely to make the right call.

This relates back to Neil Levy's standard: "A conspiracy theory that conflicts with the official story, where the official story is the explanation offered by the (relevant) *epistemic authorities*, is *prima facie* unwarranted."[76] The epistemic authorities might include researchers, scientists, and government officials. There are compelling grounds to support his position.

Whether designing medicines, materials, or governments, science has done an impressive job enriching people's lives. Certainly there is luck in these achievements, but not much magic. Good science is accessible and replicable and represents the collected wisdom of history. Experts know what they know because of the serendipitous discoveries and appalling errors accumulated over centuries. They are a decentralized community of smart people with strong incentives and deep resources to ferret out errors. Scientific methods have evolved by using the most demanding tests to address the most demanding problems. In their fields of expertise, scientists and experts have a much better batting average than other groups of people.

That does not stop experts from being wrong. They are, quite often, and the scientific method corrects for this by valuing transparency and replication. The idea is that false findings are likely to be amended over time, but by all accounts this takes time. If one were to accept all scientific findings as equally true, then this would be as anti-intellectual as rejecting all scientific findings.

There are outstanding instances of upstanding experts straightening out official narratives. When the U.S. government presented specious data on terrorism in the world, it was diligent academics who detected and corrected it.[77] There were errors in the *9/11 Report*, but they were not systematic, there is no evidence that they were made from malice or malpractice, and experts rooted them out using ordinary methods. When the United States girded its loins to escalate conflicts with North Vietnam and Iraq using flimsy claims, prominent political scientists were early and vocal opponents.

Nonetheless, conspiracy theorists often choose to selectively ignore the knowledge generated by experts and rely on more elastic evidence from unconventional sources and amateurs. (Non-conspiracy theorists are often no different on this score.) Despite an overwhelming number of studies attesting to the safety of vaccines, genetically modified (GM) food, and AIDS prevention drugs, many people reject these findings and cling to conspiratorial beliefs instead.[78]

But, like the devil citing his purpose in scripture, conspiracy theorists comfortably glom onto government information when it is convenient.

For example, much of the evidence to support 9/11 conspiracy theories comes from government reports.[79] The same logic applies to the rejection of scientific findings. Repudiations of scientific consensus are no more principled than the selective acceptance of convenient government information. Those claiming that vaccines are part of a conspiracy involving pharmaceutical companies, the government, and doctors do engage the scientific literature and present scientific studies and analyses of their own.[80] When a study supports a link between vaccines and ill effects, it is lauded as exemplary science. But when a study fails to find a link between vaccines and illness, it is jeered as bad science, bad faith, and further evidence of the plot.[81] When it comes to science and authority, conspiracy theorists look little different than the rest of us; they cheer the evidence that fits with their previously held views and boo evidence that does not.[82]

Why are people so resistant to authoritative explanations? It may be because people tend to overestimate their ability to explain phenomena.[83] Or because, in a democracy, people tend to view themselves as equals even in realms where they are not.[84] Or it could merely be that people value their autonomy highly and care less about being right than being left alone. No one likes to be condescended to, and experts, with their stores of specialized knowledge and lack of commonalities with average people, can come off as (and be) contemptuous. Or, it could be costly signaling where the goal is not veracity but solidarity.

A more troubling reason to be skeptical of experts is that no spectator is truly impartial or independent. Scientists get involved with issues they care about. Like everyone else, scientists avoid cognitive dissonance, and they may bend their published findings to fit their predispositions.[85] One biologist complained that GM researchers depend on the success of GM crops for their livelihood, which stifles doubts about the crops: "Whether it's conscious or not, it's in their interest to promote this field, and they're not objective."[86] Authorities could have a vested interest or take bribes. Government officials can impede access to evidence or funding.

A blind acceptance of all authorities puts a great deal of power in their hands and makes them susceptible to corruption. Sometimes there are few experts in an area, and then opportunities for collusion increase. Or it could be that the experts are all driven by the same set of institutional incentives. In addition, the gears of science grind slowly, and it takes years to catch errors and fabricated data. Excessive skepticism may be crippling, but moderate skepticism is healthy.

When conspiracy theorists question expert accounts, they often base their theories on what are called errant data. These may fall into two classes: data that are unaccounted for by the official story or data that contradict the official story.[87] An example of unaccounted-for data would be that Jack Ruby shot and killed Lee Harvey Oswald—the lone gunman explanation does not account for Jack Ruby's erratic actions. An example of contradictory data would be that witnesses to the Kennedy assassination reported hearing shots from places other than the book depository—this evidence would directly contradict the findings of the Warren Report. One might take errant data to suggest that the experts were wrong, or that the official story needs amending, or even that the official story is a cover-up of a conspiracy. No story explains everything, but official stories should explain as much as possible. If they do not, it is reasonable to toss them aside and search for a better theory. It is in the eye of the beholder how many errant data should exist before an official story is repudiated.

All theories have anomalies because all theories simplify complexity. Errant data do not prove much on their own. Most of life is unexplained. The fact that we cannot explain all data with crisp theories suggests nothing. Noam Chomsky chastises Truthers for this reason:

> If you look at the evidence, anybody who knows anything about the sciences would instantly discount that evidence. I mean there are plenty of coincidences and unexplained phenomena—why did this happen, and why didn't that happen? And so on. But, if you look at a controlled scientific experiment, same thing is true. When somebody carries out a controlled scientific experiment at the best laboratories, at the end, there are lots of things that are unexplained. There are funny coincidences and this and that.[88]

If errant data refer to evidence that could disprove a theory, then fortuitous data represent evidence that supports the official story but is "too good to be true." This evidence may provide a reason for accepting conspiracy theories over official stories. An example is one of the 9/11 hijacker's passports recovered at the scene. Conspiracy theorists suggest the passport was planted because it is impossible that anything inside the plane could have survived the crash, never mind a paper document.[89] But such a standard creates an impasse: if we reject stories because evidence supports them, then we will never be able to support *any* story.

In brief, we believe that the impartial spectator test is a powerful tool—but one would expect to hear that coming from two PhDs. Experts undoubtedly play a significant role in the production, verification, and dissemination of knowledge, but there are abiding reasons why the power of experts is and should be circumscribed. First, the lines between expert/non-expert and partial/impartial are sometimes unclear. People are free to decide who is an impartial expert and who is not. Second, it is problematic what constitutes a decisive expert consensus, and, whatever the threshold is, consensuses of that size have been wrong in the past. As guides go, impartial experts are less fallible than most in their area of expertise, but they are nowhere near infallible and are subject to the same biases and temptations as everyone else. Still, it does not follow that if no one is perfectly impartial, then everyone is incorrigibly partisan. The best antidote to bad experts and questionable findings is better experts and fairer tests.

CONCLUSION

This chapter has defined terms and looked over several of the best tests for verifying the truth in conspiracy theories. We contend there are at least six standards for evaluating conspiracy theories:

Occam's Razor
Falsifiability
The Worst Intentions Test
The Cui Bono Test
The Eternal Recurrence of the Same Test
The Impartial Spectator Test

Conspiracy theories are like conventional theories on steroids; their features make them difficult to challenge. Yet this is no reason to shy away from them. Every test has shortcomings, and there is no agreed-upon standard to evaluate conspiracy theories. However, several tests *seriatim* offer a demanding gauntlet that the best ideas should run. Regardless, even the best assemblage of standards will have false positives and false negatives, and no theory can withstand the unblinking scrutiny of deeply skeptical minds. What separates the theoretical wheat from the chaff is how theories fare relative to each other.

Everyone has different needs, and we leave for the reader to decide which of the six standards he or she wishes to employ. Individuals may prefer less scrutiny on their infant ideas so those notions have a chance to grow up hale and hearty (and should then face a fuller battery of tests) or more scrutiny to toughen their ideas up. It is hard to give blanket advice on which route to travel, though we lean toward more demanding tests as a loose rule. Society depends on the innovations of outsiders and oddballs, and creativity is a notoriously nonlinear process. It is inarguable that some sloppy theories have led to felicitous outcomes. Americans have no desire to apologize to the British for the conspiracy theory that spurred the American Revolution, and Fourth of July celebrations are unbothered by what are, technically, some astonishing leaps in logic. But exceptions should not make the rules.

For ourselves, we like to think of the standards as judges, and, if a conspiracy theory cannot convince a majority sitting *en banc,* it should be found guilty until such time as new evidence exonerates it. But if people prefer their ideas to endure a smaller number of tests, they should say so plainly, justify their view, apply it consistently to their beliefs, and understand that they will not persuade more discerning audiences.

Over the long term, information, evidence, and logic matter. The story of our species has been one of constant discovery, new technology, and increasingly better information. Unfounded beliefs tend to go away over time. Better information chases out errant beliefs. Namely, few people rub butter on burns or believe Alfred Dreyfus treasonous. But in the short term and at the individual level, epistemology is only important at the margins. Like the composition of the Earth, rationality is a thin crust that sits with deceptive calm on a molten core of passions. With proper incentives, people will not overly concern themselves with the niceties of science. In later chapters we will build the case that conspiracy theorists are not primarily concerned with reflective judgment[90]—they are more interested in power, threat, and unity. Allegiances and worldviews come mainly from social-psychological processes, which are not the product of sweet reasonableness.[91]

Even if people tend to trample intellectually honest standards, it is not to say that they should do so or that standards serve no purpose. From this perspective, it makes sense that most of the people who care about epistemology are in the academy: they are the rare people protected from political forces. The academy is set up to shelter unpopular opinions and solitary seekers.

Before moving on to the chapters that describe, explain, and predict, we must pause and make a normative plea. Nothing can save humanity from errors, but an even-handed and open-minded evaluation of ideas could help minimize mistakes. Everyone inside debates would benefit from considering that he or she might be wrong; and everyone outside debates would benefit from the free and fair competition of ideas. Conspiracy theories are not a large fraction of theories, but they are a particularly thorny incarnation of theory, and the study of them yields wider lessons. The characteristics of conspiracy theories are unique when compared to those of other theories, but it is not so much the flexibility of the theories themselves that attracts adherents. It is the substance that entices us all sooner or later. Chapter 3 is where we begin our search to understand why.

Where Our Facts Come From

History is much more the product of chaos than of conspiracy.

—Zbigniew Brzezinski[1]

When they get a new gadget, some people like to sit down and read the owner's manual. Most people, however, prefer to plug it in and start playing. This chapter is for the owner's manual kind of people. Before many of you skip ahead to the chapters that address substantive questions, though, it may be worth your while to see if reading the manual first might spare you some problems.

The most compelling reason to read this chapter is that data drive the reliability of arguments. How would we know if Brzezinski's epigram was correct? Maybe history is the product of conspiracy. Without a good sense of the strengths and weaknesses of various data sources, it is not clear how robust claims and findings are.

Unquestionably there have been lots of studies on conspiracy theories that have advanced our understanding. Yet there are serious drawbacks to depending solely on existing approaches. Sociologists have done a penetrating job understanding the culture of particular varieties of conspiracy theorists, but they have been less helpful in capturing a full spectrum of conspiracy theories in the same frame. Historians have immersed themselves in the details of conspiracy theorists, but they privilege the specific over the general and are not entirely clear about their causal models and case selection criteria. Political scientists have been adept at public opinion polling, but these polls have focused on the largest conspiracy theories—and then only intermittently. All told, there is a need for long-term, nationally representative data that measure conspiratorial views and the characteristics of the people who hold them.

To fill gaps in our understanding, we provide three original data sources that shed light on unexplored aspects of the subject. The first is an opinion survey, which is the most powerful tool to access people's beliefs and thoughts. Using a battery of questions, we uncover what conspiracy theorists have in common, how they differ from others, and how they think and behave politically, socially, and economically. The second is a sample from 121 years of letters to the editor of the *New York Times* and the *Chicago Tribune*—more than 100,000 in total. This affords the only consistent public record of conspiracy talk over a century and allows us to gauge the overall level of conspiracy theorizing and which conspiracy theories are most popular at any given time. The third is 3,000 articles and posts from Internet blogs and news outlets. The benefits of this data source are that it highlights the information environment and permits some educated guesses about how conspiracy theories are discussed in the Internet age.

To do its job, this chapter/manual is set up for ease of operation and concision. We go from data source to data source cataloging what they are, how we collected them, and the advantages and disadvantages of each—with some entertaining examples thrown in to sweeten the deal. First is polling, then letters to the editor, and finally Internet data. The conclusion sums up the foregoing and touches on the frontiers of the field. Navigate as you see fit.

POLLING

In surveys, researchers ask respondents questions designed to elicit their beliefs, predispositions, and characteristics. Unfortunately, there is a disadvantage to the use of existing survey data. First, polls have only been employed since the 1940s. So even if relevant questions had been asked consistently (which they were not), the polls would only do justice to the period following World War II. Questions on specific conspiracy theories have been sporadic and questions on conspiracy theorizing in general have been exceptionally rare. As occasional and somewhat unpredictable snapshots, extant data work well. As a regular measure of change over time, however, they work less well: there is no reason to think that fluctuation in the belief in any one conspiracy theory is an accurate bellwether for conspiracy theorizing writ large—any more than the stock price of General Motors is a prime indicator of the stock market.

To alleviate these problems, we commissioned our own national poll. Drawing from past literature, we designed several questions that tapped underlying conspiratorial predispositions. We also developed new questions to draw out particular conspiratorial beliefs.[2] To check for correlations, we also asked questions about basic demographics, partisanship, political ideology and behavior, social conduct, and economic activity. The survey was administered over the Internet to a nationally representative sample of 1,230 Americans.[3] This was part of a larger survey, the 2012 Cooperative Congressional Election Survey (CCES), based at Harvard University. Because this was an Internet survey, all respondents had to be Internet users, so the survey gives little leverage on how Internet use affects conspiratorial beliefs.[4]

LETTERS TO THE EDITOR

For centuries people have put pen to paper to send letters to newspapers. These letters form a public sphere in which citizens communicate on the issues of the day.[5] For slightly less long, analysts have scrutinized letters to the editor as a way to better understand public opinion. What people care enough to write about—and what editors think people care enough to read—reveals part of a community's beliefs.

Although some studies show that letters to the editor correlate well with survey measures of public opinion, we are after something slightly different.[6] Polls seek private opinions, but letters to the editor provide purchase on opinions in the public sphere.[7] Letters to the editor are for public consumption. Deciding to write a letter and deciding to publish it indicate that the ideas expressed in the letter are worth writing about and worth sharing widely. Hence, letters to the editor are an unbeatable source for measuring the resonance of conspiracy theories over a long period of time.[8] For this reason they are a mainstay of our project and deserve extended treatment.

Collecting and Collected Letters

How did we go about this process and what did we find? Our target was a sample of 1,000 letters from the *New York Times* for each year from 1890 to 2010, stratified by month for more even sampling.[9] Altogether we coded a total of 104,823 letters over a period of 121 years.[10] We picked the *New York Times* because it boasts one of the largest circulations historically and at present, is often referred to as America's "paper of record," and is a staple of academic study.[11]

It would be reasonable to object that the *New York Times* has ideological prejudices and does not speak to the hinterland. Newspapers, like all media outlets, emphasize different stories and have differing slants.[12] This could spring from the mode of ownership, the style of ownership, the editorship and news-making bureaucracy, the journalists, or the demands of a specific market.[13] To obviate these concerns, we constructed a validating sample from the equally old *Chicago Tribune*. Where the *Times* is caricatured as liberal, elitist, and coastal, the *Tribune* is caricatured as conservative, blue-collar, and heartland. In fact, the *Tribune* sample mirrored the *Times* sample both in terms of the relative amount of conspiracy talk and in the distribution of various types of conspiracy talk.[14] Moreover, we employed statistical models that account for the *Times'* changing ownership, editorship, circulation, and competition and found that these factors did not affect the data.[15] On balance, the *New York Times* is a solid source of national attitudes.

We (and by that we mean ourselves and a phalanx of stalwart research assistants) used content analysis to manually code the sampled letters. Content analysis is a process by which researchers place text into categories. The objective was to select out letters about conspiracy theories from the sample. Research assistants were trained in what counted as a conspiracy theory letter, and they read every letter. To check for consistency, we made sure that many of the letters were read multiple times.[16] The set of rules used to place each letter into a category, known as the scheme (pun unintended), asked coders to examine each letter on two basic dimensions.

The initial dimension was whether the author was an elite. We define "elites" as any person who currently or in the past (a) held high governmental office, (b) served as an executive or spokesperson for a large corporate body, (c) was a member of the news or entertainment media, and (d) was a member of a foreign government. Not known for their bashfulness, elites were easy to spot in the wild given their tendency to include their title in the body or signature of the letter.

The next dimension was whether the author engaged in conspiracy talk or not. These letters either proffered or discounted a conspiracy theory.[17] For a letter to be coded as engaging in conspiracy talk, the letter had to include all four elements found in standard definitions of conspiracy theory: (1) a group (2) acting in secret (3) to alter institutions, usurp power, hide truth, or gain utility (4) at the expense of the common good.[18] These four conditions are restrictive enough to omit sharp critique and heated political rhetoric but permissive enough to capture a wide range of conspiratorial allegations. Our coding scheme therefore has the benefit of netting a sampling of both the big and little fish of conspiracy theories.

In total, our coders identified 875 letters engaging in conspiracy talk. Of these, 240 were from elites and 635 from non-elites.[19] It is striking that less than a thousand out of a hundred thousand letters discussed conspiracy theories, but then it probably should not be.[20] Editorial pages are open to almost any subject. People write letters to discuss cooking, comedy, music, traffic, science, entertainment, and gardening. Any particular topic or set of topics is likely to garner only a small percentage of published letters. Of the letters that discussed conspiracy theories, the roster of conspiracies is lengthy. Table 3.1 provides a partial list of conspiracy theories discovered in our sample.

Table 3-1. SAMPLE OF CONSPIRATORIAL PLOTS

1890s–1920s

1890	England and Canada conspiring to take back territory in the United States
1890	Unnamed group purchased the election for Harrison
1892	Republicans who conspired to fix 1888 election now conspire to alter outcome of 1892 elections, knowing they will not be able to control Cleveland
1892	Tammany secretly manipulating the nomination process to ensure its unnamed candidate will be nominated
1894	Roman Catholics seek to control American government through authority of Rome
1895	Rulers of the Mormon church rig elections in favor of Republicans
1900	Populists plotting in secret to erode and wreck financial institutions
1903	Corporations manipulate local elections on behalf of the Republican Party, which they control
1906	Japan sending disguised soldiers to Hawaii in advance of a plan to seize the island
1908	Fires intentionally set so that firefighters could receive financial incentives
1917	Sheep protective bill passed with intention of killing off all domestic dogs
1918	Radicals/socialists/Bolsheviks seek to overtake/mislead American people and destroy U.S. government and create class struggle
1922	U.S. financiers brought about WWI for own financial interests

continued

Table 3-1. (CONTINUED)

1925	KKK conspires to control the entire lawmaking/enforcing branch of state/federal government
1927	Small boards and secret groups within the government are hampering democracy and discussing advantages of benevolent dictator
1930s–1950s	
1934	American Communists and Russian government plot to overthrow U.S. government and social order
1935	Communists have infiltrated Washington and are trying to establish a new social order called "State-Capitalism"
1936	Organization trying to destroy U.S. government and replace with fascist leaders
1936	Roosevelt administration betrays United States and is a communist
1937	WPA using children's play to spread Russian communist propaganda
1942	CBS radio misinforms public about war to increase bond sales
1947	Communists assaulting any citizen who discloses information about the Moscow conspiracy against the United States
1950	President Truman and Democrats protect communists in government by not investigating them, with the excuse that investigating them aids Russia
1950	American communist movement is a conspiracy to deliver the American nation into the hands of Soviet Russia under a system of world communism
1951	American writers and officials caused communist triumph in China and communists are running U.S. government
1954	Roosevelt/Truman covered up extent of communist infiltration into federal government
1956	The Communist Party in the United States is a conspiracy for the seizure and retention of power in the name of a class dictatorship and organized treason on behalf of Russia
1958	American scientists trying to find method for controlling the weather to take over enemy territory
1960s–1980s	
1963	Elections are fraudulent and under control of local dominant party, where dead people still vote

Table 3-1. (CONTINUED)

1963	U.S. government suppressing truth of Vietnam war/violations of Geneva agreements to protect economic interests in that region
1968	John Wayne movie "Green Berets" is a government-funded propaganda tool used to promote anti-communism
1969	American psychiatric establishment perpetuating male supremacy by brainwashing women who seek careers rather than motherhood into believing themselves neurotic
1971	Conservationists engaged in a conspiracy to increase world hunger
1973	Lesbianism is a CIA-inspired plot
1975	The Watergate affair was a politically inspired vendetta by the arrogant and unethical liberal media to destroy the Republican Party and discredit Nixon
1976	Lawyers and judges provide light sentences for crime to encourage crime so they can have more work
1978	Catholics for Christian Political Action are trying to "take over the world"
1980	The Abscam trials are an FBI scheme to inflict terror on Congress in order to pass the FBI Charter Act of 1979 to legitimize illegality
1981	The government designed Social Security to hurt the poor while the rich are given the benefits
1984	A global conspiracy against the U.S. dollar causes it to be abnormally strong
1986	CIA influencing public opinion through propaganda in government-financed books
1988	West Germany and Japan attempting to influence U.S. elections by raising the value of the dollar
1990s–2010	
1991	President Taylor did not die of natural causes; he was assassinated by the Capitol physician
1994	Mayor Giuliani's program to reform tort laws against New York is a hidden agenda to abolish trial by jury and eliminate civil damage suits
1997	Christian Coalition trying to take over Republican Party with political agenda to enshrine one religion and impose it on all; goal is to Christianize America
2001	Government is controlled by corporate masters who fixed elections to put administration in office

continued

Table 3-1. (CONTINUED)

2002	9/11 attacks were an American conspiracy to smear the Saudis
2005	Medicare and HMOs have conspired to prevent doctors from making a profit
2008	Obama is a Muslim with plans to undermine America as a political strategy
2010	Republicans attempting to increase unemployment and foreclosures to win back Congress

Our method furnishes the first representative sample of conspirato-rial beliefs. Some of the conspiracy theories in Table 3.1 have a familiar ring to them—plutocratic and socialist subversion standing out as hoary leitmotifs. And mirror-image conspiracy theories make their requisite appearance, too. Watergate was not a conspiracy perpetrated *by* Richard Nixon, it was a conspiracy perpetrated by the liberal media and trial law-yers *against* Richard Nixon.

Arguably, though, what is most stunning about Table 3.1 is how common the ostensibly uncommon conspiracy theories are. Little atten-tion has been paid to fears that scientists use weather control to conquer territory or firefighters set blazes for profit. Congress, it seems, did not pass a bill to protect sheep; it was really an underhanded bid to slaughter the nation's pet dogs. The reading is racy and sundry: foreign invasion, electoral fraud, religious tyranny, brainwashing, propaganda, murder, and intrigue.

Simply in list format, much becomes visible. However, we must break the information down to fairly compare it. Like faces and snowflakes, every conspiracy theory is unique, yet it would be foolish to claim there are no general concepts that are commensurable. By definition, all con-spiracy theories posit a knave out to subvert the common weal. The victim remains the same stock character (the innocent public), but it is the moustache-twirling mountebanks that seem to cycle through in great multiplicity. This is where the plot thickens.

Table 3.2 furnishes a selection of those accused of conspiring. Again, the breadth of those accused is staggering, far beyond the well-known

Table 3-2. SAMPLE OF CONSPIRATORS

Adolf Hitler	Cigar manufacturers	General Electric
African National Congress	City employees	General Motors
Agricultural Adjustment Administration	Clinton administration	Gerald Ford
Allies	Colleges	Germany
American Psychiatrists Association	Colonel Charles Lindbergh	Gandhi
American scientists	Columbia	Global conspirators
Amusement parks	Conservationists	Great Britain/England
Anti-Communists	Construction workers	Greece
Anti-Islamics	Croatian extremists	Guatemala
Anti-Saccharin men	Cuba	Harry Truman
Anti-Saloon League	Czechoslovakia	Health industry
Anti-war movement	Dairy producers	Herbert Hoover
Arab countries	Defense contractors	Hollywood
Argentina	Democrats	Ice companies
Austria	Domestic anarchists	Immigration and Naturalization Service
Banks	Domestic communists	India
Beef companies	Domestic Germans	Indonesia
Belgium	Domestic Hungarians	Institute of Pacific Relations
Belligerents	Domestic Nazis	International bourgeoisie
Big wealthy corporations	Dow Chemical	International Labor Defense
Black Panthers	Drug Enforcement Administration	Iran
Boers	East Germany	Iraqi government
Bootleggers	Egypt	Ireland
Bosnian government	Ethiopia	Isolationists
Boston Federal Reserve Bank	Europe	Israel

continued

Table 3-2. (CONTINUED)

Brazilian political parties	Evangelicals	Italy
Bulgarian government	Evil hands	Japanese
Bulgarian revolutionaries	Extreme Right	Jews/Zionists
Bush Jr. administration	Farm Board	Judiciary
Bush Sr. administration	Fascists	KGB
Canadian miners	FBI	KKK
Capitol physician	FDIC	Labor leaders
Catholic Benevolent Legion	Fifth columns	Landlords
Catholics for Christian Political Action	Finland	Latvian consul
Cereal industry	Firefighters	Lawyers
Childcare industry	Foreign anarchists	Leon Trotsky
Chile	Foreign communists	Liberal media
China	Fox News	Liberia
Christian Coalition	France	Life insurance companies
Christian scientists	Franklin Roosevelt	Lithuanians
Christian terrorists	Freemasons	Local government
Christians	Fruit suppliers	Lord's Day Alliance
CIA	Gangs	Lutheran newspapers
Macedonia	Politicians	Steel industry
Magyar Press	Populists	Subversive agents
Male publishers	Post office	Sudanese officials
Media	Potato companies	Suffragists
Medicare	Power brokers	Sugar growers
Methodists	Power companies	Sweden
Mexico	President Carter	Tammany Hall
Military juntas	President McKinley	Teachers
Milk committee	President of Egypt	Terrorists
Money interests	President T. Roosevelt	Textbook publishers
Mormon church	Prime Minister of Hungary	Tunisia
Muslim rebels	Prime Minister of Malta	Turks

Table 3-2. (CONTINUED)

Muslims	Pro-life supporters	Ukraine
Mussolini	Protectionists	Unions
Napoleon	Puerto Rico	United Nations
National Rifle Association	Radicals	United Parents Association
National Security Agency	Railroad companies	United Service Organization
Nazis	Reagan administration	Unknown assassins
Neo-Nazi groups	Republicans	U.S. Congress
Neville Chamberlain	Rich people	U.S. Dept. of Agriculture
New Deal programs	Roman Catholics	U.S. Dept. of Education
Nicaraguan dictatorship	Romania	U.S. Dept. of Health
Nihilists	ROTC	U.S. Dept. of Justice
Nixon administration	Rubber merchants	U.S. Dept. of State
Non-Nazi Germans	Russia	U.S. Forest Service
New York Times	San Francisco	U.S. Government
Obama administration	Saudi Arabia	U.S. Military
Oil companies	Savings and loan industry	U.S. Supreme Court
Otto Von Bismarck	School board	USSR
Pacifica Foundation	Secret groups	Wall Street gamblers
Pakistan	Secretary Garfield	Walt Disney Company
Palestine	Secretary of War	Washington bureaucrats
Pacifists	Senate Printing Office	Weapons makers
Pentagon	Serbia	West Germany
Persian ministers	Shipping companies	Wilson administration
Peru	Silver interests	Wolfgang A. Mozart
Filipino friars	Socialists	World Health Organization
Phone companies	South Africa	Writers
Plumbers	Spain	Young Americans for Freedom
Poland	Special interest groups	Yugoslavia
Police	Stalin	Zionist villagers

examples. Foreign villains come from all over the globe. Domestic villains hail from nearly every region, religion, and group. Clearly conspiracy theories are equal opportunity and cosmopolitan. Indeed, the data suggest that everyone plays the antagonist eventually. Everybody is in on it! Even gentle, genial sorts, like professors, pacifists, actors, and Jimmy Carter.

With so many villains running around, it is useful to categorize conspiracy talk based on who plays the antagonist, when, and how often.[21] We classified villains into eight major categories: political actors on the right, political actors on the left, capitalists, communists, government institutions, media, foreign actors, and other.[22] Such distinctions capture political (left/right) and economic (communist/capitalist) cleavages, as well as institutional (government/media) dimensions.

These rubrics dovetail with salient and enduring groups in American society and previous research showing which groups are suspicious of which. For instance, those on the right are suspicious of the left and communists, while those on the left are suspicious of the right and capitalists. Both the left and right are suspicious of government, the mass media, and foreign actors.[23] To illustrate the eight categories, Table 3.3 provides synopses of some conspiracy theories within each.

In our categorization, actors on the right include domestic right-wing political parties, members of those parties, and other right-wing groups. Falling under this heading are Theodore Roosevelt, Republicans, the radical right, Young Americans for Freedom, and the Christian Coalition. Actors on the left include domestic left-wing political parties, members of those parties, and other left-wing groups. Specific examples include Franklin Roosevelt, Democrats, William Jennings Bryan, New Deal Administrators, liberals, and unions.

The capitalist category includes large for-profit corporations and the wealthy. Specific embodiments are banks, financial institutions, defense contractors, oil companies, food producers, insurance companies, the Walt Disney Corporation, and "corporate masters." The communist category picks up domestic communists and socialists.[24] Exemplars here are professors (present company excluded, of course), "subversives," anti-war demonstrators, writers, and the American communist movement.

Table 3.3 SAMPLE OF CONSPIRATORIAL PLOTS BY CATEGORY

Left	Right	Communist	Capitalist	Government	Media	Foreign	Other
- President Roosevelt trying to convert the U.S.A. to communism (1934)	- Republicans using beet sugar industry as front for annexing Cuba (1902)	- Socialists infiltrated public schools to spread propaganda (1919)	- Major oil companies are running a conspiracy to get Congress to deregulate gas by artificially constraining gas supplies (1975)	- Fires intentionally set so that firefighters get financial incentives (1908)	- Newspapers suppress media stories for their own benefit (1938)	- French government working with socialists to destroy Catholic church (1906)	- Catholic Church using members to control global politics (1929)
- President Roosevelt trying to become a dictator (1937)	- President Roosevelt manipulating elections with bribes (1904)	- Child Labor Amendment is a plan for communists to control U.S.A. school system (1924)	- Corporations such as Lockheed use the media to conceal their crimes (1976)	- Elections are fraudulent and under the control of the local dominant party (1963)	- The *New York Times* wants to impose a totalitarian regime (1940)	- France secretly conspiring to conquer the rest of Europe (1932)	- American Medical Association has totalitarian ties (1945)
- Liberals conspire to bring about Soviet dictatorship in U.S.A. (1949)	- Herbert Hoover made secret business deals to bankrupt the U.S.A. (1924)	- Professors brainwashing college students with communism (1936)	- Childcare industry control government policy, hurting thousands of children while feeding fairy tales to the public (1979)	- Lesbianism is a CIA-inspired plot (1973)	- NBC is broadcasting shows that cause tension between the East and West to prevent agreement on ending nuclear tests (1959)	- UN is a terrorist organization that aims at world imperialism (1977)	- Former Nazis are taking over civil service and threatening witnesses to prevent indictment of Nazi criminals (1949)
- Northern liberal politicians attempting to gain control of the South and destroy America from within (1957)	- Extreme right is institutionalized in government and corporations; it is funding anti-democratic organizations (1962)	- WPA is using a children's play to spread communism (1937)	- Wealthy are growing babies on farms for organ transplants (1992)	- Prosecutors, lawyers, judges impose light sentences for crimes knowing that it will encourage crime so they can have more work (1976)	- *Conservative Digest* publisher is using communist hysteria to hide racist support for apartheid (1985)	- West Germany and Japan manipulating currency to influence U.S.A. elections (1988)	- Catholics conspiring to "take over the world" (1978)
- President Carter is an agent for the Soviet Union (1978)	- Radical right seeks to remove civil liberties and repeal Bill of Rights (1980)	- Mozart's music is socialistic, with intent to lead youths into battle (1941)	- Government is controlled by corporate masters who fix elections (2001)	- Government wants to finance mandatory registration, which is a plot to draft soldiers, which will lead to nuclear war (1980)	- Press working with government officials on disinformation campaign (2005)	- Japanese are waging economic warfare against the U.S.A.—they caused the 1987 stock market crash to test their strength (1989)	- Freemasonry is an international conspiracy (1981)
- Obama is a Muslim with plans to undermine America (2008)	- Young Americans for Freedom are hidden fascists who plan to take over government (1981)	- Communists have brainwashed Americans to withdraw from South Vietnam (1967)					- Polio vaccine is an anti-Muslim plot to spread autism in Africa (2007)

The government category includes institutions at all levels that are not affiliated with, or accused of acting at the behest of, an actor on the left or the right.[25] Our sample includes institutions such as the CIA, FBI, police, post office, and military. The media category includes media institutions, like the *New York Times*, John Wayne movies, public relations firms, and the radio commission. If the media were accused of working for either the right or the left, then they are coded as right or left.

The foreign category refers to foreign states and actors.[26] This category includes countries and subnational groups from every region on the globe, plus the United Nations and other international organizations. Finally, we call the remaining catchall category "other." It comprises hard-to-classify groups, which are less overtly political, economic, or ideological. These include scientists, the American Medical Association, Jews, Christian terrorists, Italian Catholics, and the Mexican Catholic Church.

The Letters Ledger

The chief advantage of letters to the editor is their longevity. American newspapers have carried letters to the editor sections for nearly 300 years; no other data source offers such leverage on conspiratorial beliefs over such a long time. They also offer an unparalleled window into the national resonance of conspiracy theories in general and particular. Nevertheless, letters to the editor must be handled with care: there are potential sources of distortion in the writing and selection of letters, and there are potential sources of bias in the structure of the marketplace of ideas.

First, unlike surveys, which randomly sample people to represent the broader population, letters to the editor are not random. Two factors may skew letters to the editor: who writes them and who edits them. To begin with, writing a letter to a newspaper requires time, talent, and passion, which many people lack. Letter writers as a whole might be exceptional within the population and therefore may have exceptional opinions.[27]

Surprisingly, previous research demonstrates that if the opinions of letter writers and non-letter writers differ at all, those differences are small.[28] As Sidney Verba and his colleagues conclude in their study of letters to the editor: "basically letter writers are not different from non-letter writers" and "they are no more likely to take extreme positions than the rest of the public."[29] Other studies have found that published letters hew quite closely to public opinion.[30] How can this be? The answer, paradoxically, comes from another potential source of contamination.

Editors arbitrate which letters get published, and this could slant the sample. One way this could happen is that editors weed out letters they think are written by cranks. Conspiracy theories may appear extreme and get excluded from the public sphere for this reason. However, excluding fringe opinions from open deliberation violates editorial norms. As Thomas Feyer, Letters Editor of the *New York Times*, avows: "no subject is off limits, within the bounds of good taste."[31] Laudably, Feyer and his predecessors practice what they preach. For such a stately mainstream paper, the *Times* is admirably welcoming of offbeat perspectives. We came across a writer who claimed to have personal relationships with leaders from other planets, another thoughtfully debated the racial demographics of alien abductees, and, wherever else he may have been sighted, Bigfoot has made many appearances in the *Times*.

Yet another potential source of bias is that editors may disproportionately print letters addressing stories reported in the news sections. This would help reinforce the audience's interest in particular stories and maybe sell more papers. However, editors acknowledge that the letters column is a place for free speech and not just a place to discuss items in the newspaper.[32] A final potential source of bias is editorial taste or ideology. Evidence for this objection is wanting as well. Scholarship shows that regardless of a paper's official editorial position, editors allow dissenting opinions to be heard, and that the viewpoints in published letters are little different from the viewpoints in non-published letters.[33]

The upshot of the available research is that "little support is found for the hypothesis that newspaper policies bias letter opinion."[34] If topics resonate in society, editors have a stake in providing a platform to their advocates in the letters section. This is not merely a principled position to uphold deliberative democratic norms: giving the public a mouthpiece to speak to galvanizing issues is good for business. Even were there slight bias in letters to the editor—and all sources of data have some bias—it is unlikely to vary systematically over time. With a large sample over a long duration, the data are likely to be an accurate measure of change over time.

Second, the marketplace of ideas has changed a lot in the last century. These changes involve the segmentation and consolidation of markets, on top of the introduction of radio and television. Recently, many have claimed that the Internet is a magnet for conspiracy theories.[35] This could mean that the overall level of conspiracy theories is spiraling up as more people use the Internet more often; or it could mean that the Internet is crowding out other media as the forum for conspiracy theorizing. Using letters to the editor, then, may miss a great deal of the prevalent conspiracy theories and underestimate the amount of conspiracy theorizing after the introduction of the Internet. These worries are overdrawn.

All topics of discussion have found a home on other media—politics, sex, sports, cars, home improvement, etc. If topics migrated away from newspaper letters to the editor to other media, then newspaper letters sections would have died long ago. New media technologies largely replicate the issues in newspapers, just like the innovations in e-books have not much changed the content of books. And empirically, the introduction of previous communication technologies has not had much of an impact on conspiracy talk across time. As we will see in Chapter 5, there is no decline in conspiracy theorizing in our measure coinciding with the increased usage of the Internet or other media sources.

In brief, the disadvantages of letters to the editor are potential prejudices in authors and editors and changes in the marketplace of ideas. These are worrisome but not paralyzing. The private bias in authors is corrected by a public bias in editors. Changes in the marketplace of ideas has no doubt made some impacts on newspapers, but making letters to the editor significantly different than they were in the past is not likely to be among them. Despite the possible flaws, letters to the editor offer the best available hold on a slippery subject like conspiracy theories.

INTERNET DATA

Our final source of data comes from content analysis of the Internet. The Internet has provided fertile territory for a warren of websites on conspiracy theories. People post about them on blogs, personal pages, public forums, and more. Some credit the Internet for ushering conspiracy theorizing into a new era but others suggest that the Internet has not been so kind to conspiracy theories.[36] A prerequisite is to draw on sturdy samples of traffic in cyberspace.

We harnessed Google Alerts to collect Internet news posts containing the term "conspiracy theory." While not all stories featuring conspiracy theories will use this term, this sample tracks how the information environment treats logic that is expressly conspiratorial. From July 2012 through July 2013 that amounted to about 3,000 items—about ten a day. Like the letters to the editor data, the content of these articles was analyzed by coders. Again, content analysis is a process by which coders categorize text within a scheme. Yet unlike the letters data, the coding focused more on the treatment of the conspiracy theory than on the inherent details of the conspiracy theory. The scheme coded posts based on the tone the author applied to it: was the author friendly, neutral, or hostile to the conspiracy theory in question?[37] This coding speaks directly to the role that the Internet plays in fostering or deterring conspiratorial beliefs as well as addressing the information environment.[38]

The news items and blog posts captured in our sample focused on conspiracy theories such as those surrounding the Boston Marathon bombing, the resurrected TWA Flight 800, Egypt's political turmoil, and communism. But there are many minor conspiracy theories that are mentioned as well: the LGBT movement is trying to turn America gay, schools are teaching jihad, sports are rigged, and, most disturbingly, *American Idol* is not what it seems.

In addition to the larger Internet data collection effort, we also examined Internet traffic patterns and social media discussion. The upside of the Internet data is that they are contemporary, they are relevant to policy, and they provide purchase on the overall tone of today's conspiracy talk. However, the downside is the short time span. Since the Internet has only been in widespread use since the late 1990s, even the best Internet data open only a small window.

CONCLUSION

The study of conspiracy theories has been hampered by a lack of long-term systematic data.[39] The data collection efforts detailed above are the first attempt to rectify this gap in the literature. We rely primarily on three original data sources: a national survey, letters to the editor, and an Internet sample. Each set of data clarifies different facets of conspiracy theorizing, but each has its drawbacks. Polling reveals opinions well, but the available data lack historical reach. Letters to the editor have colossal coverage across time but are a somewhat crude indicator. The Internet data capture the tone of conspiracy discussions adroitly, but they do not pick up on more granular preferences or offer longstanding analytical traction. We contend that combining all three offers a layered defense against the baffling complexities of conspiracy theories.

The data collection labors in this project were exhausting, but no one should be under any illusion that they are exhaustive. With automatic text readers, the dawn of Big Data, and innovations just coming onto our radar screens, the next wave of conspiracy theory researchers will use tools that look like dynamite and bulldozers compared to our picks and shovels. That is the spirit of science, and we are excited to see how the frontiers of knowledge extend in our lifetimes. Still, antiquated as we will soon look, we make a plea to our successors for multi-method, coauthored, interdisciplinary scholarship. No field has a monopoly on wisdom, no tool is the master key, and no individual can match a good team.

Who Are the Conspiracy Theorists?

America is a vast conspiracy to make you happy.

—John Updike[1]

For all the attention lavished on conspiracy theories in the media, we know precious little about conspiracy theorists. Forced to conjure up an image of one in our mind's eye, we might settle on an unwashed, middle-aged white male, fiddling with a police scanner in a cramped garage. But if we had to answer some elementary anthropological questions about them—their preferences, their social habits, how they differ from non-conspiracy buffs—we could do little but hazard guesses. Updike might be on to something; the country could be a vast expanse of natural-born conspiracy theorists.

This chapter chips away at the mystery by employing a 2012 nationally representative Internet survey. The questions expose underlying conspiratorial predispositions and beliefs about who is conspiring against whom. In addition, the survey allows us to correlate specific beliefs and general predispositions with demographic data, political opinions, and self-reported behaviors. We warn that our survey is cross-sectional, and this does not do justice to the effects of long-term factors. But it does provide excellent coverage at the individual level, and Chapters 5 and 6 backstop the survey data with long-term perspectives.

We develop two central points. First, there is an ideological belief system that determines how likely a person is to see conspiracies and believe in conspiracy theories. This belief system, the conspiracy dimension, exists on a separate plane from political ideology and partisanship.[2] Second, conspiracy theorists are systematically different. Polling data reveal the kinds of differences and the degree of difference in beliefs and behaviors. There is an underappreciated collection of traits conspiracy theorists share, which gives them a familial resemblance.

To develop these points, the chapter devotes a section to each. The first section is largely conceptual and explains conspiratorial predispositions as an autonomous factor in politics. It establishes the importance of these predispositions and how people who score high on the conspiracy dimension differ from others. The second section is largely descriptive and details the demographics, beliefs, and behaviors of the conspiratorially inclined.

THE CONSPIRACY DIMENSION

In the early twentieth century, political science, or government as it was called then, tended to focus on institutions. When scholars conceptualized voting and political activity, they thought of them as existing apart from people's predispositions and opinions. Institutionalized actions came first and then came personal affiliation. If a person voted for a Democrat, then that person must be a Democrat. Psychology was a young field; it had yet to fully pollinate with politics.

This changed in the 1950s with the advent of the behavioral revolution. Scholars began to look at social backgrounds and psychological processes. The basic model is that social psychological processes lead to partisanship and ideology, and these lead to more specific beliefs and actions. Now scholars consider people Republicans if they self-identify with, or have a sense of belonging to, the Republican Party, rather than if they are registered as Republicans or voted for one.[3]

These larger beliefs systems—partisanship and ideology—are the biggest drivers of other political opinions and behaviors. Consider the public's perception of the restaurant chain Godfather's Pizza. When Republican Herman Cain ran for president in 2011–12, his successful tenure as CEO of Godfather's became a campaign talking point. Before the campaign began, Republicans and Democrats viewed the chain equally on YouGov's BrandIndex score, which measures public opinion toward brand names.[4] As Democrats and Republicans learned of his involvement with the pizza chain, opinions of Godfather's began to polarize: Democrats adopted a negative view of the chain while Republicans became more positive. By the end of 2011, Republicans and Democrats differed by 25 points (on a scale ranging –100 to 100) in their view of the pizza chain.

The same is true of opinions addressing the independent and nonpartisan Federal Reserve. During the Bush Administration, Gallup polls showed that 61 percent of Republicans had confidence in Reserve Chairman Ben Bernanke while only 40 percent of Democrats did. A year later when Obama took office, these numbers flipped: 64 percent of Democrats claimed to be confident in Bernanke while only 36 percent of Republicans did. Given the non-partisan nature of the fed and Godfather's, the only reason for attitudes to polarize along party lines is because of the effect that partisanship has in shaping other beliefs.[5] The basic point is that new events and information are interpreted in light of larger preexisting partisan and ideological views so that if we know a person's partisanship and ideology, we can better predict many of his or her other opinions.[6]

So, too, with conspiratorial beliefs: social psychological processes (socialization) lead to conspiratorial predispositions. The strength of these predispositions then leads people, more or less, to specific conspiratorial

beliefs, and perhaps actions. Given that beliefs in specific conspiracy theories are a result of underlying predispositions, we argue that researchers
have placed too much emphasis on beliefs in specific conspiracy theories
and ignored the underlying predispositions that drive those beliefs. This
would be akin to studying opinions toward President Obama and his 2012
rival Mitt Romney without accounting for partisanship. The important
point is that conspiracy theorists can be studied like anybody else, and
conspiratorial opinions should be studied like other opinions.

Ideally, we would explore how socialization translates into conspiratorial thought and action. But that would take decades of repeated panel
studies and deeper pockets than we have. Of necessity, our sketch must be
partial, and it starts with existing predispositions.

Setting a Baseline

How common are conspiratorial beliefs? To get a rough sense, we asked
how much respondents agreed or disagreed with some statements. The
media, a much-derided and distrusted American institution, seemed like
a fine point of departure. Respondents were asked: "Much of the news
we get from mainstream news sources is deliberately slanted to mislead
us." A majority of Americans (51 percent) agree, and a scant 17 percent
disagree (Fig. 4.1).

Most Americans are skeptical about the media. In a minimal sense
then, conspiratorial beliefs are run of the mill. Yet as the details get more
specific and radical, belief in the conspiracy theory falls off drastically.
When asked immediately prior to the 2012 election: "Some people currently have the fear that the elections will be cancelled. How likely do you
think this is?" only 6 percent said very or somewhat likely. Eighty-seven
percent bet correctly that the elections would be held (Fig. 4.2).

So conspiratorial beliefs are prevalent but bounded. As conspiracy
theories become more extreme in their accusations and less tethered to
evidence, they tend to have fewer adherents. We often hear reports of
doomsayers and apocalyptic visionaries, but such figures are exceptions.

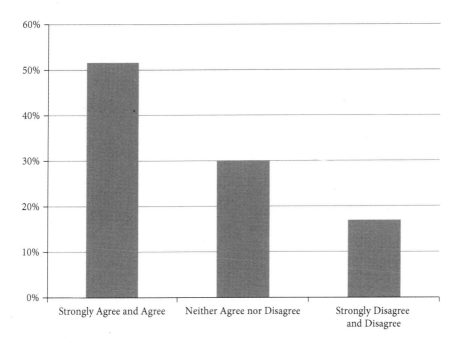

Figure 4.1 Is News Deliberately Slanted?

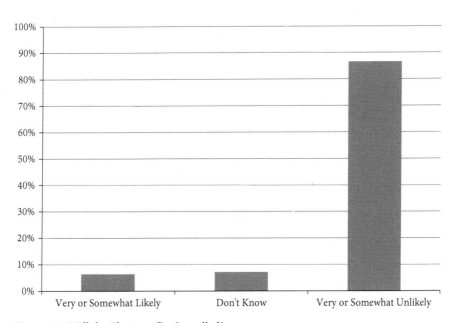

Figure 4.2 Will the Elections Be Cancelled?

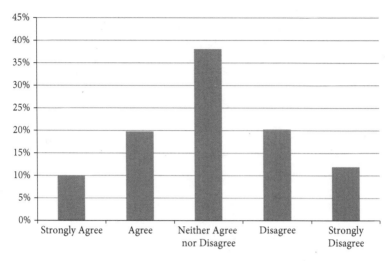

Figure 4.3 Do Secret Groups Control Events?

Another statement about the role of conspiracies in world events high-lights this: "Big events like wars, the current recession, and the outcomes of elections are controlled by small groups of people who are working in secret against the rest of us." We find a normal curve (Fig. 4.3). Thirty percent agree with the statement, 30 percent disagree. A plurality in the middle, 38 percent, neither agrees nor disagrees.

Keep in mind that conspiratorial predispositions are like height: some people have a lot, some have a little, but few are in the extremes. It is prob-ably for their rarity that the high end is so memorable, yet the exotic is not a fair frame of reference. Most of the analyses contained in this chapter speak to predispositions and beliefs that are shared by large swaths of the public.

Zooming in on Conspiracy Theorists

Given previous polling data, we suspect that everyone believes in at least one conspiracy theory, and most people believe in several. So everyone is a conspiracy theorist at least some of the time, and the term should not have a negative connotation. We do not intend to suggest that those who are more prone to conspiracy theories are right or wrong. Because our goal is to examine widely held beliefs and behaviors, we do not separate people who invent, improve, impart, or embrace conspiracy theories from each other. In this chapter, we make our definition more analytically precise and use the term "conspiracy theorist" to refer to those who are most strongly predisposed to believe in conspiracy theories.

To measure respondents' predispositions toward conspiratorial thinking, we adapted three survey questions that previous scholars have used to measure underlying conspiratorial predispositions.[7] The questions were selected because they address general concepts and get to the heart of conspiratorial thinking: powerful groups covertly controlling events against the common good.

Some researchers tend to work backward from specific conspiratorial beliefs to induct predispositions. But this opens the possibility for specific beliefs to gravely bias the estimates of predispositions. For instance, a researcher who asked about beliefs in death panels, Hawaiian birth certificates, and communist plots and then created a summary measure to represent conspiratorial predispositions would find that conspiratorial predispositions afflict solely right-leaning people. Hence, we measure conspiratorial predispositions as impartially and broadly as possible and then use those estimates of predispositions to explain other beliefs.

Agreement with each of the three statements below was measured on a five-point scale, strongly agree to strongly disagree. The statements were:

"Much of our lives are being controlled by plots hatched in secret places."
"Even though we live in a democracy, a few people will always run things anyway."
"The people who really 'run' the country are not known to the voters."

For some readers, the three statements above are completely true, but for others they are preposterous. Figure 4.4 shows the distribution of answers to the three questions. We are less concerned with the amount of truth behind each of the three statements than with the variation in how much

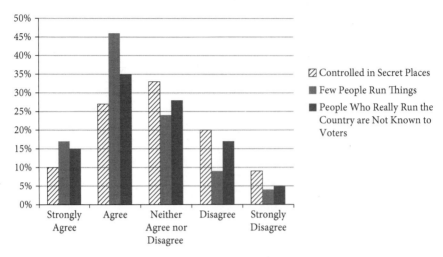

Figure 4.4 Measures of Conspiratorial Predispositions.

people agree or disagree with them. Melding the three responses, we created a composite measure of each respondent's predisposition toward conspiratorial thought.[8]

Based on the strength of their predispositions toward conspiratorial thought, the respondents were divided into thirds—low, medium, and high.[9] We maintain that those in the high category are more likely to view events and circumstances through a conspiratorial lens and believe that powerful groups are plotting against society. Those in the low category will share little of this worldview. Classifying into thirds is arbitrary but useful because it speaks to broad portions of the populace and addresses mass attitudes.

Because scientists are not a trusting bunch, we thought it fitting to verify our composite measure to see how well it gauges a predisposition to see conspiracies. If the respondents falling into the high, medium, and low categories exhibit different opinions in predictable directions, then it would suggest our measure is valid. To establish validity, respondents were requested to state their level of agreement with three questions.

The first prompt was: "The government can be trusted most of the time." If our measure of conspiratorial predispositions is sturdy, we should detect major differences between the three groups. That is in fact what happened: 61 percent of those high on the conspiracy dimension disagreed,

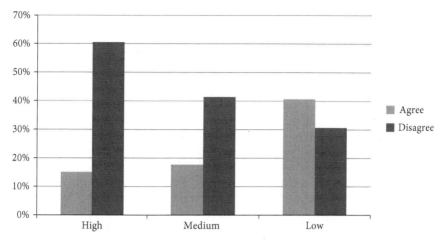

Figure 4.5 Trust in Government and Conspiratorial Predispositions.

41 percent of those with medium predispositions disagreed, and 31 percent of those with low predispositions disagreed (Fig. 4.5).[10]

The second validity check returned to the "big events controlled by small groups" question above. Comparing our measure of conspiratorial predispositions to responses, sure enough, there is tremendous separation between the thirds: 57 percent of those high on the conspiracy dimension, 20 percent of those medium on the dimension, and 11 percent low on the dimension agree with the statement (Fig. 4.6).[11]

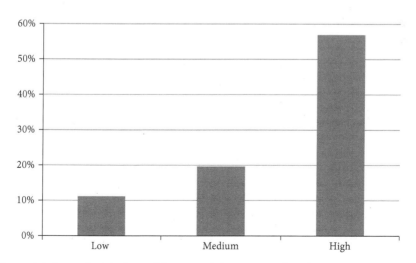

Figure 4.6 Secret Groups Control Events and Conspiratorial Predispositions.

For the third and final check, we asked respondents to name names. They were told to identify from a list the groups they felt were "likely to work in secret against the rest of us." The groups were corporations and the rich, Republicans and other conservative groups, Democrats and other liberal groups, communists and socialists, the government, foreign countries, international organizations, fraternal groups, labor unions, and other. Those high on the conspiracy dimension identified an average of 3.5 groups, compared to 2.4 and 2.1 for the medium and low groups.[12] These are all good indications that the high group is exceptionally primed to see conspiracies, and as measures of general conspiratorial thinking go, ours appears sound.

YOUR FRIENDLY NEIGHBORHOOD CONSPIRACY THEORIST?

Now that we have distinguished those especially prone to conspiracy theories, what do they have in common? How much do they have in common with you? This section describes the list of traits, beliefs, and behaviors they tend to share for a more intimate view of conspiracy theorists. The opening section investigates their basic demographics and the sections that follow explore their ideology and party ties, political participation, perspectives on violence, social habits, and economic behavior.

Describing Conspiracy Theorists

Pretend you are an advertising executive hired to sell a product to conspiracy theorists. Who is your target demographic? You have to get the average conspiracy theorist's gender, race, age, and education right. Stereotypes suggest a 40-something awkward white man with some higher education and a penchant for books and talk radio.[13] Think Mel Gibson's wild-eyed protagonist in *Conspiracy Theory* or Dan Aykroyd's daffy paranoid in *Sneakers*. But how accurate are those stereotypes?

Mostly not. Starting with gender, women are about as likely as men to be conspiracy theorists. Figure 4.7 shows the gender distribution across

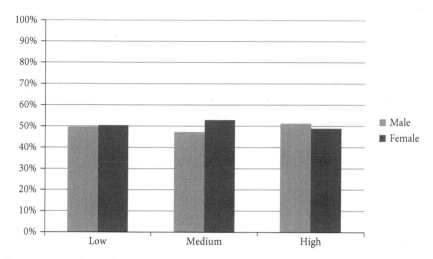

Figure 4.7 Gender and Conspiratorial Predispositions.

each level of conspiratorial predisposition. While socialization for boys and girls differs in many ways, it likely does not differ in terms of the propensity to see potential conspiracies, and this is likely why men and women show similarity. The hosts of *The View* are nice exemplars. Jenny McCarthy believes in vaccine conspiracy theories; Rosie O'Donnell has espoused Truther theories; Star Jones has suggested a conspiracy theory involving George Zimmerman; and Whoopi Goldberg believes the moon landing was faked.[14]

As for race, the findings are mixed. Whites have the highest rate of falling into the high category compared to Hispanics and blacks, but only by about 4 percentage points. However, when we look at the high and medium categories together, 89 percent of Hispanics and 86 percent of blacks fall into the medium or high category compared to 72 percent of whites (Fig. 4.8). And, whites are twice as likely to have low conspiratorial predispositions. In relation to whites, being black or Hispanic is a significant and positive predictor of conspiratorial predispositions when accounting for level of educational attainment and family income.[15]

Blacks are an interesting case study in generational change. Our argument suggests they would exhibit higher rates of conspiratorial thinking

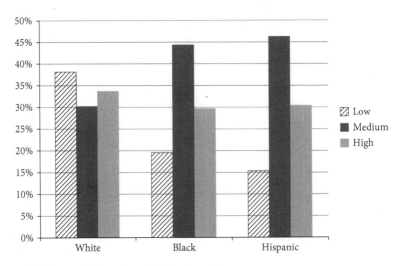

Figure 4.8 Race and Conspiratorial Predispositions.

than whites because of their minority status and a long history of racist conspiracies perpetrated against them. History, however, is not destiny. Comparing predispositions by age, we find that older blacks are more conspiratorial than younger blacks, presumably because they experienced more discrimination and were socialized by parents who experienced still more discrimination.[16] With the election of Barack Obama and other strides blacks have made up the social ladder, we expect blacks to become less conspiratorial over time as they gain power.

Of the other minority groups—Native American, Asian, "other," and Middle Eastern—upward of 80 percent fell into the medium or high categories. This broadly jells with our claim that minority groups are more prone to conspiracy theorizing, and suggests that the smaller a group is, the more conspiratorial it will be. However, the sample sizes are not sufficiently large for definitive statements to be made about smaller minorities groups. Future research would be doing a great service by collecting more reliable data.

There is some truth in the age stereotype: conspiracy theorists tend to be about middle-aged, but this may not be a product of the life cycle.[17] Instead, we look at age through the lens of generations, which refers to people born around the same time and exposed to similar circumstances in their formative years. Because they were socialized in similar conditions, people within a generation should exhibit similar worldviews.[18]

We compared all currently populous generations in terms of their levels of conspiratorial thinking: the Silent Generation, Baby Boomers, Generation X, and Millennials. Of those four groups, members of Generation X appear to be the most conspiratorially minded. Gen Xers have the highest percentage of people high on the conspiracy dimension and of people both high and medium on the conspiracy dimension (Fig. 4.9).[19] These findings support our argument that conspiratorial predispositions stem from socialization.

People have long suspected Gen Xers of excessive cynicism.[20] Every age sees scandals, but Gen Xers grew up in a somewhat anomalous age of less innocence: in the wake of shocking assassinations, galling FBI and CIA revelations, Vietnam, Watergate, and Iran-Contra. Levels of trust in the government sank from a high in 1960 to historic lows during the 1970s, rebounding only slightly for a few years in the early 1980s.[21] This "period effect," or short-term reaction to events, was imprinted on impressionable Gen Xers. Polling bolsters the claim; asked in 1994 if they thought Social Security would still exist when they retired, by 18 percentage points Gen Xers thought it more likely that UFOs existed.[22]

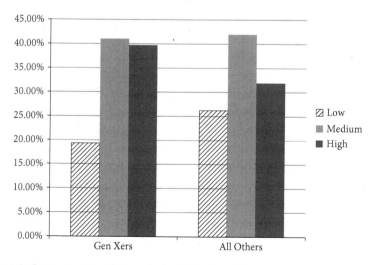

Figure 4.9 Generation X and Conspiratorial Predispositions.

Then the reaction to this reaction set in. Now Millennials are more trusting of government and more likely to participate politically, to wit, high levels of youth turnout in the 2004–12 elections. Culture has shifted. Take, for example, two comparable television shows aimed at different generations: the *X-Files* (1993–2002), aimed at Gen Xers, and *Fringe* (2008–2013), aimed at Millennials. Both center on FBI agents chasing paranormal phenomena and conspiracies, but in *Fringe* the U.S. government is benign, while in the *X-Files* it most certainly is not.

When it comes to schooling, having fewer years of formal education correlates with more conspiracy theorizing. Forty percent of those without a high school degree have high conspiratorial predispositions, and that drops steadily as educational attainment rises (Fig. 4.10). Only half as many postgraduates are high on the conspiracy dimension.

The fine print is important: it is impossible to know from our data that education causes or cures conspiratorial predispositions, but we have reasons to believe that it helps. After all, education is just another form of socialization. Nonetheless, there are also selection effects in play. Distrusting the system, the more conspiratorially inclined may shy away from educational institutions. Likewise, self-replicating educational elites might not attract, reward, or retain conspiracy-minded people. Whatever

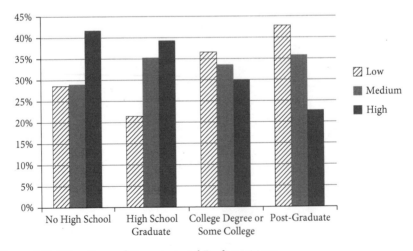

Figure 4.10 Education and Conspiratorial Predispositions.

the direction of effects, and we suspect it is complex, education remains a marker for lower conspiratorial predispositions.

In a nutshell, the profile of the average conspiracy theorist has a barely passing resemblance to many prevailing notions. Instead of a bookish middle-aged white man, the next conspiracy theorist you meet is just as likely to be a poorly educated, 40-something minority woman. Yet these are only rough demographic descriptors and averages; the meat of the matter is in beliefs and behaviors. Continue with caution: our data are self-reported and there is no way to leap from beliefs to behaviors with high confidence (on the subject of self-reporting, a full disclosure on the authors is available in the following note.)[23] We cannot observe these behaviors ourselves; who do you think we are, the NSA? But we present what evidence we have, and the reader shall judge.

Ideology and Party Ties

Everyone has partisan predispositions of some sort or another, and these nudge us to hold baskets of certain values and focus on some information over others.[24] Often this is healthy and functional. But sometimes what is politically expedient is intellectually indefensible. And when party affiliation interacts with conspiracy theories, sharp people are prone to make dull attacks.

Each side of the spectrum seems convinced that the other side routinely spawns conspiracy theories in a febrile delirium while its own conspiracy theories are reasonable and factual, if not self-evidently true. The other side, they say, dangerously welcomes conspiracy theories into the mainstream while their own side safely relegates them to the lunatic fringe. Chapter 6 will provide further reasons why it is easy, at any point in time, to single out one side or the other for conspiracy theorizing. But for now, we are confident claiming that much of this is the result of partisanship driving perception.

Below we single out some illustrations—not to hassle the authors but to demonstrate that even smart, successful, well-intentioned people fall for conspiratorial optical illusions. No one better personifies this than liberal Nobel Laureate and *New York Times* columnist Paul Krugman. His general thesis is that conservatism is a "cult, very much given to conspiracy theorizing." In comments that come close to cornering the market on virtue, he remarks: "Unlike the crazy conspiracy theories of the left—which do exist, but are supported only by a tiny fringe—the crazy conspiracy theories of the right are supported by important people: powerful politicians, television personalities with large audiences. And we can safely predict that these people will never concede that they were wrong."[25] Later Krugman adds:

> Why does such stuff flourish? Probably because there is no punishment for it—as long as you're on the right, and I mean right, side. Let Michael Moore point out, entirely correctly, the close ties between the Saudis and the Bush family, and he's blasted as a crazy conspiracy theorist. On the other hand, let Donald Luskin suggest, in 2004, that George Soros is planning to engineer a financial crisis to defeat Bush, and he gets to publish front-page articles in the *Washington Post* Outlook section declaring that there isn't a recession.[26]

In fairness, competitors tend to resemble each other, and the right side of the aisle makes similar claims about the left as well. Commentary from the conservative *Washington Times* echoes Krugman in reverse: "Yet in a liberal Hollywood where to express skepticism about man-made global warming is to be labeled—with all its obvious connotations—a 'denier,' [the] insinuation that the U.S. government was complicit—by its silence, if nothing else—in the destruction of the Twin Towers and the murder of 3,000 people has elicited nary a peep in condemnation. Where, one is compelled to ask, is the outrage on the left?"[27]

Such claims are unencumbered by rigorous evidence. The distribution of those low, medium, and highly predisposed to conspiratorial thinking falls fairly evenly across the five-point liberal–conservative spectrum (Fig. 4.11).[28] Interestingly, conspiratorial predispositions do not increase as we move away from the middle; in fact, those identifying as moderates have the lowest percentage of respondents falling into the low category.

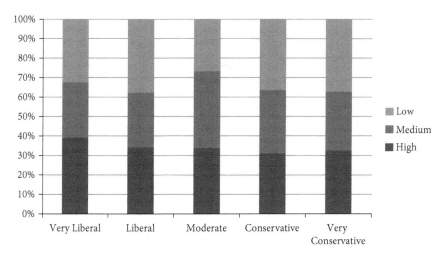

Figure 4.11 Political Ideology and Conspiratorial Predispositions.

While ideology and party greatly overlap, one must look at conspiratorial predispositions across party identification as well. The evidence lines up similarly. On a seven-point scale from "strong Democrat" to "strong Republican," those ranking high on the conspiracy dimension range between 24 and 40 percent on the Democratic side and between 27 and 33 percent on the Republican side (Fig. 4.12). In short, the empirical evidence suggests that conspiratorial predispositions appear nearly flat across political ideology and partisanship.

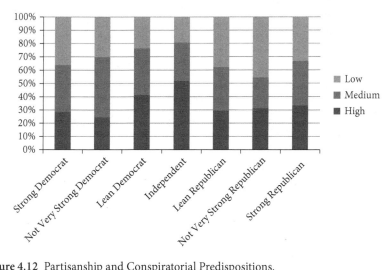

Figure 4.12 Partisanship and Conspiratorial Predispositions.

Each side is similarly conspiratorial but throws accusations in different directions. The right accuses liberals and communists of conspiring, and the left accuses conservatives and corporations. When asked to identify from a list which groups they believed were conspiring, Republicans and Democrats diverged in predictable order. Fifty-one and 33 percent of Democrats thought corporations and conservatives were conspiring, respectively. As for Republicans, 58 percent pointed the finger at communists and 42 percent indicted liberals (Fig. 4.13).

Moving from general predispositions to particular conspiracy theories, consider MSNBC host Chris Matthews, who denies symmetry: "I don't buy that it's symmetric [between the two parties], there are a lot more Birthers than there are Truthers."[29] Matthews may not have been aware of the data. A Scripps Howard University poll from July 2006 shows that 45 percent of Democrats believed that 9/11 was a conspiracy by the federal government, and a CNN poll from July 2010 showed that 41 percent of Republicans believe that Barack Obama was born in another country.[30] Truther and Birther beliefs have been polled extensively, and results vary based upon question wording, polling methodology, and timing. But symmetry seems to be the overarching trend.[31]

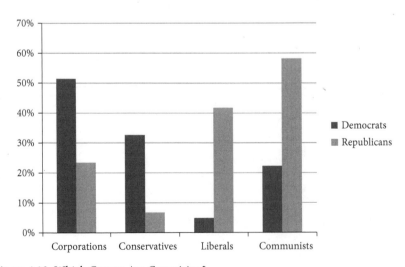

Figure 4.13 Which Groups Are Conspiring?

Finally, consider comments by Jonathan Chait, Senior Editor of *The New Republic*, who argues that the right "evinces a kind of paranoid thinking that . . . cannot be found in the mainstream left." In discussing conspiracy theories, he focuses on those involving electoral fraud: "Bizarre, counterfactual beliefs about massive electoral fraud exist on both right and left. The important difference is that left-wing electoral conspiracy theories are almost completely marginal, rejected by even highly partisan outlets like *Daily Kos*, whereas the right-wing equivalent enjoys mainstream support."[32]

This is a testable proposition, and the results undercut Chait. When we asked respondents how likely voter fraud would have been involved if their preferred presidential candidate did not win the election, 50 percent of Republicans said it would be very or somewhat likely, compared to 34 percent who said it would be very or somewhat unlikely (Fig. 4.14). For Democrats, 44 percent said fraud would have been likely compared to 37 percent who said it would be unlikely to have played a role. Again, it is about a tie.

Other data sources confirm this symmetry. A 2013 national poll asked about fraud in specific presidential elections. Thirty-seven percent of Democrats believed that "President Bush's supporters committed

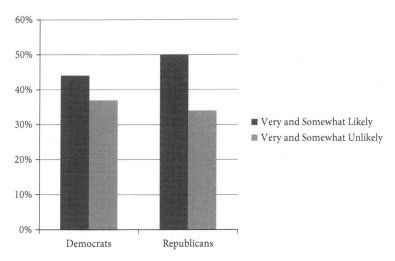

Figure 4.14 Electoral Fraud and Conspiratorial Predispositions.

significant voter fraud in order to win Ohio in 2004." This is compared to 36 percent of Republicans who believe that "President Obama's supporters committed significant voter fraud in the 2012 presidential election."[33]

Each side believes that when the other side wins cheating is to blame, and they believe it about equally. These beliefs rebound upon each other. Democrats, responding to the belief that their voters had been suppressed in 2000 and 2004, made herculean efforts at voter registration and mobilization in 2008 and 2012. Republicans saw these efforts as an attempt to commit voter fraud by stuffing ballot boxes. Responding to their perception, Republican governors and legislatures across the states attempted to institute tougher restrictions on voting, including requiring voter identification. In response to this, Democrats accused Republicans of manufacturing phony assertions of voter fraud as part of a wide-ranging conspiracy to curtail Democratic voters' access to the polls.[34] This spiral of hostility is bound to continue.

While both sides accuse the other of being a bunch of credulous crackpots, our observation is that such accusations are made more against conservatives. This may be because, for mundane reasons, the accusations are coming from the media and the academy. Since the beginning, that is since Richard Hofstadter, the claim has been that there is partisan asymmetry because the right is more authoritarian, anti-intellectual, and tribal.[35] Although there are differences between the left and right,[36] scholars and the media should be circumspect about overdrawing them in this instance. We believe the notion of asymmetry has persisted because academics and journalists align largely with the left.[37] This pushes these two institutions to disproportionately dwell on conspiracy theories held by the right but overlook conspiracy theories closer to home. Hofstadter himself was a leftist with Marxist sympathies—it is perfectly understandable why he picked up a pen in the wake of the Red Scare.

When we presented parts of this work at an academic conference panel in 2013, the other academics presented papers addressing the theory that Obama was born in a foreign country, the theory that Obama is a Muslim, and the theory that Obama fakes Bureau of Labor Statistics data. All are valuable contributions, but the audience could be forgiven for thinking

Republicans were more susceptible to conspiracy theories than Democrats. In political science at least, much of the study of conspiratorial beliefs has focused on conspiracy theories accusing actors on the left, especially since Obama's election in 2008. Searching through the conference archives of the American Political Science Association (2002–13) and Midwest Political Science Association (2004–13), we found many papers studying conspiratorial beliefs held by those on the right and nearly none studying conspiratorial beliefs held by the left.

The cumulative effect is that our knowledge-generating and knowledge-disseminating institutions make the right look chock-full of cranks and the left look sensible and savvy. There is no conspiracy here; ideology drives the worldviews of professors and journalists just like it does everyone else.[38] But that does not make it just. There is not much evidence that either side is significantly more prone to conspiracy theorizing. Yet this has not stopped either from slinging slurs at the other side while understating the conspiracy theorists on their own side. This may be an adaptive behavior in the rough-and-tumble world of political discourse, but it should not pass muster as science.

Strikingly, it is the oft-overlooked outsiders who are the most conspiratorial. Who are they? Sixty percent of those who identify as "other" are high on the conspiratorial predispositions dimension. That is more than 20 points higher than the next most highly predisposed group, independents. Those identifying as "other" also boast the smallest percentage of people with low conspiratorial predispositions (Fig. 4.15). This builds on previous studies showing that third-party voters tend to be much more distrustful.[39] We want to be clear, however, and note that very few people claim to be a member of a minor party (about 4 percent).

There is one additional point to make regarding partisanship and liberal–conservative ideology. While we use both as blanket terms to caricature large blocs of people, there is great heterogeneity within parties and ideologies. Some of this can be explained by conspiratorial predispositions. Support for the Iraq war came largely from Republicans, but there was dissent within that camp. When asked if it was a mistake to invade Iraq, 33 percent of those with high predispositions, compared to 25 and

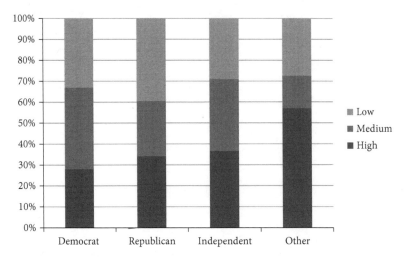

Figure 4.15 "Other" Parties and Conspiratorial Predispositions.

15 percent of those with medium and low predispositions, thought the Iraq war was a mistake.[40] Most Democrats, regardless of conspiratorial predispositions, were against the invasion of Iraq.

This flips when we look at the Afghanistan war. Where George W. Bush "owned" the Iraq war, voters saw Afghanistan as Obama's war.[41] Similarly, dissenting Democrats can be predicted by conspiratorial predispositions. When asked if it was a mistake to invade Afghanistan, 50 percent of Democrats with high conspiratorial predispositions said yes, compared to over a third of those with medium and low predispositions.[42] So conspiratorial predispositions predict opinions that seem counter to the opinions associated with party or ideology.

How Conspiracy Theorists Behave Politically

Are conspiracy theorists politically active? By almost every measure the answer is yes, but at much lower rates than everyone else. A few weeks prior to the 2012 election, they were almost three times as likely to not be registered to vote compared to those in the low category (Fig. 4.16). It should therefore come as no surprise that they are less likely to report

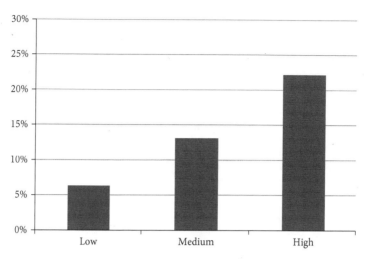

Figure 4.16 Non-Registration and Conspiratorial Predispositions.

having voted after the election. Sixty-eight percent in the high conspiratorial predispositions category, 83 percent in the middle category, and 91 percent in the low category claim to have voted after the 2012 election (Fig. 4.17). While self-reports of voting tend to be inflated, the relationship between conspiratorial predispositions and voting is pretty clear.[43] Part of the reason for lower turnout among conspiracy theorists is that they are the most likely to believe fraud will play a role in the election.

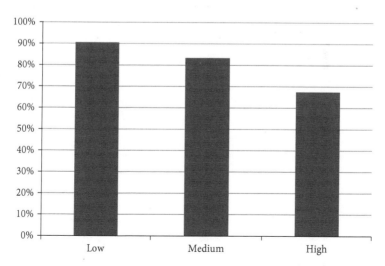

Figure 4.17 Voter Participation in 2012 and Conspiratorial Predispositions.

Fifty-two percent of those high on the conspiracy dimension thought there would be fraud, compared to 29 and 19 of the medium and low groups, respectively.

Such lack of participation obtains down the line. From putting up signs to running for political office, people in the high and medium categories participate at a lower rate than those with low conspiratorial predispositions (Fig. 4.18). Conspiracy theorists' lack of clout is most telling in terms of political donations. Thirty-seven percent of those in the low category donated money to a candidate, campaign, or political organization compared to only 16 percent in the high category.[44] Low political activity gives conspiracy theorists little reason to relinquish conspiracy theories and politicians little reason to court conspiracy theorists. Neither side has much incentive to break the cycle.

Few people run for office to begin with, but those with high conspiratorial predispositions are less than half as likely to run for office as their low conspiracy counterparts. While it is easy to point to prominent politicians when they champion conspiratorial positions (e.g., Joseph McCarthy),

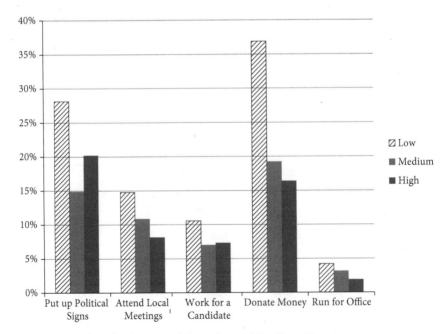

Figure 4.18 Political Behavior and Conspiratorial Predispositions.

most politicians are not conspiracy theorists. When some in Congress wrote a letter demanding to know why the administration was purchasing ammunition, MSNBC's Rachael Maddow chastised Congress for falling into conspiracy hysteria. She need not have: of 435 representatives, only four signed the letter.

Ah yes, but whom do conspiracy theorists vote for? It is about a wash, but only among the two main parties. While the percentage of highly pre-disposed people voting for Romney was slightly higher than for Obama, the percentages of those in the high and medium categories were identical for both candidates (Fig. 4.19). Both candidates have their share of conspiracy theorists. Of the small amount of people who voted for a third party, 98 percent are in the high or medium category and 71 percent are in the high category.

From Voting to Violence

Are conspiracy theorists more disposed to violence? Probably, but not by much. Following revelations that the Boston Marathon bombers were Truthers, Rachael Maddow emphatically said yes: "[p]ick your poison,

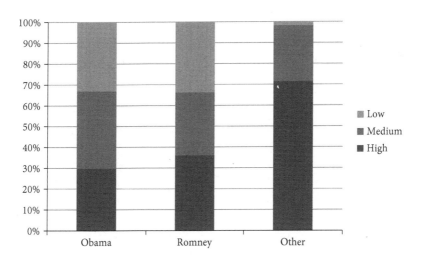

Figure 4.19 Presidential Choice and Conspiratorial Predispositions.

right. It's the Protocols of the Elders of Zion . . . or it's 9/11 Truth . . . there has always been an appeal to this necrotizing conspiracy theory radicalism, which almost always butts up against justifying violence."[45]

Anecdotes and conspicuous cases are unnerving, but they do not necessarily represent the rule. Broader research notes the difficulty in correlating conspiracy theories to violence. Jamie Bartlett and Carl Miller capture the puzzle deftly: "There are many extremist groups that do not believe conspiracy theories as far as we can tell, such as the Real IRA or the Unabomber. Conspiracy theories are not a necessary condition for extreme beliefs or action. Equally, conspiracy theories do not always lead to extreme or violent behavior. There are many peaceful, even moderate groups that believe conspiracy theories."[46]

The good news is that massive majorities object to violence, and the kind of violence we are concerned with here, politically motivated violence, is a miniscule fraction of all violence. Still, those with stronger conspiratorial predispositions are more likely to be inclined toward violent action. Sixteen percent of those high on the conspiracy dimension agree with the statement: "violence is sometimes an acceptable way to express disagreement with the government." This is in contrast to 11 percent and 6 percent of lows and mediums, respectively (Fig. 4.20). Eighty percent of

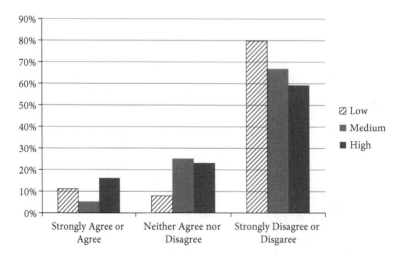

Figure 4.20 Acceptance of Violence Against the Government and Conspiratorial Predispositions.

those low on the conspiracy dimension disagree with the statement than violence is sometimes an acceptable way to express disagreement with the government, but only 59 percent of those high on the conspiracy dimension do.[47]

The same pattern holds when respondents are asked to express agreement with the use of "violence as an acceptable way to stop politically extreme groups in our country from doing harm." Twenty-one percent of the highly predisposed agree compared to 15 percent of the medium and low groups. And 56 percent of those low on the conspiracy dimension disagree with the statement, while only 42 percent of those high on the conspiracy dimension disagree.[48]

But it is the extremists we should be most worried about. To inspect them more closely, we isolated the 50 people at the top and 50 people at the bottom of the conspiracy dimension. Almost 20 percent of the high group says violence is an acceptable way to express disagreement with the government. This is more than double the less than 8 percent of the low group that does. Only about 50 percent of the high group disagrees with the use of violence for this reason, while 80 percent of the low group does.

It might sound reassuring that not even 20 percent of the 50 most predisposed respondents say violence is an acceptable way to express disagreement with the government. But regard these results warily; there are a number of limitations to the data. Surveys are suggestive, and they cannot reveal who will actually resort to violence. The most eager to utilize force are the least likely to submit to a survey or answer honestly on this score. There are so few people who view violence as acceptable in our sample that we cannot glean much about them as a group. The survey is designed to measure preferences, not preference intensity, and intensity is important when talking about violent proclivities. So is the permissiveness of the domestic context. If only 1 percent of the population agreed with the statement strongly enough to take forceful action, there would be blood in the streets daily.

It is disconcerting that, when asked about gun control, around half of those with higher conspiratorial predispositions wanted less strict gun laws (about double the other categories) while other scholars have shown that those who are predisposed to believe in conspiracy theories are also predisposed to agree with the use of conspiracies to achieve ends.[49] This follows logically: if powerful forces are out to get you, you are going to need a full array of firepower for self-defense. The prototypical example is Timothy McVeigh: obsessed by conspiracy theories, opposed to gun restrictions, and willing to conspire to parry his perceived enemy.[50] In brief, highly inclined conspiracy theorists are about twice as likely to agree with political violence in principle, but that is still a relatively small number of people. From our perspective, the danger lies less in their dispositions than in the favorable political conditions that allow them to act out their fiercest fantasies. Chapter 6 expands on this.

Social Life: Relations with Friends, Spouses, and God

Returning to our caricature of conspiracy theorists, they are often portrayed as isolated and socially awkward. But are they? Not really. Conspiratorial predispositions do not seem to predict the number of friends people claim to have. No matter their predispositions toward seeing conspiracies, people seem to have the same number of friends. Likewise, in looking at marital status, there were few differences along the conspiracy dimension.

The one difference is that conspiracy theorists are somewhat more tight-lipped with those closest to them. Those low on the conspiracy dimension reported talking to an average of seven people about important matters in the last month, but those with medium and high conspiratorial predispositions reported discussing important matters with an average of six people.[51] This difference is marginal and hard to interpret. Fewer discussants does not mean less discussion, and it may be that people high on the conspiracy dimension are not disposed to divulge the full extent of their social circle. If conspiracies are afoot, reticence is prudent.

Are those with stronger conspiratorial predispositions more or less in touch with public affairs than those lower on the scale? Slightly less in touch. Those higher on the conspiracy dimension reported less interest in news and public affairs by a clear margin. Forty-three percent of those high on the conspiracy dimension reported being interested against 62 percent of those scoring low. They are also less likely to go to church. Thirty-one percent of those high on the conspiracy dimension report never attending religious services versus a third fewer of those low on the conspiracy dimension. The net result of this evidence is that conspiracy theorists might be somewhat less social than less predisposed people, but not by much.

Homo Conspiratus Beats *Homo Economicus*

On the surface, conspiracy theorists have it all figured out. For feats of sheer intellectual chutzpah, few can top them: they have unmasked big secrets by powerful agents that the rest of the world blithely ignores. Wall Street dreams of such profit opportunities! But the reality is that conspiracy theories are hazardous to your wealth. Conspiracy theorists tend to be poorer than average (Fig. 4.21) and about 20 percentage points less likely than the other two groups to report owning stocks (Fig. 4.22).[52]

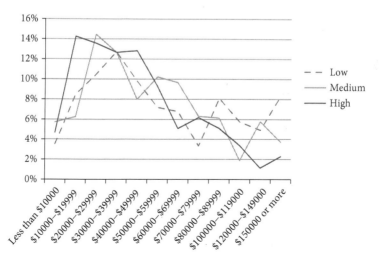

Figure 4.21 Income and Conspiratorial Predispositions.

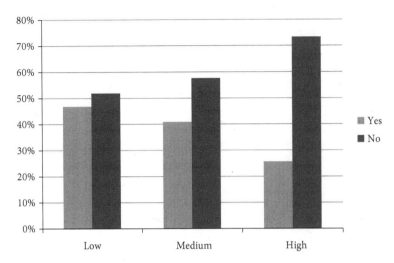

Figure 4.22 Stock Ownership and Conspiratorial Predispositions.

Even accounting for income, those with high predispositions are significantly less likely to invest in the market. Conspiracy theorists might claim that the market is rigged so they should not invest in it. This makes some sense. But on the other hand, the stock market is one of the largest generators of wealth, and anyone who had even a slight edge on the motives and goals of powerful actors should be able to reap handsome profits.

Conspiracy theorists are less likely to have jobs in the financial industry, military, and public administration (Fig. 4.23), exactly the institutions that conspiracy theorists tend to accuse. This is somewhat unexpected given that jobs in the financial industry, government, and military might foster conspiracy theorizing because of their size and complexity. Conspiracy theorists are not drawn to sectors of the economy where money and power are concentrated. This suggests that conspiracy theories are more useful in protecting the self than in dominating others.

Combining our findings, conspiracy theorists differ substantially from their stereotypes. They are less wealthy, less politically engaged, less conservative, less white, and less likely to be male than perceptions suggest. Socially, they appear to be pretty average, except they are somewhat less

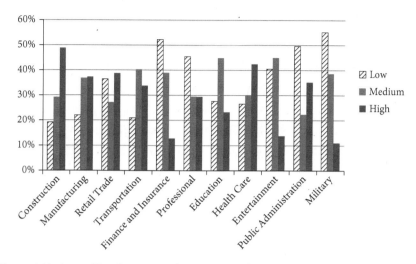

Figure 4.23 Area of Employment and Conspiratorial Predispositions.

engaged in their communities and more approving of violence. They do not cluster in economic sectors where money and power accumulate and avoid the stock market. But again, these are averages that conceal crucial details.

CONCLUSION

This chapter has developed two ideas. First, there is an underlying predisposition toward seeing conspiracies called the conspiracy dimension. It captures how predisposed people are to conspiracy theories and is independent from political ideology or party identification. Second, those highly predisposed to conspiracy theories look differently than the popular perception suggests they should. On average, they tend to be about as likely to be men as women and Republicans as Democrats, poor in terms of formal education and money, less likely to participate politically, more accepting of violence, and less apt to work in financial services, government, or the military. On the whole, they appear to deserve their reputation as outsiders.

The conspiracy dimension has political implications and an underpinning logic that we have only just begun to explore. One of the more noteworthy facets of it is a partisan blindness toward the conspiracy theories of one's own group and sensitivity to the conspiracies of others. It is also notable that fringe groups, third parties, social movements, and the alienated are the most likely to indulge in conspiracy theorizing because conspiracy theories are for losers—a theme we shall return to shortly.

The Ages of Conspiracy

In 1690 Frenchmen and Indians razed the town of Schenectady
and struck forts on the coast of Maine, sending a frisson of fear
through New York and New England. . . . That deplorable military
situation and the panic it caused provided the context for one of
the most infamous episodes in colonial history: the Salem witch
trials.

—Walter McDougall[1]

Conspiracy theories are permanent fixtures on the American landscape.
But for such popular perennials, no one seems to agree on when their peak
season is. Journalists have not been shy about perpetually proclaiming an
age of conspiracy. In 2013, *New York Times* Editor Andrew Rosenthal
saw a poll on U.S. conspiratorial beliefs and summed it up in five words:
"No Comment Necessary: Conspiracy Nation." Two years prior, the *New
York Daily News* breathlessly declared: "It's official: America is becoming
a conspiratocracy. The tendency for a small slice of the population to

believe in devious plots has always been with us. But conspiracies have
never spread this swiftly across the country. They have never lodged this
deeply in the American psyche. And they have never found as recep-
tive an audience." In 2010, *The Times* columnist David Aaronovitch was
confident the West was "currently going through a period of fashionable
conspiracism."[2]

Six years before that, the *Boston Globe* suggested that we were then
living in the "golden age of conspiracy theory."[3] A decade previous, in
1994, the *Washington Post* claimed that Bill Clinton's first term "marked
the dawn of a new age of conspiracy theory" when only two years earlier it had posited that we then lived "in an age of conspiracy theories."[4]
Back in 1977, the *Los Angeles Times* concluded the United States had set
a world record: "we have become as conspiracy prone in our judgments
as the Pan-Slav nationalists in the 1880s Balkans."[5] Rewinding to the fall
of Camelot, the *New York Times* was sure 1964 was the age of conspiracy
theories because they had "grown weedlike in this country and abroad."[6]
Jonathan Kay, Managing Editor of the *National Post*, hedges and suggests
twin peaks in the 1960s and 2000s.[7] Presumably we could multiply examples back to Salem in 1692, but you understand the point: conspiracy
scares are ubiquitous.

Academics sing in similar cacophony. Film scholar Gordon Arnold
and historian Robert Goldberg assert that conspiracy theorizing in the
United States rose markedly after World War II, while another historian,
Daniel Pipes, counters that conspiracy theories reached a crescendo
at the outbreak of World War II but declined steadily afterward.[8] Ac-
claimed historian David Brion Davis claimed that conspiracy theories
were widespread in the nineteenth century but are confined to "only
a few crackpots and extremists" in modern times. Davis has since re-
pented, claiming that "a world-weary pessimism and cynicism" has
driven a new era of heightened belief in conspiracy theories.[9] So who
is right?

We argue that none of them is. This chapter has dual purposes: positive
and negative. On the positive side, we develop an argument to explain the

level of conspiracy talk in the United States over the last century. Conspiracy theories, in our view, ought to be relatively stable over the long haul because socialization and power shifts drive them, and these change slowly. Certainly there are short-term fluctuations, but these are likely to net out over time. Most of the time, the conspiracy dimension interacts with party affiliation, which means that Chicken Littles can electrify at most a third of the country at once.

The only exception is when domestic coalitions are realigning to face novel threats. Without an ideological brake on half the country, there can be surges in the overall level of conspiracy talk. Also, with growing U.S. relative power, the chances of citizens dying violently at the hands of international actors has fallen, and with it one of the preeminent sources of conspiracy talk. For these reasons, it is understandable that the chief upswings in overall prevalence happened in the 1890s and 1950s, with the unique perils of monopoly trusts and partisan realignment in the former case and nuclear weapons and bipolarity in the latter case. Beyond that, the total level of conspiracy talk should correspond to information environments suggesting that an actual conspiracy has transpired or may transpire.

On the negative side, we investigate the logic and evidence behind several conventional wisdoms on when conspiracy theories flourish and find them wanting. This casts a shadow over some of the more captivating explanations (including one of Parent's pet theories, leaving him to dejectedly scapegoat Uscinski for its defeat). The bottom line is that many of the explanations for the supposed rising levels of conspiracy theorizing should come with warning labels.

To develop these points, the chapter is organized in the following manner. The first section elaborates the logic of our argument and extracts testable implications from it. The second section presents an overview of our letters to the editor data and shows the results of time-series regression analysis. The third section tests seven popular claims about conspiracy theorizing and finds that only one of them, the information environment, works. A conclusion summarizes the findings.

THEORY: THE LOGIC OF THE ARGUMENT

Our central claim is that the total amount of conspiracy theorizing ought to be stable over long periods of time. There are two forces behind this stability, and they typically keep national conspiracy theories on a fairly even keel: socialization and the distribution of power. Socialization is straightforward in theory but complicated in practice. The fundamental notion is learning during one's childhood; people tend to share many of their family's values because they were immersed in them during their formative years.

To reiterate, individuals tend to take on ideological casts in their youth. One of these casts is the conspiracy dimension, the subject of Chapter 4, which is the underlying propensity to see events through a conspiratorial lens. People highly predisposed to see conspiracies are approximately equally distributed between the major political parties. Another of these casts is political ideology, whether one leans more liberal or conservative, and which party one tends to identify with. Because people hate cognitive dissonance, these ideologies have to largely harmonize. Individuals high on the conspiracy dimension will not pounce on all potential conspiracy theories, but only those consonant with their political beliefs. Therefore, there is bipartisan balance in the distribution of conspiracy theorists.

Beyond socialization lay shifts in the distribution of power. As some groups or coalitions fare better, others lose out, and those on the losing end will experience feelings of threat, lack of control, and powerlessness. This will push them to express their conspiracy theories as conspiracy talk. Conspiracy talk by those on the losing end will tend to pick up the slack from the diminution of conspiracy theories from the winners who perceive less threat and feel less need to communicate conspiracy theories. The American government has effectively been a two-party system since the beginning, and there is rough partisan parity in the alternation of political power. This suggests that over time, while the types of resonant conspiracy theories will change in response to shifts in domestic power, the overall resonance of domestic conspiracy theories should be flat because mostly out-of-power people will sound conspiratorial alarms at any given time.

Internationally, the system performs similarly but the implications are less balanced for U.S. conspiracy theories. True, one country's rise in power will have to come at the expense of others, but the repercussions inside the United States are not as simple as the domestic narrative above. As a country rises in power, its foreign policy interests and threats rise in proportion, though as a rule larger states are safer than small states. The reverse happens as states fall in the hierarchy of great powers. But if threat is the core variable, we have only a crude understanding of how the concept changes over time, coarse measures of power only loosely correlate with it, and it is mediated by factors such as international norms, technology, and military doctrine.[10] When a state is safer from international predation, conspiracy theories about outsiders recede. However, humanity being better at problem creating than problem solving, a drop in international conspiracy fears is largely replaced by a rise in domestic conspiracy fears.[11]

On balance, our depiction of conspiracy theorizing is hydraulic; conspiracy theories are a liquid that, when displaced, soon find its level again. But although our story is predominantly one of continuity, any long-term model needs a dynamic element, and our model has two. First, information environments that suggest the existence of conspiracies can drive the perception that a conspiracy is afoot. The more information suggesting a conspiracy is afoot, the more people will believe and communicate conspiracy theories.[12] Second, sometimes there are shocks to the system that cause displacement. Our model predicts that bipartisan threats can energize predisposed people on both sides of the political spectrum and the country might then experience a major uptick in conspiracy talk.

Bear in mind that our model is pitched at such a level of abstraction that we can say little about what form these infrequent moments will take, other than that they are likely to be novel and take place when coalitions are fluid. While this may rule out a great deal of change and be compatible with critical juncture narratives, it is not as specific an explanation as we would like. Nevertheless, our claims are original and consistent with the logic that runs through this work, and proto-theory must start somewhere.[13]

EMPIRICS: OVERALL CONSPIRACY TALK ACROSS TIME

So much for theory; what does the evidence say? In this section we examine some of the most accepted explanations for the total amount of conspiracy talk. As described in Chapter 3, we rely on letters to the editor of the *New York Times* from 1890 to 2010. The data yield an annual number, in 121 yearly observations, with higher values indicating higher prevalence of conspiratorial beliefs in the public and lower values indicating lower prevalence of conspiratorial beliefs in the public. We express this as the proportion of non-elite letters engaging in conspiracy talk to total non-elite letters in our sample each year (Fig. 5.1).

The line initially looks bumpy, but the major trend and a few spikes are swiftly discernible. Beginning with the major trend: despite popular hoopla, the prevalence of conspiracy talk has waned in the United States since 1890. Choosing the Kennedy assassination as an arbitrary halfway point, conspiracy theorizing seems to have entered an incremental descent. From 1964 on, conspiracy theories average 0.5 percent of the letters per year, while before 1964 conspiracy theories are more than double. The data suggest one telling fact: we do not live in an age of conspiracy theories

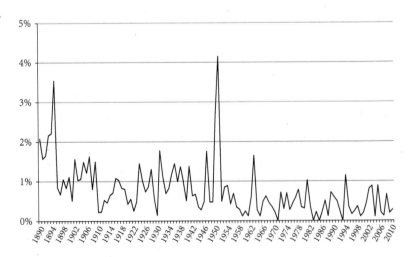

Figure 5.1 Time-Series of Conspiracy Letters.

and have not for some time. The major exceptions to the overall steady decline are spikes in the mid-1890s and early 1950s. It is only during these two periods that letters with conspiracy talk rise above 3 percent of the letters.

Broadly, the data are consistent with our argument. The central feature of the graph is that most of the time it does not fluctuate much. Socialization and shifts in the balance of power suggest that continuity will trump change, and that is what we almost always see. What about the two main anomalies? The answer has to do with who is being accused.

In the 1890s, business had become a very powerful actor both economically and politically, but still it had yet to fall squarely into one of the two party coalitions. Without a doubt business interests have been a chief component of U.S. politics from the founding. But the 1890s are an unusual era in American capitalism because of the prominence of monopolies and trusts—vast concentrations of wealth on a whole new scale—and the government's desire to bust them.[14] People belonging to both parties could easily be suspicious of business because such opinions would not conflict with partisanship. This essentially left all people prone to conspiracy thinking prone to accusing business. From 1890 through 1896, a hefty 30 percent of all conspiracy talk each year was on average aimed at business.

But this changed with the 1896 presidential race between Republican William McKinley and Democrat William Jennings Bryan. McKinley made a strong effort to pull business interests into the Republican Party, a pillar that remains a core part of the Republican coalition to this day.[15] With business solidly in sympathy with Republicans and vice versa, it became more difficult for Republicans to accuse business of conspiring. Following 1896, accusations at capitalists occupied an average of only about 10 percent of the conspiracy talk in our data. This pattern continues to the present; recent conspiracy theories about Halliburton, a multinational firm, came nearly universally from the left.

In the 1950s, it is no mystery that the data pick up the second Red Scare. A large portion of the conspiracy talk is driven by fears of communist entrenchment. For the years 1947 through 1957 (generally considered the years of the Red Scare) accusations against communists make up an average of 20 percent of conspiracy talk. During 1950 and 1951, they make up a third. To put this in perspective, the amount of conspiracy talk aimed at communists during those two years was six times the average during the entire 1890–2010 period. Why?

These were the most dangerous years of superpower rivalry and an unprecedented period in American foreign relations. Few knew what to make of the postwar era: bipolarity was a distribution of power no one had experienced and nuclear weapons were a revolutionary technological advance with unknown implications. The collapse of the German, and to a lesser extent British, empires brought the two superpowers toe to toe, and a series of events frightened American decision makers: Soviet moves on Greece and Turkey, the Czech coup, the Berlin blockade, the fall of Nationalist China, the loss of the nuclear monopoly, the outbreak of the Korean War (mistakenly blamed on Stalin), and the sensational trials and convictions of scores of Americans for being Soviets spies, two of whom were executed for treason.[16] These shocks were enough to galvanize elites from both parties, who in turn mobilized the public against new dangers. With bipartisan support, the federal government passed laws to combat communism at home and abroad. But as time passed and new evidence came in, the communist threat turned out not to be so towering, and conspiracy fears abated.

As for lesser swells, the Watergate era makes a prime example. News and Congressional hearings of the Watergate break-ins and other wrongdoings by the Nixon administration created an information environment ripe for conspiracy theorizing. During the late 1960s the overall resonance of conspiracy theorizing drops, but it quickly ticks up during Watergate, then drops a few years after once the threat was quelled.

The principal point is that conspiracy talk in the United States is not all that variable over more than a century. The story is mostly one of stability and gradual decline. If there were golden ages of conspiracy theorizing in the United States, they subsided in the 1890s and 1950s. We contend that socialization and power shifts account for this steady story, but that on rare occasion there are massive shocks that jolted both sides of the aisle into paying attention to conspiracy theories.

ANALYSIS: EVALUATING POPULAR EXPLANATIONS

Whenever conspiracy theories make national news, some brave soul must make sense of it. Pity the poor pundit who ventures guesses to momentous questions bereft of decent data. There are fine reasons why previous accounts disagree on the apogee of American conspiracy theorizing—measuring beliefs is difficult and costly—but now that better evidence is available, how much merit is there in the prevailing wisdoms?

That depends on the wisdom: not all of them appear baseless. To get to the bottom of the matter, we turned concepts that might cause conspiracy theorizing into numerical measures so we could make statistical comparisons. The goal is finding true and non-trivial causes, which entails identifying non-random relationships between variables with strong reasons for why a correlation should be there. Using the letters to the editor data discussed in Chapter 3, we use multivariate regression to search for correlations. The results are in Table 5.1.[17]

In the table, asterisks indicate that the explanatory variable is significantly correlated with our dependent variable. The variable we wish to explain is our time-series of conspiracy letters in yearly observations from 1890 to 2010. To be clear, this measure refers to all conspiracy talk rather than talk about any one conspiracy theory. It is intended to reflect the overall resonance of conspiracy theories and provides leverage on understanding the forces that drive conspiracy theories, en masse, to resonate more or less over time. Regardless of the specific conspiracy theories proffered, what makes conspiracy theories resonate? The sign (+/−) of each coefficient indicates the direction of the correlation: an increase in a variable with a positive sign leads to an increase in the levels of conspiracy talk, and the reverse with a decrease. The table being a bit abrupt, the following sections unpack the logic(s) and evaluate the theory and evidence behind each of them.

Table 5-1. Time-Series Regression Results

Variable	Coefficient
NYT front page	11.2*
	(8.2)
NYT total	−29.3
	(29.6)
Elite rhetoric	4.4*
	(1.8)
Defense spending	−.02*
	(.02)
Polarization	−.2
	(.85)
Federal outlays	.00
	(.00)
Women representatives	−.04*
	(.03)
Black representatives	.04
	(.03)
Unemployment	.00
	(.02)
GDP	.00
	(.01)
GINI	1.2
	(2.4)
Patents	−.04
	(.42)
Television	.00
	(.00)
Internet	.01
	(.01)
Films	−.05
	(.07)
TV shows	.00
	(.11)
Books	.00
	(.00)
Adjusted r^2	.16
Observations	121

NOTE: *$p < .1$; (one-tailed). Prais–Winsten regression; coefficients and standard errors rounded to two decimal places.

It's the Economy, Stupid!

> I think that at a time when the country is anxious generally and going through a tough time, fears can surface, suspicions, divisions can surface in a society.
>
> —BARACK OBAMA[18]

> The false belief that Obama was not born in the U.S. or that he is a Muslim has been tracking upward with economic uncertainty and individuals' worries about the economy. Plenty of conspiracy beliefs go hand in glove with worries and fears about globalization and unexpected/unpredictable economic shocks.
>
> —JAMES T. LAPLANT[19]

Perhaps the most common explanation for widespread conspiracy theorizing is the economics of tough times.[20] The underlying logic is psychological: the trauma of financial catastrophe wreaks havoc on people's psyches. Financial losses and insecurity can lead to feelings of loss of control, powerlessness, and uncertainty—the psychological states that can trigger conspiratorial beliefs and cause them to be communicated. This explanation has the advantages of being intuitively plausible and having some empirical support. Small, short-term studies find that those who view the economy as worsening are more likely to believe in conspiracy theories, and those who feel insecure about their employment are more likely to believe in conspiracy theories.[21]

Yet the logic and evidence have problems. Modern economies are complex; individuals affected by economic downtimes may not have a specific villain to accuse. So while people affected by a bad economy may become temporarily disposed toward conspiratorial thinking or more likely to communicate a conspiracy theory, they may not gravitate toward or ever communicate specific theories. Furthermore, conspiracy theorizing is costly, risky, and unlikely to resurrect one's fortunes. People may care little for truth, but they do care about getting rehired or promoted, and burning precious resources that could be used for more needful tasks in lean times seems unwise. If anything, the negative feedback of financial failure should encourage clearer thinking and harsh truths. Logic cuts both ways.

To test the proposition that economic downturns drive the resonance of conspiracy theories, we measure economic misery. It is easy to say that the economy affects people's beliefs, but what parts of the economy exactly? Is it employment rates, economic growth, or something else? Rarely do commentators specify. To make the best of it, we track the economy with three yearly measures: the unemployment rate, changes in GDP, and the GINI coefficient of income inequality.[22] If economics drives the overall resonance of conspiracy theorizing, it ought to show up in one of these indicators. It does not.

Despite the frequency with which the economy is blamed for conspiracy theories, it does not predict conspiracy talk over long periods of time. Although economic conditions may well explain some infamous cases of conspiracy theories, such as post-WWI Germany's embrace of the "stab in the back" myth when its middle class was wiped out, economic explanations appear inoperative in the United States. Consider the Great Depression with its devastating levels of economic distress. The percentage of letters espousing conspiracy talk is not much higher during this period than during other periods. What we do see is that, as these conditions persisted over time, accusations aimed at the right dissipated and then turned on Roosevelt and his administration. No economic group may be powerful enough to work well as a national fall guy.

It's Big Government

Across the country, activists with ties to the Tea Party are railing against all sorts of local and state efforts to control sprawl and conserve energy. They brand government action for things like expanding public transportation routes and preserving open space as part of a United Nations-led conspiracy to deny property rights and herd citizens toward cities.

—LESLIE KAUFMAN AND KATE ZERNIKE[23]

The United States has a long history of fearing central authority and its trappings.[24] This is based on one of the sturdiest axioms of politics: concentrations of power corrupt. The growth of the American state may allow authority to run amok and suffocate freedom.[25] But even short of tyranny or usurpation, concentrations of power could lead to insensitive and unresponsive actions by remote officials.[26] Under such conditions, conspiracy theories represent a defense mechanism: citizens are proclaiming their alertness against burgeoning concentrations of power and their resolve to oppose them.

Anecdotal evidence of this thesis is not hard to find. The Declaration of Independence is a celebrated instance of big government conspiracy theorizing, and there was plenty of concern during the Constitution's drafting and ratification about excessive concentrations of power, cabals, and subversive factions. More recently, we have witnessed conspiracy theories erupt around nearly every type of government policy, big and small.

There are fine reasons to doubt this narrative. One is that, in a democracy, the majority gets the size of government it deserves. For every person who wants the government to stop keeping him down, another wants the government to give him a hand up. Focusing on disgruntled small government types is a very partial accounting of public opinion. Another reason to doubt is that objections about size may only be a subterfuge for objections about substance. States are merely means to ends, and few are so principled that they would take exception to an oversize tool if it were performing good works on a grand scale. On this view, governmental girth is not the problem, leadership is. People tend to complain about the size of government only when they do not control it.

There are two ways to test this hypothesis: one easy, one hard. The easy way would be to look at annual U.S. government spending as a percentage of GDP. The problem with this approach is that people might acclimate to high state spending and, like boiling frogs, not notice the overall level. Just as a matter of ocular trauma, this approach is easy to dismiss. Federal outlays have expanded for 230 years under all parties, and if conspiracy talk correlated with it we would now talk about nothing but conspiracy theories.

The hard way is to look at the percentage change in annual federal outlays. This is a more sensitive measure and a more demanding test, so we
adopt it. It does not work either. State size is not a significant predictor of
conspiracy theories. As the next chapter's data will suggest, perhaps this
is because no party seriously fears big government when they control it. If
big government is such a menace, Republicans at least ought to be just as
worried when a Republican is in the White House as when a Democrat is.
But they are not.

It's Social Change

> The driving force behind the dogged unwillingness of so many
> to acknowledge that Obama was born in the United States is not
> just simple partisan opposition to a Democratic president but a
> general ethnocentric suspicion of an African-American president
> who is also perceived as distinctly "other."
>
> —MICHAEL TESLER AND DAVID SEARS[27]

Maybe conspiracy theorizing is less about money and power than status.
Individuals may fall prey to conspiratorial thought when they lose social
standing.[28] On this view one would expect conspiracy theories to arise
during times of heightened social change.[29] Believers blame their diminished place in society on cheating opponents, rather than losing fair and
square. This coping strategy brings the benefits of cutting unflattering
corners off reality and absolving personal responsibility for negative outcomes. The logic resembles the first explanation we examined, but there
the impetus was economics and here it is ego-nomics.

Even if status were crucial, though, there is the distinct possibility that
changes in status may just substitute one group's conspiracy theories for
another. Status is a positional good, and the rise of one group may come at
the expense of others. That would cause new conspiracy theories to arise
but would not alter the total level of talk. Or it could be that social change

is not a zero–sum game and everyone's rights can be protected. With no harm there is no foul, and no need for conspiracy theories.

Measuring social change is tricky because it is nebulous and slow and involves a broad set of factors. For instance, how would one measure the progress of African Americans: nominal political rights, effective political rights, economic security, physical security, educational attainment, representation in corporate boardrooms, or some combination? The more factors that are thrown into the mix, the more indeterminate the concept becomes. We must make a choice. Because our theoretical commitments privilege politics, we go with political gains. Ultimately, citizens signal social acceptance by how frequently they elect particular groups to office. In the American context, arguably the most relevant and sensitive indicators of status are the number of women and minorities in the House of Representatives.

Yet we see no correlation. Tellingly, the content of the letters suggests status shifts are not paramount concerns. It is hard to contest that the 1960s were a time of great social ferment and huge strides in social change, yet conspiratorial letters in this period seldom address the civil rights movement. More damningly, just as women and minorities revolutionized American politics in the civil rights era, levels of conspiracy talk dip and continue to slide. Taken as a whole, this suggests that status anxieties and social issues do not rank high on the scale of threats.

It's Technophobia

Facebook—the social networking monster that everyone's on—may have been created by secretive US government agencies hell-bent on mining the personal information of millions, according to one theory. Part of Facebook's funding supposedly came—very indirectly—from the CIA, and from the DARPA's Information Awareness Office, which had the following mission statement: "... to gather as much information as possible about everyone, in

a centralized location, for easy perusal by the United States government, including (though not limited to) Internet activity, credit
card purchase histories, airline ticket purchases, car rentals, medical records, educational transcripts, driver's licenses, utility bills,
tax returns, and any other available data.

—*New Zealand Herald*[30]

Even before the fires were extinguished at the World Trade Center
and the Pentagon, conspiracy theories began flooding the Internet. A few quickly spilled out of Web sites and were widely circu-
lated by e-mail before fading into oblivion.

—Alan Riding[31]

It's traditional for conspiracy theories to flood the Internet after a
major crime—and sure enough, there are a few bouncing around
following the mass shooting in Aurora last week. One that's gained
some traction in the digital world is that the US Government is to
blame for the shooting. It staged the massacre, the theory says, to
gain power over the population by having an excuse to disarm it.

—Ted Thornhill[32]

Technology could trigger an uptick in conspiracy theorizing via two
routes. One could be that rapid change alienates older generations and
sparks fears of retrograde progress, unchecked innovations, and uto-
pian innovators. Citizens may feel overwhelmed by change and believe
that technology erodes their autonomy.[33] The other route could be that
increased communication may accelerate the spread of conspiratorial
ideas in confined spaces, achieving a sort of echo chamber effect of
balkanized politics. With newer, more efficient methods of communicating to large geographically disparate audiences, many surmise that
conspiracy theories should spread farther and faster than ever before.[34]
Hardly an article on conspiracy theories goes by without mentioning
the Internet.

There is, however, a firm basis for skepticism. First, the use of technologies in this country has increased at an amazing rate, and the quality of the technology grows at an exponential rate. Computer processing speed, memory capacity, and digital pixels are doubling roughly every two years. If technology correlated with conspiracy theories, conspiracy theorizing should be off the charts by now.

Second, communication technologies are not necessarily gateways to conspiracy-drenched informational environments. Despite the widespread assumption that conspiracy theories dominate the Internet, there is little evidence to support this. Conspiracy theories certainly have their allure, but the U.S. websites with the most traffic are not devoted to conspiracy theories and conspiracy theory websites are not highly visited.

For example, the main Truther site, 911Truth.org, ranks as the 79,824th most trafficked site in the United States. Glenn Beck's news site, which sometimes features conspiracy theories among other hard news, ranks 131st in the country in terms of Internet traffic. And the Info-Wars website, run by radio host Alex Jones, comes in at 306 in terms of traffic; it is the most trafficked website devoted specifically to conspiracy theories. But this is a far drop from the traffic more popular sites receive. People are on the Web looking for news, dates, plane tickets, and movies far more often than conspiracy theories.[35] And the information environment on the Web may not be as hospitable to conspiratorial logic as some assume.[36]

We examined the information environment on the Internet over the period of a year to see how it discusses conspiracy theories. Our data came from Google Alerts and was detailed in Chapter 3. Of just under 3,000 stories pertaining to conspiracy theories, 63 percent discussed a conspiracy theory (or theories) negatively, 17 percent were neutral, and 19 percent were positive.

This indicates that someone simply seeking out news from the Internet would get a negative portrayal of conspiracy theories. Many are surrounded by words like "fantasy," "bizarre," or "debunked." And our data suggest that their treatment is not much different in news blogs than it is on the Internet sites of traditional news outfits. Of course, there are plenty of sites for people to find information supporting conspiracy theories, but people not predisposed to believing in conspiracy theories will likely not seek out them out. Technology could just as easily decrease conspiracy theorizing because it increases access to anti-conspiratorial information.

If technology were to drive conspiracy talk, we would expect this effect to show up in variables related to innovation and communication technology. Consequently, we employed three variables. The first was the percentage change in the number of approved patents. This provides a rough rate of technological advance. As more products flood the market, the downstream effect should have modern-day Luddites up in arms. The second and third were the percentage of the population with a television and the percentage of the population with an Internet connection. As more and more people bring the marvels of technology into their living rooms, the amount of conspiracy talk should go up.

And still none of these registers. The rate of patent approval goes up and the rate of patent approval goes down, but not in step with the amount of conspiracy talk. This may be because quantity is not the same as quality. Lots of little inventions may not be as psychologically jarring as one mammoth invention. Still, it would take a very selective accounting of epic inventions for this version of the explanation to work. The level of conspiracy talk descends steadily over the last few decades; that would imply that there have been no big inventions for some time.

So, too, with television and the Internet. Although TV may irritate conspiracy theorists, it appears not to do so more than word of mouth or radio ever did. And although the Internet may make it possible for self-selected groups to find and encourage each other's worldviews, they appear to be self-contained enough not to influence the broader population appreciably. Of course, the Internet does not seem to have decreased conspiracy theorizing either.[37] The data show that technology is unrelated to the level of conspiracy theorizing.

It's Popular Culture

> The volume and influence of stigmatized knowledge have in-
> creased dramatically through the mediation of popular culture.
> Motifs, theories, and truth claims that once existed in hermeti-
> cally sealed subcultures have begun to be recycled, often with great
> rapidity, through popular culture.
>
> —MICHAEL BARKUN[38]

Few whipping boys are so obligingly whippable as the entertainment
media. The attack angle of choice for cranky critics is that mass media
stoke the flames of conspiracy theorizing for fun and profit. Back in the
day, producers had scruples, but nowadays the slimy pied pipers purvey
far-fetched stories of schemes and skullduggery—anything for a buck.[39]
When hacks blur the boundaries between reality and entertainment, unsuspecting audiences get gulled into believing conspiracy theories are
conspiracies. Considering the average American watches at least four
hours of television a day, even a small amount of conspiratorial content
could cumulate to toxic levels in short order. Some studies attribute supposed increases in conspiratorial beliefs to films such as *JFK* and television
shows like the *X-Files*.[40]

But then again, there are good reasons why the entertainment media
may not have a noticeable impact. Entertainment, much like the seg-
mented cable news market, bears a serious potential for self-selection and
preaching to the choir. In the Darwinian quest for ratings and revenues,
TV, movies, and books have to give target audiences what they crave, not
what the creators want the audience to want. There may not be much
room for self-selected messages to change opinions.[41] And if conspiracies
sell, they tend not to sell particularly well. *JFK* and *X-Files* were memorable, but hardly as profitable as anti-conspiracy material like *The Wizard
of Oz* or *Law & Order*. In fact, when we examine how conspiracy theory
entertainment is treated in the broader information environment, we find
that it is often mocked. Many reviews of *JFK* were hostile to Oliver Stone's

depiction of conspiracy and may have cut short any chance Stone had of convincing the previously unconvinced.[42]

To test the effect of entertainment, we measured the number of movies considered to be conspiracy theory movies released each year, the number of television series featuring conspiracies airing each year during prime time, and mentions of the term "conspiracy theory" in books released each year using Google's Ngram.[43] Although the number of shows and movies may be driven by other factors, our regression model should be able to isolate how much correlates with the entertainment media. There is no evidence that any of these drive conspiracy talk.

It's Fears of Foreign Intrigue

> [M]ost of the great powers were agreed, most of the time, that these eruptions were the expression of some deeply subversive streak in European and colonial society which might unhinge the established order and the state system. Metternich, in particular, was obsessed with the idea of an international revolutionary conspiracy orchestrated by a mythical central *Comité Directeur*.
>
> —BRENDAN SIMMS[44]

When foreign dangers loom large, there is a strategic logic that suggests conspiracy theorizing may be an adaptive response. With high outside threats, citizens are extremely vulnerable to treachery and in such times it makes sense to put a premium on conformity, be especially on guard against treachery, and be particularly alert to potential plots.[45] On this logic, conspiracy theories are a tripwire alarm, a way of economizing attention and energy on the most menacing perils to protect the most sensitive areas. The second Red Scare is the apogee of this.

On the other hand, conspiracy theories have their drawbacks in terms of threat perception and response. False alarms have costs and, as the Red Scares showed, scapegoating inflicts real damage on a country. Then there is the problem that articulating one's darkest fears and greatest vulnerabilities may incite enemies to seize on them. And then there is the issue that mass-level threat perception may not be an effective mechanism for group protection because elites often have access to higher-quality information.

As for measurement, threats are subjective and empirically elusive. Our best approximation is to measure defense spending as a percentage of GDP. This roughly indicates the amount of threat the United States faces in a given year because societies reveal their preferences by making costly tradeoffs between consumption, investment, and security (sometimes referred to as "guns versus butter" decisions.) Curiously, threat has but a miniscule and likely coincidental impact on the total amount of conspiracy talk.

This spurious finding is curious because we see a clear upsurge in conspiracy theorizing during the most dangerous period of the Cold War, and in the next chapter we see clear evidence of foreign threat coming to the fore during the gravest conflicts. It may be that the United States is relatively insulated from foreign threats because of its remote geography, large landmass, enormous GDP, and unmatched military expenditures. Yet this seems like only a partial explanation. Evidently Americans are sometimes threatened by foes abroad and react somewhat differently when that threat is elevated, but for some reason that does not alter the aggregate amount of conspiracy talk.

It's Polarized Elites

In polarized political debate, the very fact of polarization tends to provoke doubt about the availability of any solution that would be widely acceptable. If people disagree so vehemently and persistently about a matter of policy, and if some even seem to reject the value of public justification itself, then it becomes tempting to say that no solution will avoid the political domination of one group by another.

— Eamonn Callan[46]

Political polarization has been increasing in the United States for decades and there is reason to think that polarized politics raises the incentives to see one's opponents as conspirators.[47] If you have less and less common ground with your opponents, you are more likely to believe their actions will harm the (read "your group's") common good. This can lead Americans to view the political solutions as black and white. The germane hypothesis is that as elite factions spread farther apart in their preferences rhetoric will intensify and accusations of conspiracy will escalate. On the other hand, we showed in the last chapter that extreme partisanship does not drive conspiratorial beliefs; instead, a separate dimension of conspiratorial thought does.

We use the gold-standard measure of American political polarization—Keith Poole and Howard Rosenthal's DW-NOM scores[48]—and it yields no statistical relationship between polarization and conspiracy talk. This non-finding on polarization is actually quite fascinating. First, it adds to our argument that partisanship/ideology does not drive conspiratorial thinking. But second, it signals that although politicians have an incentive to level conspiracy charges and countercharges at each other, either they refrain from doing so for mysterious reasons or the public fails to respond to them when they do. Thus, the total level of conspiracy talk is unaffected.

The Information Environment

> If you were a person who watched FOX News all day, it is possible you have been marinating in this conspiracy theory for long enough now that this seems feasible.
>
> —RACHEL MADDOW[49]

> But what I am focusing on tonight is sitting members of the United States Congress, people in important positions of power, who are pointing fingers at individuals working in this government, making allegations or spreading innuendoes about them

without any direct evidence. They're dragging people's names and reputations through the mud.

—ANDERSON COOPER[50]

A commonsensical claim is that conspiracy talk grows more frequent as credible information of conspiracies becomes readily available. People are generally rational, and when changes in the information environment support conspiratorial beliefs, they will be expressed more.[51] Those most predisposed will be quick to communicate their beliefs when evidence becomes more available. And when trusted national media and opinion leaders give credence to a conspiracy theory, even those moderately predisposed will pick up the conspiracy theory for the same reasons. A canonical case is Watergate. Few paid attention to early allegations of a break-in, but as the evidence stacked up, the story became nationally absorbing. Although there will always be diehards who cannot be convinced, most people are not like this. Tests of truth matter, and people do not have to be epistemologists to make informed guesses about what is likely correct.

The news media are the most prominent way that citizens hear about conspiracy theories, and elites, with their access to visible platforms, are in an obvious position to influence views on conspiracy theories (and much else besides). How journalists and elites talk about domestic and foreign foes could cast a long shadow on public opinion because they are presumed to be in possession of the best information.

Beginning with the news, front-page stories are perhaps the best stories from which to estimate news discussion of conspiracies and conspiracy theories—these stories are the most visible to the public and should have the most impact.[52] We also examined the full body of the *Times*. We searched the *New York Times* Historical Database for the term "conspiracy" and tallied up the percentage of articles on the front page and in the full paper mentioning conspiracies per year. We measured elite rhetoric the same way we measured everyone else's rhetoric, with letters to the editor written by elites.

The results for both are striking. A one-standard-deviation increase of conspiracy-related discussion on the front page of the *Times* predicts an impressive increase of .26 standard deviations of conspiracy talk in the public. Mentions in the full body of the paper are not predictive. The model estimates that a one-standard-deviation increase in elite rhetoric predicts a .23 standard deviation increase in conspiracy talk in the public. These are substantial relationships.

However, causation is seldom straightforward; news content and elite rhetoric may be responding to audience opinions, rather than the reverse. To analyze the direction of causation between the public and the news, we performed additional testing using lags. The data suggest that the information environment is the driver, but we caution that with yearly units of time, more testing is needed. So while the causal direction remains speculative, at least we now have some promising space to direct future labors.

One question that arises from our findings is that if elites can influence the public to believe in conspiracy theories, why not do it all the time? As with partisan politics and the information environment, crying wolf is costly in the competitive game of politics. Rabblerousing elites (this means you, Donald Trump) can catalyze conspiracy theories in the minds of highly predisposed partisans, but that is unlikely to spread further. Demagogues are usually successful for only brief periods of time in the United States, and then the fundamentals of the information environment win out. Elites are well positioned to get access to conspiratorial evidence and to publicize it, but they cannot create it from scratch. Information quality is critical.

CONCLUSION: AGELESS CONSPIRACY THEORIES

There is a strong temptation to proclaim every year the "age of conspiracy." This is somewhat true; conspiracy theories never really go out of fashion. Yet if the question is when U.S. conspiracy theorizing peaked, the answer is: not now and not for decades. The contribution of this chapter is that it can identify the 1890s and 1950s as the real ages of conspiracy in the United States. The prevalence of conspiracy talk in the United States has diminished slightly across time, especially since the mid-1960s.

The most marked trend in the data, however, is stability. We believe this is largely due to the interaction between conspiratorial predispositions, partisan commitments, and shifts in the distribution of power. The high watermarks for conspiracy talk likely happened because of anomalous circumstances, when novel threats alarmed people on both sides of the aisle. Monopoly trusts were collusive in the 1890s; communist subversion was a pressing possibility in the 1950s. But the country passed measures to manage these problems, signs of danger grew less intense, coalitions changed their positions, and life went back to normal.

Comparing the long-term data against the most popular explanations, most of the comforting stories we use to explain away supposed surges in conspiracy theorizing seem as baseless as conspiracy theories themselves are often held to be. This includes such usual suspects as economic hard times, big government, new technologies, social status, partisan politics, and foreign intrigue. Each of these explanations may explain one or a few conspiracy theories, but they do not explain the overall level. It may also be that there are other ways to measure these explanations, and their relationship to conspiracy talk is more complicated than we know. As always, more testing helps.

As for the positive findings, the information environment and elite cues appear most promising. This tells us that the next time people scramble for big-picture answers about conspiracy theories, they could do worse than starting with the quality of evidence. We should all keep in mind that information is never inert, and everyone interprets it through his or her own political and conspiratorial predispositions and perspectives. But large numbers of people over long periods of time do not do this estranged from reality. Separating the more from the less true is an inescapably arduous, messy, but imperative process.

6

Conspiracy Theories Are for Losers

There seems to be a curious American tendency to search, at all times, for a single external center of evil to which all our troubles can be attributed, rather than to recognize that there might be multiple sources of resistance to our purposes and undertakings, and that these sources might be relatively independent of each other.

—GEORGE F. KENNAN[1]

Had early Americans been asked to put a thumbtack on the map where their conspiratorial fears originated, many of those tacks would have landed on Great Britain, with a few on France, fewer on Spain, and occasional outbreaks of concern about Bavarian Illuminati and Freemasons—wherever they furtively congregated. Decades later, those thumbtacks would have come closer to home with fears of abolitionist and slave power conspiracies. Decades after that, tacks would have scattered around monopoly trusts, socialists, and anarchists, then clustered around Germany and the USSR. If Americans are determined to find an epicenter of evil, why is it so mobile?

Nowadays, most people fail to see what much of that fuss was about, but many of them feel compelled to pin conspiratorial blame on new domestic and foreign foes. Why? To answer this question, this chapter examines the resonance of conspiracy theories over time. In the sense we will be using it, "resonance" refers to how natural, useful, or acceptable an idea appears to society.

We argue the targets and timing of resonant conspiracy theories follow a strategic logic, based on foreign threat and domestic power. In this way, conspiracy theories are used by vulnerable groups to manage perceived dangers: they are early warning systems that keep watch over the most sensitive areas and prepare solutions to potential attacks. At bottom, conspiracy theories are a form of threat perception, and fears are fundamentally driven by shifts in relative power. Because defeat and exclusion are their biggest inducements, conspiracy theories are for losers (speaking descriptively, not pejoratively).

To make our case, the chapter unfolds as follows. The first section presents the logic of our argument. The second section details some technical specifications and the methods used for our macro-level analysis. The third section reports the results of our inquiry. The fourth section takes a more granular approach, applying macro-level findings to the use of conspiratorial rhetoric by minor parties and movements. The final section summarizes our findings and discusses implications.

A POLITICAL VIEW OF CONSPIRACY THEORIES

Our basic claim is that conspiracy theories are essentially alarm systems and coping mechanisms to help deal with threats. Consequently, they tend to resonate when groups are suffering from loss, weakness, or disunity. But nothing fails like success, and ascending groups trigger dynamics that check and eventually reverse the advance of conspiracy theories.

Like atoms in science, groups are the foundation of our argument. By "groups" we mean stable aggregates of individuals who share political interests and seek cooperation with other members. In our model, we assume groups compete for power. All groups perform at least two functions: coordination and distribution. To vie against others, groups coordinate individuals to create or capture resources, broadly interpreted, and then distribute those spoils authoritatively. These tasks are in tension; there are always incentives to cooperate to expand the size of the pie and to compete for a greater slice of the pie. The ratio between the two is primarily a product of external threat.[2] More threat means more unity until the threat becomes so large that no amount of unity could manage it, at which point unity falls apart.

So the larger outside dangers loom, the more in-group cooperation and less distributional strife there is likely to be. In such situations, groups tend to behave like unitary actors. But as external threat relents, conditions allow the indulgence of infighting. In these periods, internal subgroups compete for a greater share of collective resources. Because present victory brings relative gains that may leverage future victories, defeated subgroups have strong incentives to be especially vigilant and vigorous.

Whether or not conspiracy theorists realize it, their talk must conform to the present distribution of power to resonate widely. In this way, conspiracy talk has a strategic logic. Sharing conspiracy theories provides a way for groups falling in the pecking order to revamp and recoup from losses, close ranks, staunch losses, overcome collective action problems, and sensitize minds to vulnerabilities. Emerging groups, minor groups, and social movements will turn to conspiracy talk for similar reasons. ·

Successful conspiracy theories can meet these goals because they have an infectious effect and function as mental inoculation. Conspiracy talk provides a unifying narrative of a terrifying enemy. Communicating conspiracy theories heightens alertness to avert tragedy. The tendency of conspiracy theorists to scapegoat, however reprehensible, channels anger, avoids internecine recriminations, and aims at redemption.

We assert that that perceived power asymmetries drive the direction of resonant conspiracy talk. Two types of asymmetries are especially noteworthy: those between domestic political groups and those between the United States and foreign actors. During periods of low external threat, domestic groups jockey fiercely for distributional benefits. In a democracy, power is allocated through elections, and winners allocate resources. Victory being a lax disciplinarian, large winning groups feel less anxiety, more in control, and less need for conspiracy theories. But losses may be cumulative, and conspiracy talk is most likely to issue from domestic groups who fail to achieve power, objectives, or resources.

During periods of elevated external threat, coordination issues displace domestic distributional concerns. Thus, as external threats increase, conspiracy talk about international foes rises in relation to conspiracy talk demonizing domestic opponents. Anxiety and a perceived lack of control will come from foreign actors rather than domestic opponents. In both cases, though, balancing against threats is the crux of conspiracy theorizing.

Translated into the American context, the most important factors are domestic political power and foreign threat. Domestically, the largest concentrations of power are in the presidency, Congress, and the Supreme Court, in that order. The party in the White House should have the strongest effect on conspiracy talk because the presidency is the most powerful, visible, and unified institution in government. No individual has as large an impact on national policy as the president, and his or her supporters should receive favored policies and preferential access to resources. The flipside of this is that parties outside the president's, left in the shade, have good reason to worry that their inferiority will be used against them, and they will be touchy about encroachments on their power. Conspiracy theories are one manifestation of that, and they should track the party of the president (Republican or Democrat) and the perceived members of their coalition (big business or socialists, respectively).

Next, the party controlling Congress exerts considerable influence over the distribution of resources and should also affect conspiracy talk. The legislative branch is much more decentralized than the executive branch and so less able to move with speed and secrecy. With unified government, the party in power should attract more conspiratorial allegations because it exercises more authority. A corollary of this is that the longer a party predominates, the more conspiracy theories should swirl around it. Divided government—defined here as the party opposite the president having majority control of at least one house—allows the party opposite the president a significant voice and veto. This should soothe some of the sores that cause conspiracy theories to resonate against the president.

Lastly, the Supreme Court should have a small effect on the resonance of conspiracy theories. This may seem counterintuitive. As the highest court in the land, the Supreme Court should be a lightning rod: justices are appointed, declare laws unconstitutional, and have lifetime tenure. Throw in cloaks, rituals, arcane incantations, and hushed deliberations, and conspiracy theories should be bound to strike. Yet by most accounts the judicial branch is the weakest of the three, with no executive powers and oversight on only a small number of cases per year. In addition, appointments are made by the president and approved by Congress, making the court derivative of the other branches in a sense. With less power, the judicial branch is likely to be a bit player in conspiracy theories.

Internationally, conspiracy theories resonate with urgent threats abroad. Threat perception is a much-studied but still dimly understood topic in international relations, but largely threats revolve around the ability to project capability across space.[3] The next section discusses measurements, but for now the conceptual distinction is that citizens assess foreign threats based on material capability, proximity, and military expenditures.[4]

Here we should pause and make some caveats. Our argument is structural and depends on threats to the distribution of power, but it says little about the rationality and motives of groups—other than that they seek power and are sensitive to loss. Like Charles Darwin or Adam Smith's theories, actors in our model need not understand their incentive structure but are punished if they fail to follow it. Conspiracy theorists do not need to know when the right time for a particular theory to resonate is, nor, for that matter, do they need to know why they turn to conspiratorial rhetoric. But theories not following this logic will not resonate as well as those that do. Because they forge central tendencies, incentives are critical for our argument, not intentions.

Structural arguments can operate behind the backs of actors, who are more likely to know *that* a behavior is rewarding than *why* it is rewarding. This makes evidence on the ground problematic, but examples abound. Despite the loosening of gun control regulations, gun rights supporters objected to the president's gun policies because they were, as Wayne LaPierre, Executive Vice President of the National Rifle Association, put it, "all part of a massive Obama conspiracy to deceive voters [in 2012]."[5] This accusation of conspiracy resonated when it did because it came from out-of-power Republicans assaulting in-power Democrats. It resonated so well, in fact, that it spurred massive NRA fundraising.[6]

Compare the popularity of conspiracy theories *aimed at* in-power groups to the popularity of conspiracy theories *made by* in-power groups. During the impeachment trial, the Clinton administration gained little sympathy blaming a "vast right-wing conspiracy" for their troubles; indeed, the phrase became a punch line. The opening salvo of President Obama's 2012 reelection campaign also garnered little support: the commercial accused "secretive oil billionaires" of distorting the president's record. It is hard to view the most powerful person in the world as a defenseless victim of spectral forces, and for this reason the ad's message did not catch on.

What is the value added of this argument to the literature? To psychological approaches, it contributes another layer of detail in how environmental cues convert personality traits into conspiracy theories. Psychologists have linked conspiracy theories to feelings of uncertainty, anxiety, and lack of control in the face of high stakes.[7] But our hypotheses are more specific about how and why the environment elicits conspiracy theories. Although the underlying psychological dynamics are more or less constant in the population and lead us to predict that conspiratorial beliefs are fairly static, political factors draw out conspiratorial beliefs and convert them into resonant conspiracy talk. Previous works by sociologists and political scientists have done an able job showing that conspiracy theories are aimed at outsiders and adversaries.[8] Yet they do not do as good a job explaining which outsiders will be scapegoated, when, and why. We hope to highlight that the quintessence of conspiracy theories is political threat assessment. Shifting threats activate different political boundaries.[9]

TECHNICAL SPECIFICATIONS AND METHODS

To spell out the fundamentals, we are trying to explain why different conspiracy theories resonate at different times. Rather than examine internal thought and beliefs that may not be expressed, we are interested in the outward expression of conspiratorial beliefs. (Given the scarcity of relevant survey data, we are forced to examine the resonance of recorded conspiracy talk.) Therefore we return to our letters to the editor data, which give purchase on long-term trends in the resonance of conspiracy theories. Our main claim is that power asymmetries drive the ebb and flow of resonance over time. To measure changes in the distribution of domestic power, we track the party of the president, control of Congress, and the ideological tilt of the Supreme Court. These are straightforward measures and need not be belabored.

To operationalize international power asymmetries, we look at foreign threat. There are many ways to measures changes in foreign threat, but we opt to examine the most exigent kind: great power wars. These come in two varieties: hot and cold. Hot wars are serious enough to warrant a declaration of war, and after 1890 these include the Spanish–American War, World War I, and World War II.[10] For WWI and WWII, we include the full span of the war because, with the balance of power in the balance, U.S. interests were severely affected and American foreign policy, though formally neutral, was significantly involved soon after hostilities commenced.

Second, there is the Cold War, which did not warrant a formal declaration of war but overshadowed half of last century. We define this as 1946 to 1991, from Winston Churchill's "Iron Curtain" speech to the USSR's collapse. We expect these great power conflicts to increase the proportion of foreign conspiracy theories and drown out domestic conspiracy theories. If foreign conspiracy talk does not increase during great power conflicts, it invalidates this claim.

One could object that we omit other disputes, from small actions, such as Beirut and Panama, to regional contingencies, such as Vietnam, Iraq, and Afghanistan, to more diffuse conflicts, such as the wars on drugs or terror. While worrisome, these conflicts are qualitatively different than declared wars and the Cold War and are poor comparisons based on how we conceive of threats. The destructive potential of middling to weak states, narcotraffickers, and terrorists pales in comparison to great power capabilities.[11]

It is imperative that our timeframe encompass a period in which group identities are fairly stable because our arguments rest on claims about distinct groups. To minimize controversy, we confine this chapter's scope to the period 1897 to 2010. The reason is that 1897 is often considered the start of the modern party system, when business and labor interests solidified into the Republican and Democratic parties, respectively.[12]

In this slightly shorter timeframe, our coders identified 800 letters engaging in conspiracy talk. The 800 letters identified in the sample made 836 accusations of conspiracy (36 of the letters identified two groups). The analysis focuses on the villains accused rather than the number of letters. Below, we present findings directly from the raw data. Note that we have subjected many of the findings here to severe statistical scrutiny, partially to account for the potential mediating effects of the *New York Times* staff, ownership, competition, and circulation, and also to account for changes in the media market and in society as a whole over the course of the 114-year timeframe.[13] Technical analyses are in the online appendix for motivated readers.

WHAT AMERICAN CONSPIRACY THEORIES DO AND DO NOT LOOK LIKE

With 836 alleged villains spread among eight categories during this time period, the distribution is strikingly hierarchical. The largest category is "foreign," with 37 percent of villains. This makes sense because outsiders are proverbially untrustworthy and unlikely to share norms or interests with insiders. Within this category 39 percent are European, 24 percent Russian/

Soviet, 12 percent Latin American, 11 percent Asian, 9 percent Middle Eastern, and 5 percent others. Almost two thirds are European or Russian—not
surprising considering the United States fought three hot wars against Europeans and a cold war against the USSR. We predict that the distribution
of foreign villains will shift as geopolitical power pivots to Asia.

Outside of "foreign," the next largest categories are "right/capitalist," with
22 percent of the villains, followed by "left/communist," with 20 percent—
if one combined the partisan political groups, they would be the largest
total group, with 42 percent. Readers should also note the over-time symmetry between accusations aimed at these groups. "Government" com-
poses 13 percent, "other" amounts to 7 percent, and "media" accrues a
scant 2 percent. Figure 6.1 presents the proportion of each category within
our sample.

So much for the preliminaries—what are the results? As predicted, conspiracies aimed at the right and capitalists increased as a proportion of
total conspiratorial allegations each year when a Republican was president
and decreased when a Democrat was president (and vice versa). Figure 6.2
shows that during the years a Republican was in the White House (black
columns), conspiracy theories about the right and capitalists increased to
16 percent and 18 percent, respectively, while conspiracy theories about

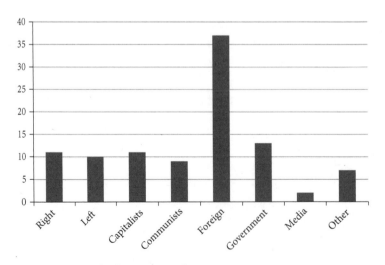

Figure 6.1 Proportion of Villains in Sample.

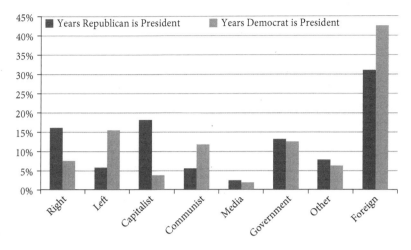

Figure 6.2 Proportion of Villains by Party of President.

the left and communists decreased to 6 percent each. When a Democrat was in the White House (gray columns), conspiracy theories about the right and capitalists decreased to 5 percent and 4 percent, respectively, while conspiracy theories about the left and communists increased to 15 percent and 12 percent, respectively.

This pattern becomes clearer when we combine the right and capitalists into one category and the left and communists into another. Figure 6.3

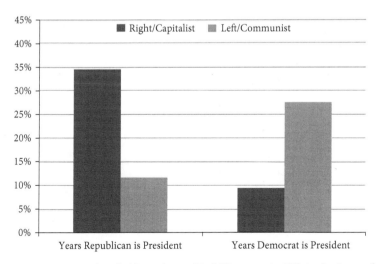

Figure 6.3 Proportion of Right/Capitalist and Left/Communist Villains by Party of President.

shows that during Republican administrations, conspiracy theories targeting the right and capitalists averaged 34 percent of the conspiratorial allegations per year, while conspiracy theories targeting the left and communist averaged only 11 percent. During Democratic administrations, *mutatis mutandis*, conspiracy theories aimed at the right and capitalists dropped 25 points to 9 percent while conspiracy theories aimed at the left and communists more than doubled to 27 percent. Who controls the White House invites conspiracy theories.

For illustrations, compare consecutive years when executive power changes party. In 1968, Democrat Lyndon Johnson was president and accusations against the left and communists were 17 percent of total conspiracy talk while accusations against the right and capitalists were zero. Republican Richard Nixon won the 1968 presidential election and took office in January 1969. That year, accusations of conspiracy against the left and communists dropped from 17 percent to 0 percent while accusations against the right and capitalists increased from 0 percent to 25 percent. A similar pattern cropped up after the 2008 presidential election. When Barack Obama took office from George W. Bush, accusations against the right and capitalists dropped by 40 percentage points while accusations against the left and communists increased by 10 percentage points between 2008 and 2009.

So far we have examined the effect of party control of the White House, but does the picture change if we look beyond party? We find that over the course of presidential terms, the balance between the right and capitalists versus the left and communists is fairly consistent. In looking at party control of the White House, which ranges between four years (Carter) and 20 years (F. Roosevelt/Truman) in our sample, there is evidence that as parties hold on to power longer, they bear an increasing brunt of conspiratorial attacks.

This likely indicates that Americans find living with power asymmetry more uncomfortable as time goes on. Anecdotally, 9/11 Truther theories began to strongly resonate not immediately after 9/11/2001, but in the beginning of Bush's second term. And President Obama's administration seemed to become especially prone to conspiratorial scandals in its second term.[14] This is an interesting finding, but because of the small sample size (we have only four instances where parties have maintained control of the White House for more than eight years) one ought to be cautious about drawing conclusions from it.

Divided government also conforms to expectations. Figures 6.4 and 6.5 compare periods of divided and unified government. When a Republican was president (Fig. 6.4), united government showed a difference of

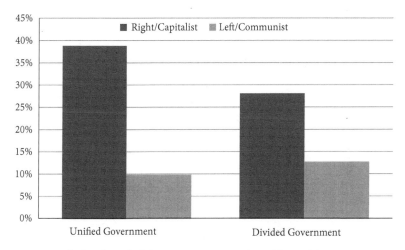

Figure 6.4 Divided and Unified Government During Republican Administration.

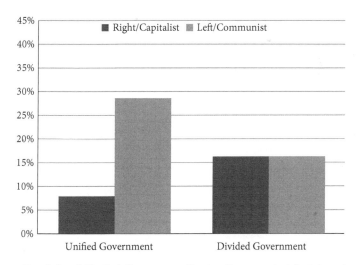

Figure 6.5 Divided and Unified Government During Democratic Administration.

29 percentage points between the right and capitalists and the left and communists. During divided government the difference dropped to 15 percentage points (the right and capitalists decreased by 10 percentage points while the left and communists increased by 2.6 percentage points). When a Democrat was president (Fig. 6.5), united government showed a difference of 21 percentage points between the right and capitalists versus the left and communists. During divided government the difference dropped to zero (accusations against the right and capitalists increased by eight percentage points while accusations against the left and communists decreased by 12 percentage points).

Juxtapose recent years when Congressional majorities changed hands. In 1994, the Republicans won a majority in the House of Representatives for the first time in 40 years; Democrat Bill Clinton was president. In 1994, when the Democrats controlled the White House and both houses, accusations of conspiracy against the right and capitalists were 18 percent of the conspiracy talk. After the Republicans entered office, accusations against the right and capitalists increased to 43 percent of the conspiracy talk in 1995. When the 2006 election changed the House from Republican to Democratic control during Republican George W. Bush's second term, accusations of conspiracy against the right and capitalists plummeted from 100 percent of the conspiracy talk in 2006 to 0 percent in 2007.

When actors attempt to grab power, they are often accused of conspiring. Think of Franklin Roosevelt's 1937 court-packing plan, which would have given the Democrats control over all branches of government. In response to Roosevelt's unveiling of the plan, conspiracy theories aimed at the left increased to 50 percent of the conspiracy talk for that year. Authors argued that Roosevelt was attempting to set up a dictatorship. One letter dated February 10, 1937, stated, "If the President has his way and is permitted to emasculate the Court, the United States may class itself as a nation of puppets." On September 10, 1937, a writer claimed that while the president "declares for democracy," he in fact uses the "methods of a dictator." Another letter, dated October 30, 1937, plainly claimed Roosevelt was setting up a "political oligarchy." Credible threats to alter the domestic distribution of power led to more conspiracy theories against the dominant group.[15] In total, the evidence argues that the balance of power in the executive and legislative branches of government drives the waxing and waning of domestic conspiracy talk. The more power a group has, the more other groups will oppose it.

As for the effect of international perils on conspiracy talk, wars exert a significant effect. We compared the Spanish–American, WWI, WWII, and Cold War era years to the other years in our timespan (Fig. 6.6). During these years of acute threat, the proportion of foreign conspiracy theories increased by 17 percentage points, from 28 percent to 45 percent. Figure 6.7 shows the over-time volatility of foreign and the summation of the domestic right, left, capitalist, and communist villains. Foreign and domestic actors peaked and troughed opposite each other with a stark relationship (a correlation coefficient of –.71). This zero–sum element comes as no surprise because the measures are percentages of a whole and must come at each other's expense.

Having previously demonstrated the stability of conspiratorial thinking at the individual level, we have shown that the conspiracy theories fluctuate over time. This creates an apparent tension between volatility in partisan accusations and stability in overall conspiracy theory levels. Both

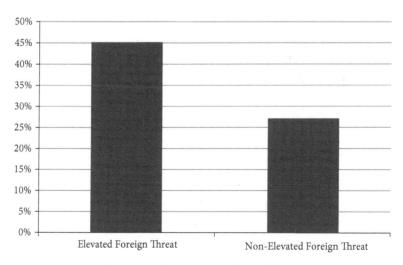

Figure 6.6 Proportion of Foreign Villains During Elevated Threat and Non-Elevated Threat.

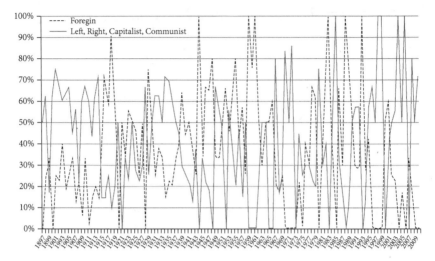

Figure 6.7 Proportion of Foreign Villains Compared to Left, Right, Capitalist, and Communist Villains.

can be true at the same time. The findings on partisan resonance refer to conspiracy theory beliefs while the findings on total prevalence refer to conspiracy talk. Each picks up slightly different phenomena.

THIRD PARTIES AND FRINGE MOVEMENTS

So far, we have demonstrated how the resonance of domestic conspiracy theories alternates in response to major shifts in power. Now we circle back to the finding from Chapter 4 that it is the individuals outside the major parties who are most liable to conspiracy theories. This supports our logic that conspiracy theories are a weapon of the weak used most by embattled minorities who perceive themselves under threat. Political parties are durable, dominant institutions and likely to be punching bags for this reason. If one has been on the business end of a governmental decision, one of the two parties is usually responsible for it, if not morally then as part of a causal chain.

But the relationship may go in a different direction (or a combination of both directions): those who see value in third parties, or who do not support either party, are bound to be almost completely shut out of policy and discourse. Voices and preferences outside the two-party system are seldom heard. If they are going to be heard, outsiders need to concentrate their efforts and explain away their failures. Conspiracy theories perform both functions.

Our argument is not that losing reflexively causes groups to conspiracy theorize; it is that losing stokes a propensity to conspiracy theorize. Some powerful groups conspiracy theorize more and others less, and the same can be said for weak groups. We are not determinists and there is room for individual choice across the board. Yet the more a group loses, the more likely it will conspiracy theorize, and typically the more tortured the conspiracy theories get. This section examines several instances of this phenomenon, but it also showcases the limits of our argument. Some minority groups are ambivalent about conspiracy theories or fail completely to avail themselves of conspiracy theories.

First, let us look at instances of fringe movements and third parties who primarily rely on conspiracy theories for their rhetoric. Because no book on conspiracy theories would be complete without him, we start with tireless activist Lyndon LaRouche and his group LaRouchePAC. In the 1980s, LaRouche argued that AIDS had been created by either the "'Soviet War Machine via the World Health Organization (WHO) to conquer America, or by the International Monetary Fund to wipe out the 'excess eaters' in starving Africa" and that reports that the HIV virus could not be spread through casual contact were "lies."[16]

Times have changed, but at 91 years old, LaRouche's doomsday clock remains eternally one minute before midnight. The rhetoric warns of danger from powerful groups who subvert normal processes and calls for action to organize and oppose:

The real danger of global thermonuclear war comes from the fact that the present global monetarist system is doomed. The empire is the global monetarist system, and the British Monarchy plays a particular role within that global imperial system. . . . The British Empire is not contained within the United Kingdom. It is a true empire, a global system.... The imperial blackmail game is very simple: Russia and China capitulate, or there will be thermonuclear war. So long as Barack Obama remains in office as President of the United States, the global imperial game is rigged. Remove Obama from office, and the United States can break out of the vise-grip of the British monetarist system, return to a credit system, and once and for all, wipe out the imperial system.[17]

As a matter of fact, the projection of all trends is that the human species is being reduced, by the order of the Queen of England, to a rapid reduction of the human population from 7 billion persons to less than 1! And the time has come when we can no longer submit to that evil. So therefore, we have to have the resolution, to oppose this evil, which I've just partly described. But that's not enough. What we're doing now, based on the Basement operations in the way we organized it, the water system which had been planned during the time of John F. Kennedy, the NAWAPA policy based on water management. Since that time, changes in technology, since the 1944-45 period, now enable us to shoot ahead, and create an entirely new opportunity for mankind, through thermonuclear power.[18]

What is curious about radical conspiratorial writings is that they are only a more intense version of mundane political discourse. Where regular politicians highlight problems, advocate solutions, and call for concerted action soon, conspiracy theorists highlight an abysmal state of affairs, advocate titanic policies, and call for concerted action right now.

Another prototypical conspiratorial movement involves those opposed to genetically modified organisms (GMO), in essence a protest against the genetic engineering of food. Not everyone who opposes GMOs is a conspiracy theorist; reasonable people can disagree about research and fail to see small groups of people covertly working against the common good. But the most visible and vocal members of this movement, however, are conspiracy theorists. They believe that genetically modified foods are a corporate plot, led by the giant multinational Monsanto, to profit off unhealthy food.

Of course, everyone knows that artisanal producers of cheese and bacon also profit off unhealthy food, many organic products can kill you, and the life expectancy of our ancestors who lived in all-organic environments was agonizingly abbreviated. Nature's record of beneficence is about as checkered as humanity's. What incenses anti-GMO protesters is the belief that Monsanto uses its size to co-opt the U.S. government, and fraud to tamper with the food supply.

Here is the flavor of their Facebook postings: "Monsanto hates Democracy. They'd rather work somewhere where corporations have exclusive access and everything is kept secret from the public." Another chimes in: "It's time we ask ourselves: How long will we tolerate the growing monopolization and genetic engineering of seeds by a monopolistic pesticide company that poses a deadly threat to our health, our environment and the future of our food?" In an interview with reporter John Stossel, Jeffrey Smith, a representative for the movement, and the Executive Director of the Institute for Responsible Technology, declares that the conspiracy has gone global:

> **John Stossel:** So Monsanto has captured the FDA, this thousand-person agency, and they're just in the tank with big business?
> **Jeffrey Smith:** Monsanto has not only captured the FDA, but as I traveled to 36 countries, they've done the same to many, many countries . . . [19]

This is not about the prosaic world of science and methods; this is about the diabolical world of power and money. There are no shades of gray. The corporate conspiracy has infiltrated and enslaved the scientific and political establishments alike. According to conspiracy narratives, the only reasonable response is to close ranks and act in the face of danger. From the Millions Against Monsanto by OrganicConsumers.org Facebook page: "Nothing shocks me anymore except peoples unwillingness to wake up and care what they are eating and feeding their children!!! Get involved people, its the only way things will improve!!!!" Another frets: "Seeing that the head of the FDA was an executive at Monsanto, we can be sure the FDA is corrupt. I have zero faith in the FDA. I don't think they give a damn about our health, they're only interested in $$. BUT I still take action, sign petitions etc." And finally a radical plea for redemption: "[Obama] doesn't care about our health. We are a nuisance. An overgrown population that needs to be destroyed. Agenda 21. New world order."[20]

Segments of the Occupy Wall Street (OWS) movement also traffic in conspiracy narratives. As governments took action and the movement fizzled, admirers had to explain why the movement was not catching fire or gaining more sympathy. The simple explanation—that much of the country had yet to share OWS's views—was unattractive. Public intellectual Naomi Wolf took a different tack: a nationwide plot involving governments at all levels and the media was to blame:

> I noticed that rightwing pundits and politicians on the TV shows on which I was appearing were all on-message against OWS. Journalist Chris Hayes reported on a leaked memo that revealed lobbyists vying for an $850,000 contract to smear Occupy. Message coordination of this kind is impossible without a full-court press at the top. This was clearly not simply a case of a freaked-out mayors', city-by-city municipal overreaction against mess in the parks and cranky campers. As the puzzle pieces fit together, they began to show coordination against OWS at the highest national levels.[21]

Second, let's look at a minority group that is split between conspiratorial and anti-conspiratorial factions: libertarians. The split among them appears because of the difference between libertarian thought and libertarianism as a minor party. Those who associate with the party are outnumbered and outflanked by the two major parties, and Libertarian candidates rarely win. Like other minor parties, they should be prone to conspiracy theorizing. Those who support libertarian ideals but belong to one of the major parties, though, have little incentive to do so. As libertarian and anti-conspiracy theorist Milton Friedman proclaimed, "I am a libertarian with a small 'l' and a Republican with a capital 'R.' And

I am a Republican with a capital 'R' on grounds of expediency, not on principle."[22] Libertarians like Friedman do not need conspiracy theories; their views translate into influence via a major party.

In contrast, those belonging to the fledgling Libertarian Party lack influence. They want government off their backs because they see government as an incorrigible and insidious threat to individual liberty, but they have little luck in gaining a national following. Like a minority party paragon, they explain their unexalted status as the result of a plot. Going into the 2012 election, Libertarian Party literature explained why their candidate was not garnering a significant amount of support: "The D's and R's are finally working together . . . to keep Gary Johnson out of the debates. Fight back by joining today's twitter bomb. And if you haven't already done so, please sign the petition to get Governor Johnson into the debates. TYRANNY BROUGHT TO YOU BY THE LETTER D AND THE LETTER R."[23]

Yet the libertarians not associated with the Libertarian Party promote rationalism and shun conspiracy theories. They treasure the free market because it is decentralized, they value science, and their flagship magazine is titled *Reason*. Sometimes these two strands of libertarians clash. In 2013, it was leaked that the NSA had been keeping records of phone calls made by U.S. citizens without a warrant. These meta-data were then used by the government to track patterns and supposedly foil terror plots. John Stossel, a popular figure in the libertarian movement, claimed to be unconcerned with the recordkeeping by the NSA and, as a consequence, faced widespread ire from his audience. To address this, he debated former federal judge and libertarian Andrew Napolitano:

Andrew Napolitano: yes, of course to the slippery slope. I mean, a
   single phone call in the computer of a single spy is innocuous. But
   all of our phone calls in there, revealing everything about ourselves,
   exposing our inner-most thoughts and behavior to the government
   will eventually turn us into East Germany, where the government
   knows who did wrong and the government knows who knows
   who did wrong, and the government prosecutes people who didn't

squeal on their neighbors. In the last five years of that society, the most frequently prosecuted crime was the failure to turn in one's neighbor. Do we really want that society here? That's what this will bring us to.

John Stossel: no, we do not. But then, what do you say about two respected libertarians—you know who they are, I assume you respect them—Richard Epstein and Roger Pilon, [who] wrote "the critics would be more credible if they could identify a pattern of government abuses. But after 12 years of continuing practices, they can't cite even a single case."[24]

Third, the movement for gay equality stands out because it is a rare example of a minority movement that has never had a prominent role for conspiracy theories. The most obvious cause of this may be that the adversaries of the gay movement were transparent enough to obviate the need for conspiracy theories. But perhaps more importantly, in the last 30 years at least, the gay movement in the United States has made steady progress. Despite their difficulty in statewide referendums, their messages have been widely accepted on movies and television, and they have been successful in winning legal protections and benefits. The gay movement has also become an important part of the Democratic coalition, and they have the support of the president. Although the quest for gay rights has taken decades to achieve early successes, this is relatively speedy in political affairs and the failure to adopt conspiratorial rhetoric does not appear to have delayed their progress. It is probably indicative that there are few other groups that can make similar claims.

In summary, this section argues that third parties and political movements have more need for conspiratorial rhetoric than do major parties because they are consummate losers—they never win. Those groups that achieve goals and overcome rivals, regardless of their size, may have less need for conspiracy theories. The more losses one suffers, the more tempting conspiracy theories become, though at every point one can choose to shun them.

CONCLUSION

The key finding of this chapter is that conspiracies resonate based on power and threat. The most important factor domestically is the party of the president. Internationally, great power wars are the prime movers. Foreign dangers tame internal faction and formidable foreigners are more attractive targets for conspiracy theorizing than homegrown hucksters. While many conspiracy theories may be fictitious, they speak to real perceptions of power. This is consistent with the argument that there is a strategic logic to conspiracy theories.

We can see this logic operating in many ways. When the Democrats won both the White House and Congress in 2008, conspiracy theorist Glenn Beck took over a coveted timeslot on the Fox News Network. When the Republicans regained some power by taking back the House in 2010, Glenn Beck's conspiracy talk was less relevant and his show was cancelled. The movie *The Manchurian Candidate* was produced twice in this country, once in 1962 during a Democratic administration and during heightened tensions with communist countries, and once in 2004 during a Republican administration. In the early version the villains were communists; in the later version the enemy was big business.

Beyond the subjects that resonate in culture, conspiracy-driven violence seems to respond to shifts in power as well. Timothy McVeigh blew up the Federal Building in Oklahoma during a Democratic administration, supposedly as a response to the Branch Davidian tragedy the year prior. Oddly, McVeigh could have easily taken action against the federal government prior to that, perhaps as a response to the government's handling of the Ruby Ridge incident, which occurred in the middle of George H. W. Bush's term, but did not. The FBI responded during the Clinton years by allocating resources to infiltrate right-wing groups, and when Obama came to power in 2008, the Department of Homeland Security once again sought to focus on right-wing militias.[25]

A number of intriguing implications follow. First, the data suggest that only great power wars alarm citizens sufficiently to increase foreign conspiracy theorizing. This implies that, despite drastic elite rhetoric about falling dominoes and impending terrorist strikes, the public has been quite skeptical about the threats that lesser conflicts pose. Threat mongering only appears to inflame conspiracy theorizing. During the Vietnam war, letters were less likely to get anxious about foreign evildoers than anti-war demonstrators, hippies, the Weather Underground, and the Nixon administration. Conspiracy talk may be at least a barometer and at best a bellwether of political behavior.

Second, the arguments presented in this chapter modify and challenge classical thought. According to Machiavelli, it is the weak who are most likely to engage in conspiracies, and so the strong should be the most anxious about them.[26] After all, the strong may do what they please with force; the weak must pursue their goals by craft. While we are uncertain whether in-power or out-of-power groups actually conspire the most, we dispute Machiavelli's depiction of vulnerability. Our results show the powerful are generally *thought* to be the ones conspiring. The weak, then, may be prone to conspiracies in a double sense: prone to partake in them and especially vulnerable to them. It is this vulnerability that drives conspiracy theories to come from those more apt to practice than suffer a conspiracy. Curiously, it is impossible to know how much conspiracy theories deter the powerful from malfeasance and make conspiracy theories self-denying.

Third, conspiracy theories show the limits of power and the limits of conspiracy theories. A trope of conspiracy theorists is that those in power are snake charmers, using conspiracy theories to manipulate the masses. Joseph McCarthy and Adolf Hitler come to mind. Although this chapter is not about who creates and spreads conspiracy theories, the evidence suggests snake charmer fears are exaggerated. Elites can influence conspiratorial beliefs as part of the information environment, but resonant domestic conspiracy theories are usually aimed at those in power, who, ironically, are powerless to stop those theories from resonating. There is little even presidents can do. But if conspiracy theorists are right about how powerful a villain is, it is unclear that conspiracy theories should be so extensive.

Finally, the implications for democracy are poignant. Democracy demands that power change hands, and this means that sooner or later nearly everyone will play the winner . . . and then the loser. In this respect, conspiracy theories are fair, much like an insurance plan, where pools of people make regular payments and take turns being reimbursed. Eventually, everyone savors the sweet righteousness of the prosecution before drinking the bitter draft of the persecuted.

Conspiring for the Common Good

If there were no conspiracy, the government would have had to invent one so that we would believe they are doing their work.

—Daniela Garcia[1]

Published in 1964, Richard Hofstadter's *Paranoid Style in American Politics* portrays conspiracy crazes as clownish but frightening spectacles that recurrently take center stage. As a work of descriptive history, his essay has not been equaled, but as a work of explanation, his essay makes dubious and vague assertions. Dubiously, conspiracy theorists were painted as slightly pathological right-wing extremists. Vaguely, only on the penultimate page does he speculate on causes. The paranoid disposition, he intones in the passive voice, "is mobilized into action chiefly by social conflicts that involve ultimate schemes of values."[2] In the United States, he continues, they tend to take the form of ethnic, religious, or class conflicts. Yet such conflicts are nearly constant in the American experience. Saying that conspiracy theorizing correlates with all kinds of cultural conflict explains everything and nothing.

What have we learned since Hofstadter? Quite a bit, actually. In this chapter, we give a synopsis of our work and pursue points undeveloped by other chapters. The first section summarizes the value added, key findings, and core logic. The second section investigates the prospects for making and breaking conspiracy theories. The third section discusses loose ends and avenues for future research. The fourth section is devoted to policy recommendations and implications, and the fifth engages avenues for future research.

THE CRUX: POWER AND PROOF

We aimed to advance the debate mainly by offering new leverage to explain and predict conspiracy theories. Empirically, this took the form of novel data that gathered representative samples of conspiracy theories rather than small batches of famous cases. Our intention was to make more specified and falsifiable claims to assess what we do and do not know about conspiracy theories. The final goals were to separate the more from the less powerful explanations and see if prior insights could be integrated into a more general understanding of conspiracy theories. Having reached the end, we hope to have met those goals.

First, for those who wonder whether a conspiracy theory is true, this book provides some solace. It is disconcerting that there is no infallible litmus test to separate conspiracies from conspiracy theories, and there is little comfort in how tenaciously a minority of the public clings to conspiracy beliefs. Yet these problems should be kept in perspective. There is a series of tests that, if used together, do a fair job indicating how speculative an individual conspiracy theory is. Those tests are Occam's razor, falsifiability, the worst intentions test, the cui bono test, the eternal recurrence of the same test, and the impartial spectator test. The more scrutiny given, and the more tests passed relative to rivals, the better a theory is.

Better information changes minds. Most Americans initially believed the charges against Richard Nixon were trumped up, but through tenacious reporting almost everyone now believes that the Nixon administration broke into the Watergate Hotel and attempted to cover up those and other crimes. Nixon admitted to wrongdoing, Congress issued reports, and several of the conspirators went to prison. People responded, in this case quite quickly, to authoritative information. In other instances, information takes its toll slowly. Some people continue to cling to Redemption theory, which maintains that the U.S. government uses its citizens as collateral and citizens in the know can redeem themselves to claim the money.

But overall, the information environment is surprisingly effective at tamping down conspiracy theories. This may sound implausible because the United States appears to be awash in conspiracy imagery. Television dramas like *24* and an unending stream of action movie plots attest that conspiracy theories are the lazy screenwriter's best friend.[3] Internet movies and chat rooms make conspiracy theories available to wider audiences, and even serious documentary films, such as *An Inconvenient Truth*, push conspiracy rhetoric.[4] News outlets, talk radio, music, and books all traffic in conspiracy theories.[5]

Yet simply because conspiracy theories are discussed prominently does not mean they are discussed favorably. And just because evidence of conspiracy is readily available does not mean that many seek it out or care. When exposed to conspiracy-related information, people are not affected equally.[6] Individuals selectively assimilate information in relation to their other opinions and values.[7] All of this makes broad acceptance an uphill fight for conspiracy theories.

Further, we have a pretty good idea of why diehard minorities will not relinquish their cherished conspiracy theories. People have differing predispositions to believe conspiratorial narratives, which are distinct from political commitments. It is the connection between partisan loyalties and conspiratorial predispositions that makes conspiracy theories resonate. Highly predisposed Democrats are highly susceptible to believe conspiracy theories about Republicans and vice versa. And individuals lacking a strong predisposition to see conspiracies will need more evidence to buy into a conspiracy theory. This implies that conspiracy theories cannot be eliminated, but also that they will seldom be very contagious. Few conspiracy theories are bipartisan in their appeal or able to jump high evidentiary bars.

Second, conspiracy theorists do not look as advertised. Descriptively, they are as likely to be men as women and Republicans as Democrats. They are liable to be poor in terms of finances and formal education. Some stereotypes hold up, however. Socially, conspiracy theorists appear to discuss matters with fewer friends, but that is not to say they discuss matters any less. As for participating in politics and the stock market, they do less of it. But they are more positively inclined toward guns and violence than average Americans.

This amends some of Hofstadter's portrayal of conspiracy theorists. They are, as a rule, not really paranoid or even that unusual. On the whole, nearly all Americans hold conspiracy beliefs, so it is hard to argue that nearly everyone is extreme or freakish. Moreover, the evidence in Chapter 4 suggests that, in terms of political belief, people with strong conspiratorial predispositions are about as likely as not to be moderates. As for the insinuation that conspiracy theorists are pathological, although it might be pleasing to imply that conspiracy theorists are crazy, it would be unwise. A very visible segment of conspiracy theorists are articulate and successful—preeminently the American Founders[8]—and people who are diagnosed as mentally ill rarely believe in conspiracy theories.[9] Hofstadter's privileging of cultural factors misses the possibilities that cultural differences may be an effect of previous distributions of power and current cultural conflicts may be about present levels of power. Obviously culture and power are bound up in each other, but we make the case for the primacy of the political in conspiracy theories.

Third, while alarms are continually sounded for the rising tide of conspiracy theories, the prevalence of U.S. conspiracy theorizing has not varied much. There were peaks in resonance in the 1890s and 1950s, but the aggregate amount has fallen off since the mid-1960s. For most of the country to believe a conspiracy theory, not only must it appeal to those who don't usually think in conspiratorial terms, but it must appeal to people across ideological divides. This is a rare occurrence, yet the eras of monopoly trusts and the second Red Scare qualify.

Fifth, probably the hardest finding for many to swallow is that conspiracy theorizing is approximately equal among Republicans as Democrats. This risks offending the totality of our readership, who see their group's conspiracy theories as real and other groups' conspiracy theories as absurd. But, glumly, partisan symmetry seems to us inescapable. The survey data suggest that Democrats are a match for Republicans in conspiracy theorizing, and the letters to the editor suggest that each side has mirrored the other's behavior over the last hundred years.

Sixth, foreign threat and domestic power asymmetries are the biggest spurs to conspiracy talk. The two are to a large degree substitutes; foreign threats crowd out domestic dangers, but when they recede domestic conspiracy talk reasserts itself. Because the presidency is the largest concentration of power, the party controlling the White House and members of their coalition become quarry for conspiracy theorists. The pattern is cyclical. When a Republican occupies the Oval Office, conspiracy theories swarm around Republicans and capitalists; when it is a Democrat's turn, conspiracy theories dog Democrats and socialists. But the big picture is that conspiracy theories are opportunistic and respond to shifts in domestic and international threats.

Our underlying argument throughout is that successful conspiracy theories are primarily political and conform to a strategic logic. Countless conspiracy theories occur to people, fewer are mulled over, fewer are voiced, few catch on, and hardly any attract a majority of the public. The death rate among conspiracy theories is colossal. The survivors have to appeal to the right people, at the right time, in the right way, and adapt to survive.

Conspiratorial predispositions are ingrained early in life and persist much like other orientations. But they are only widely activated in a context where the belief helps a group balance against threats. Conspiracy theories are weapons of the weak to recover from losses, improve cohesion, and coordinate resistance. In their drive for redemption (or revenge, depending on one's perspective), they absolve their proponents of blame, past and future, and dampen infighting—but at a steep cost to bystanders and scapegoats.

MAKING AND BREAKING CONSPIRACY THEORIES?

In studying the nature of conspiracy theories, it is unavoidable that one could use this knowledge to advance or attack individual conspiracy theories.[10] Here we peer down each path. On one side, imagine you wanted to advocate a conspiracy theory out of fear, honor, or greed. Your target demographic has been described above. To shoot for the stars, your model ought to be the Kennedy assassination, arguably the most successful conspiracy theory magnet of the last century. What it has to offer is glamor, secrecy, intrigue at the highest level, a period of intense threat, and villains on both the left (Fidel Castro) and right (the military-industrial complex). Because of this, Kennedy assassination theories cross the partisan divide and have more adherents than the Birther and Truther theories combined. Similarly, it may be that Hitler's anti-Semitic conspiracy theories were so disastrously effective because he engineered conditions of dire threat while convincing Germans that Jews were somehow simultaneously rapacious capitalists and subversive communists.

A small-scale case study of conspiracy theory entrepreneurship is David Icke, of reptilian shape-shifter fame. Icke spent years writing books about the reptilian conspiracy, garnering a lot of press but little following.[11] Then he widened his conspiracy theories to target more widely-loathed groups—corporations, political parties, and governments—and was able to raise almost half a million dollars in the summer of 2013.[12] But, having enlarged his reach by focusing on villains almost anyone can hate, Icke's appeal is now confined by the fact that he resonates only with those at the very high end of the conspiracy dimension. This is because all he offers is conspiratorial rhetoric, and people not overtly interested in that will not seek out his message. Glenn Beck, on the other hand, has bigger audiences than David Icke because he intersperses non-conspiratorial content with a wider appeal.

Most modestly successful conspiracy theories are hemmed in to one side of the political spectrum or the other. There is a ready-made audience for partisan conspiracy rhetoric. One need only harmonize rhetoric to the needs of the audience and have a good ear for the sounds of shifts in domestic and international power. Then play a different tune accordingly.

On the other side, imagine you would like to break a conspiracy theory. There are two major routes to do so: top-down and bottom-up. Professor Cass Sunstein, a former Obama Administration official, argues for a top-down approach. Despairing that direct appeals have not worked, he suggests that covert government agents should infiltrate online forums and convince conspiracy theorists of government narratives.[13] Sunstein's ideas have caused consternation, and this tactic would likely be self-defeating. Brendan Nyhan has more moderately suggested that journalists be more cautious in how they report conspiracy theories.[14] However, even this docile practice by journalists could raise suspicions that the media is shilling for powerful interests and blocking critical ideas. Sooner or later conspiracy theorists would catch on to any scheme and this would only deepen their distrust of government—to say nothing of the potential for Orwellian abuses of authority.

A bottom-up approach is humbler and better. Conspiracy theories cannot be crushed individually or collectively, and so there is no point in trying. A worthier goal is to contain what cannot be stopped, and that is best done by friends, neighbors, and one's self. With patience and good humor, people should use the tests laid out in Chapter 2 to see how likely it is that an idea they treasure might be wrong. They should hear out the theories of others and use rigorous logic and evidence to evaluate notions fairly. Some people are religious in their devotion to conspiracy theories and should be left in peace so long as they return the favor. Yet most people are amenable to persuasion and are worth conversing with. However flawed, that appears the most promising option.

POLICY RECOMMENDATIONS AND IMPLICATIONS

What, then, are we to do about conspiracy theories? Our answer is guardedly conservative: not much. Even if there were not compelling freedom of speech considerations—and there most certainly are—there are meager grounds to justify governmental action. One reason is that legal measures are unnecessary. Most conspiracy theories wilt for want of evidence and approbation. Like gut flora, most conspiracy theories are harmless and some may strengthen the immune system. A second reason is that there is little that can or should be done. Political scientists and psychologists are developing methods that could reverse people's conspiratorial beliefs. They have yet to make much headway. Were they to achieve a break-through tomorrow, though, it is unclear that dispensing with conspiracy theories would have a healthy effect on society or that anyone ought to have the tools to strip people of their most stubbornly held beliefs.

Nonetheless, there are always limits to tolerance. Our evidence sug-gests that conspiracy theorists on average are more accepting of violence, though little but anecdotes links them to actually committing violence. Still, caution is the better part of valor. Insofar as our work demonstrates who is likely to be targeted by conspiracy theorists (i.e., largely dominant political figures) and when, it highlights the need to protect figures who are already well protected. There will always be tactically bright but stra-tegically dim conspiracy theorists, like Anders Behring Breivik and the Tsarnaev brothers, who target the most defenseless. But such attacks are politically stillborn because they show how little their perpetrators have to offer. The most that can be done is probably what is currently being done: monitoring potentially violent individuals and groups, and intervening when they become clear and present dangers.

But while the foregoing suggests modest policy recommendations, it has greater implications for politics. Although they may look extraordi-nary and extreme, conspiracy theories can teach us a lot about everyday politics. Conspiracy theories are a declaration of values, an admission of vulnerability, and hence a strategic invitation to friends and foes alike. Un-derstanding the most popular conspiracy theories fleshes out preferences and belief structures.

For these reasons, conspiracy theories afford an opportunity for both good and evil. Adversaries may see in them a chance to take advantage of the other side, or an occasion to express sensitivity to the other side's concerns.[15] Allies may see them as a call to arms. Observers may find them useful indicators of changes in the political environment and a harbinger of the balance between international and domestic perils. The most successful conspiracy theories are like rivers, revealing the topography and moving along an efficient, if winding, path.

Paradoxically, democracy is both a salve for, and a source of, conspiracy theories. Democratic mechanisms such as elections, accountability, competition, and a free press make it extraordinarily difficult for potential criminals to launch lasting conspiracies without being subject to scrutiny and sanction. But these mechanisms cannot function without a certain level of public vigilance to drive and supervise them. A skeptical eye toward power is therefore not only sensible but also desirable, and conspiracy theories are the culmination of this attitude. Conspiracies have happened, are happening, and will continue to happen. Conspiracy theories help to combat them. Paraphrasing a well-worn saying, variously attributed, the price of liberty is eternal paranoia.

Even though most conspiracy theories are harmless (and perhaps even helpful), there is evidence that extreme manifestations may take healthy skepticism to an unhealthy degree. Compromise and respect in democracies may be hindered by persistent allegations of conspiracy. If you are convinced that your opponents are conspiring against you, it makes negotiation nearly impossible. As of this writing, the Republican-controlled House has voted to repeal "Obamacare" 40 times and pulled the country toward a financial precipice. While both sides of the aisle have identified problems in the law requiring legislative fixes, Republicans cannot compromise on a bill potentially containing "death panels." Ironically, this has led the administration to delay, change, and waive major parts of the legislation unilaterally (some say conspiratorially).

The bottom line is that conspiracy theories have profound repercussions for American politics, but there is little the U.S. government should do about them. All states must have power and keep secrets, and so long as that is the case conspiracy theories will thrive. Education and political transparency may ease the worst excesses of conspiracy theories, but they cannot eliminate them. Nevertheless, it would be no small victory if more people were more self-aware of their prejudices and predispositions.

FUTURE RESEARCH

A few loose ends remain to be tied up, or left for others to tie up. One is that that there is little exclusively modern about conspiracy theories. They can be found in the court intrigues of the Bible's Book of Esther and the diplomatic dispatches of Renaissance Florence.[16] And yet over the long term, conspiracy rhetoric may be about as popular as it ever was. Scapegoating seems to have gone secular but otherwise remains the same. In the *Iliad* it is common for the characters to ascribe their losses to divine intervention (or its withdrawal), and medieval battle losses were blamed on heavenly displeasure. Today, recourse to godly plots is less common, and it is an interesting puzzle why that might be so, but mortals and immortals still scheme to deprive us of our hearts' content. In any event, there is a good case to be made that, whomever the goat, scapegoating is an adaptive behavior with more continuity than change. But that case has yet to be made.

Another is that there is little exclusively American about conspiracy theories. We examined only the United States at a national level, but future research should inquire into the cultural differences within and across countries. With its diverse regional and local cultures, the United States is an ideal testing ground for how cultural factors affect the belief in conspiracy theories.

The results above also indicate that there are cross-national institutional dynamics, which could port over to other countries. Two come immediately to mind. First, there should be differences between democracies. States that do a better job protecting rights should feature less conspiracy theorizing than states that abuse them. In addition, proportional representation systems ostensibly give more groups a voice in government. This should make them less prone to conspiracy theories than first-past-the-post systems, and thus Europeans less prone to conspiracy theories than Americans, though the European Union may complicate matters. New Zealand would make an excellent laboratory for this sort of inquiry because of its lack of external threats and transition from a first-past-the-post system to a proportional representation system several decades ago.

Second, there should be differences between democracies and non-democracies. If conspiracy theories are for losers, then conspiracy theories should be more prevalent where people are durably disenfranchised. Anecdotes about the Arab Street suggest this, but greater study could yield interesting findings on the differences between regime types. Insofar as they are separable from democracy, less educated and poorer states should be more liable to conspiracy theorizing. Also, non-democracies vary in inclusiveness and representation. Dictators and despots delegate and devolve powers differently, as well as coming from (and appointing ministers from) larger or smaller subnational groups. Autocrats that do a better job protecting minority rights, rotating offices, and representing minority preferences, even if non-democratically, are less likely to feature prevalent and persistent conspiracy theories. It is an open question whether some non-democracies may make their citizens feel more represented (and therefore display less conspiracy theorizing) than some democracies. All of these are testable implications in search of tests.

Lastly, a captivating corollary of our data is that they open new vistas into threat perception. Threats are hard to measure, but conspiracy theories bring to the surface people's deepest political anxieties. Our measures offer additional purchase to understand how the strength and substance of perceived threats change over time. An example of this would be to chart the perceived power of international organizations by measuring the ebb and flow of conspiracy theories involving the United Nations across time and space.

Although elites have some influence over mass opinion, it is stunning how unsuccessful they are at inflating threats.[17] During the Cold War and after, elites tried to bestir public opinion to view opponents less capable than the Soviet Union (e.g., North Vietnam, Iran, and Al-Qaeda) as major menaces to U.S. interests. The war on terror, in particular, was sold as a second Cold War, the defining crusade of a new era. Nevertheless, the data support the contention that by and large the public was not buying it—and this in spite of the fact that some claimed a terrorism-hyping industry sprang up to stoke American anxieties.[18] Nor have elites exploited conspiracy theories to take advantage of political polarization.

So while conspiracy theories are about threats, not any old danger will do. Citizens must see an enemy with significant relative power readying to inflict great harm on them. One can only fool some of the people some of the time. We would never claim that conspiracy theories are materially determined—there will always be an important role for social construction in threats—but there appears to be a strong material influence on how groups perceive threat. Future work could do a better job nailing down the conditions under which ideas and material factors interact to produce threats.

OF CONSPIRACY THEORIES

The line between fact and fiction is unnervingly unpredictable. Ambiguity may be exciting when safely confined between book covers, but it is distressing when confronted outside them. Nevertheless, a major finding of this work is that, as a group, conspiracy theories are neither the vile excrescence of puny minds nor the telltale symptom of a sick society. They are the ineradicable stuff of politics. Conspiracy theories are less the lifeblood of the body politic than lymph: not an attractive feature of the system, or a thoroughly healthy one, but necessary to normal functioning within proper parameters.

On the surface, conspiracy theories may appear roundabout and risible—at least our favorites are—but the cost is high to stigmatize conspiracy theories as a class. Taken together conspiracy theories are experiments in perception and a normal part of life. They are attempts to interact with a treacherous, dizzying reality. They richly reveal both their proponents and the world we all struggle to make sense of. They divide us into bickering camps but unite us in our frailty and perplexity. And they are the most accessible way to speak unflattering truths to power. Ultimately, conspiracy theories are a timeless tactic in a timeless contest, for "the strong desire to rule, and the weak desire not to be ruled."[19]

CHAPTER 1

1. Niccolò Machiavelli, *The Prince*, trans. Harvey C. Mansfield (Chicago: University of Chicago Press, 1998), p. 72. Online appendix including data, replication materials, and additional analyses available at Joeuscinski.com.

2. Robert Middlekauff, *The Glorious Cause: The American Revolution, 1763–1789* (New York: Oxford University Press, 2005); Bernard Bailyn, *The Ideological Origins of the American Revolution* (Cambridge: Harvard University Press, 1992).

3. Pauline Maier, *American Scripture: Making the Declaration of Independence* (New York: Vintage Books, 1998).

4. Chaim D. Kaufman and Robert A. Pape, "Explaining Costly International Moral Action: Britain's Sixty-Year Campaign against the Atlantic Slave Trade," *International Organization* 53, Autumn (1999); Brion David Davis, *Inhuman Bondage: The Rise and Fall of Slavery in the New World* (New York: Oxford University Press, 2006); Paul K. MacDonald, "Is Imperial Rule Obsolete? Assessing the Barriers to Overseas Adventurism," *Security Studies* 18, no. 1 (2009).

5. Quoted in Maier, *American Scripture: Making the Declaration of Independence*, p. 106.

6. Dickinson and Burke in Gordon S. Wood, *The Creation of the American Republic, 1776–1787* (Chapel Hill: University of North Carolina Press, 1998), p. 5 [emphasis in original].

7. Stephen Betts, "Local Residents Claim Regional Road Planning is International Plot," *Waldo Village Soup* (2010); Andrew Whittemore, "Finding Sustainability in Conservative Contexts: Topics for Conversation between American Conservative Élites, Planners and the Conservative Base," *Urban Studies* (2013).

8. Patrik Jonsson, "Blackbirds Fall from Sky, Fish Die Off: What's a Conspiracy Theorist to Think?" *The Christian Science Monitor* (2011).

9. Babak Dehghanpisheh, "Conspiracy Theories with a Bite: Shark Attacks in Egypt Prompt Charges of Outsider Sabotage of Tourism," *Newsweek* (2010).

10. E.g., Uzma Jamil and Cécile Rousseau, "Challenging the 'Official' Story of 9/11: Community Narratives and Conspiracy Theories," *Ethnicities* 11, no. 2 (2011).

11. E.g., Cass Sunstein and Adrian Vermeule, "Conspiracy Theories," *Social Science Research Network* (2008): 1; Kathryn S. Olmsted, *Real Enemies: Conspiracy Theories and American Democracy, World War I to 9/11* (New York: Oxford University Press, 2008).

12. Sarah Palin, "Statement on the Current Health Care Debate," *Facebook* (2009).

13. Brendan Nyhan et al., "One Vote out of Step? The Effects of Salient Roll Call Votes in the 2010 Election," *American Politics Research* (2012).

14. Steven Rattner, "Beyond Obamacare," *New York Times* (2012).

15. Bill O'Reilly, "Who is Running Sandra Fluke?" *The O'Reilly Factor* (2012).

16. Sunstein and Vermeule, "Conspiracy Theories," p. 17.

17. E.g., Dan Cassino and Krista Jenkins, "Conspiracy Theories Prosper: 25% of Americans are 'Truthers,'" press release (2013); Ted Goertzel, "Belief in Conspiracy Theories," *Political Psychology* 15 (1994).

18. Thomas Hargrove, "Third of Americans Suspect 9/11 Government Conspiracy," *Scripps News*, August 1, 2006; Cassino and Jenkins, "Conspiracy Theories Prosper: 25% of Americans are 'Truthers'"; Adam Berinsky, "The Birthers are (Still) Back," *YouGov: What the World Thinks* (2012).

19. CBS, "CBS Poll: JFK Conspiracy Lives," *CBSNews.com*, February 11, 2009.

20. Cassino and Jenkins, "Conspiracy Theories Prosper: 25% of Americans are 'Truthers.'"

21. Adam Berinsky, "Rumors, Truths, and Reality: A Study of Political Misinformation," in http://web.mit.edu/berinsky/www/files/rumor.pdf (MIT 2012).

22. "Telling the Truth About Believing the Lies?" in *American Political Science Association* (Chicago, 2013).

23. Brendan Nyhan, "Why the 'Death Panel' Myth Wouldn't Die: Misinformation in the Health Care Reform Debate," *The Forum* 8, no. 1 (2010); "Why Conspiracy Theories Die Hard," *CNN.com* (2011), http://www.cnn.com/2011/OPINION/04/28/nyhan.birther.truth/index.html; Brendan Nyhan and Jason Reifler, "The Effects of Semantics and Social Desirability in Correcting the Obama Muslim Myth" (2009); "When Corrections Fail: The Persistence of Political Misperceptions," *Political Behavior* 32, no. 2 (2010); "Opening the Political Mind: The Effects of Self-affirmation and Graphical Information on Factual Misperceptions" (2011); Brendan Nyhan, Jason Reifler, and Peter A. Ubel, "The Hazards of Correcting Myths about Health Care Reform," *Medical Care* 51, no. 2 (2013); Berinsky, "Rumors, Truths, and Reality: A Study of Political Misinformation."

24. Nyhan, Reifler, and Ubel, "The Hazards of Correcting Myths about Health Care Reform."

25. Anna Kata, "A Postmodern Pandora's Box: Anti-vaccination Misinformation on the Internet," *Vaccine* 28, no. 7 (2010).

26. Adam Berinsky, "The Birthers Are Back," *YouGov: What the World Thinks* (2012); "The Birthers are (Still) Back."

27. Cassino and Jenkins, "Conspiracy Theories Prosper: 25% of Americans are 'Truthers.'"

28. Cass R. Sunstein and Adrian Vermeule, "Conspiracy Theories: Causes and Cures*," *Journal of Political Philosophy* 17, no. 2 (2009).

29. James H. Kuklinski et al., "Misinformation and the Currency of Democratic Citizenship," *Journal of Politics* 62, no. 3 (2000); Bryan Caplan, *The Myth of the Rational Voter: Why Democracies Choose Bad Policies* (Princeton: Princeton University Press, 2007); Martin Gilens, "Political Ignorance and Collective Policy Preferences," *American Political Science Review* 95, no. 2 (2001).

30. Christopher J. M. Whitty et al., "Biotechnology: Africa and Asia Need a Rational Debate on GM Crops," *Nature* 497, no. 7447 (2013).

31. Nicoli Nattrass, "How Bad Ideas Gain Social Traction," *The Lancet* 380, no. 9839 (2012).

32. Vickie M. Mays, Courtney N. Coles, and Susan D. Cochran, "Is There a Legacy of the U.S. Public Health Syphilis Study at Tuskegee in HIV/AIDS-Related Beliefs Among Heterosexual African Americans and Latinos?" *Ethics & Behavior* 22, no. 6 (2012); cf. April Clark et al., "Conspiracy Beliefs about HIV Infection are Common But Not Associated with Delayed Diagnosis or Adherence to Care," *AIDS Patient Care and STDs* 22, no. 9 (2008).

33. Ted Goertzel, "Conspiracy Theories in Science," *EMBO Reports* 11, no. 7 (2010) : 495; Phil Plait, "Antivaccine Megachurch Linked to Texas Measles Outbreak," *Slate. com* (2013); Ted Goertzel, "The Conspiracy Meme," *Skeptical Inquirer* (2013).

34. Alan W. Bock, "Ambush at Ruby Ridge," *Reason Magazine* (1993).

35. Mark S. Hamm, *Apocalypse in Oklahoma: Waco and Ruby Ridge Revenged* (Boston: Northeastern University Press, 1997).

36. Maryanne Vollers, *Lone Wolf: Eric Rudolph: Murder, Myth, and the Pursuit of an American Outlaw* (HarperCollins, 2006).

37. Dan Murphy, "Fort Hood Shooting: Was Nidal Malik Hasan Inspired by Militant Clerics?" *Christian Science Monitor*.

38. Adam Goldman, Eric Tucker, and Matt Apuzzo, "Tamerlan Tsarnaev, Influenced By Mysterious Muslim Radical, Turned Towards Fundamentalism," *Huffington Post* (2013).

39. David Remnick, "The Culprits," *The New Yorker* (2013).

40. Frank Rich, MSNBC, 9 p.m., May 8, 2013.

41. Given their access to up-to-date opinion data, journalists generally know where public opinion stands at any given moment, but knowing the extent to which an opinion is held does not provide any special understanding of *why* that opinion is held. Most journalists lack the specialized training needed for such endeavors. Furthermore, given the sensational nature and inherent newsworthiness of conspiracy theories, journalists have often paid unwarranted attention to particular individual conspiracy theories and in doing so have presented a distorted view of them; see, e.g., James Tracy, "An Open Letter to the *South Florida Sun-Sentinel*," memoryhole-blog.com (2013).

42. "Conspiracy Theories: Separating Fact from Fiction," *Time.com* (2009).

43. "Democrats and Republicans Differ on Conspiracy Theory Beliefs," *Public Policy Polling* (2013).

44. Joseph E. Uscinski, "Why Are Conspiracy Theories Popular? There's More to It Than Paranoia," *EUROPP: European Politics and Policy* (2013).

45. Peter Knight, "Outrageous Conspiracy Theories: Popular and Official Responses to 9/11 in Germany and the United States," *New German Critique* 35, no. 1 (2008): 797; Volker Heins, "Critical Theory and the Traps of Conspiracy Thinking," *Philosophy & Social Criticism* 33, no. 7 (2007).

46. Michael Tesler and David O. Sears, *Obama's Race: The 2008 Election and the Dream of a Post-Racial America*, Chicago Studies in American Politics (Chicago: University of Chicago Press, 2010).

47. Gary Jacobson, "Barack Obama and the American Public: The First 18 Months," in *Annual Meeting of the American Political Science Association* (Washington, D.C., 2010), p. 5.

48. CBS, "CBS Poll: JFK Conspiracy Lives."

49. Richard Hofstadter, *The Paranoid Style in American Politics, and Other Essays* (Cambridge, MA: Harvard University Press, 1964), pp. 4, 39; S. Anthony, "Anxiety and Rumor," *Journal of Personality and Social Psychology* 89 (1973); Goertzel, "Belief in Conspiracy Theories."

50. Ralph L. Rosnow, "Psychology of Rumor Reconsidered," *Psychological Bulletin* 87, no. 3 (1980); Ralph L. Rosnow, James L. Esposito, and Leo Gibney, "Factors Influencing Rumor Spreading: Replication and Extension," *Language & Communication* 8, no. 1 (1988); Ralph L. Rosnow, John H. Yost, and James L. Esposito, "Belief in Rumor and Likelihood of Rumor Transmission," *Language & Communication* 6, no. 3 (1986); Thomas Hargrove, "Third of Americans Suspect 9–11 Government Conspiracy," *Scripps News* (2006).

51. Jennifer A. Whitson and Adam D. Galinsky, "Lacking Control Increases Illusory Pattern Perception," *Science* 322, no. 3 (2008); Daniel Sullivan, Mark J. Landau, and Zachary K. Rothschild, "An Existential Function of Enemyship: Evidence that People Attribute Influence to Personal and Political Enemies to Compensate for Threats to Control," *Journal of Personality and Social Psychology* 98, no. 3 (2010); Aaron E. Kay et al., "Conspensatory Control: Achieving Order Through the Mind, Our Institutions, and the Heavens," *Current Directions in Psychological Science* 18, no. 5 (2009).

52. G. W. Allport and L. J. Postman, *The Psychology of Rumor* (New York: Holt, Rinehart & Winston, 1947); Rosnow, "Psychology of Rumor Reconsidered"; Rosnow, Yost, and Esposito, "Belief in Rumor and Likelihood of Rumor Transmission."

53. Robert Thomson et al., "Trusting Tweets: The Fukushima Disaster and Information Source Credibility on Twitter" (paper presented at the Proceedings of the 9th International Conference on Information Systems for Crisis Response and Management, 2012).

54. Sunstein and Vermeule, "Conspiracy Theories: Causes and Cures*," p. 202.

55. Philip E. Converse, "The Nature of Belief Systems in Mass Publics (1964)," *Critical Review* 18, no. 1–3 (2006).

56. See Lippman, quoted in John Zaller, *The Nature and Origins of Mass Opinion,* Cambridge Studies in Public Opinion and Political Psychology (Cambridge, UK: Cambridge University Press, 1992), p. 7.

57. Robert S. Erikson and Kent L. Tedin, *American Public Opinion: Its Origins, Content, and Impact,* 7th ed. (New York: Pearson Longman, 2005).

58. Zaller, *The Nature and Origins of Mass Opinion,* p. 6.

59. Ibid.

60. For example, see Todd K. Hartman and Adam J. Newmark, "Motivated Reasoning, Political Sophistication, and Associations between President Obama and Islam," *PS: Political Science and Politics* 45, no. 3 (2012).

61. Matthew Atkinson and Joseph E. Uscinski, "Why Do People Believe in Conspiracy Theories? The Role of Informational Cues and Predispositions" (2013)

Available at SSRN: http://ssrn.com/abstract=2268782 or http://dx.doi.org/10.2139/ssrn.2268782.

62. Milton Lodge and Charles S. Taber, *The Rationalizing Voter* (New York: Cambridge University Press, 2013).

63. Nicholas DiFonzo and Prashant Bordia, *Rumor Psychology: Social and Organizational Approaches* (American Psychological Association, 2007).

64. Herbert McClosky and Dennis Chong, "Similarities and Differences between Left-Wing and Right-Wing Radicals," *British Journal of Political Science* 15, no. 3 (1985): 346.

65. Stephan Lewandowsky, Klaus Oberauer, and Gilles Gignac, "NASA Faked the Moon Landing—Therefore (Climate) Science Is a Hoax: An Anatomy of the Motivated Rejection of Science," *Psychological Science* 5 (2013).

66. Anna-Kaisa Newheiser, Miguel Farias, and Nicole Tausch, "The Functional Nature of Conspiracy Beliefs: Examining the Underpinnings of Belief in the *Da Vinci Code* Conspiracy," *Personality and Individual Differences* 51, no. 8 (2011).

67. Robert Brotherton, Christopher C. French, and Alan D. Pickering, "Measuring Belief in Conspiracy Theories: The Generic Conspiracist Beliefs Scale," *Frontiers in Psychology* 4, Article 279 (2013); Martin Bruder et al., "Measuring Individual Differences in Generic Beliefs in Conspiracy Theories Across Cultures: The Conspiracy Mentality Questionnaire (CMQ)," *Frontiers in Psychology* 4 (2013); Atkinson and Uscinski, "Why Do People Believe in Conspiracy Theories? The Role of Informational Cues and Predispositions"; Michael J. Wood, Karen M. Douglas, and Robbie M. Sutton, "Dead and Alive: Beliefs in Contradictory Conspiracy Theories," *Social Psychological and Personality Science* (2012); Roland Imhoff and Martin Bruder, "Speaking (Un-)Truth to Power: Conspiracy Mentality as a Generalised Political Attitude," *European Journal of Personality* (2013); Viren Swami et al., "Lunar Lies: The Impact of Informational Framing and Individual Differences in Shaping Conspiracist Beliefs About the Moon Landings," *Applied Cognitive Psychology* 27, no. 1 (2013).

68. Imhoff and Bruder, "Speaking (Un-)Truth to Power: Conspiracy Mentality as a Generalised Political Attitude."

69. Atkinson and Uscinski, "Why Do People Believe in Conspiracy Theories? The Role of Informational Cues and Predispositions."

70. Ibid.

71. Ibid.

72. McClosky and Chong, "Similarities and Differences between Left-Wing and Right-Wing Radicals."

73. Imhoff and Bruder, "Speaking (Un-)Truth to Power: Conspiracy Mentality as a Generalised Political Attitude"; Berinsky, "Rumors, Truths, and Reality: A Study of Political Misinformation"; see also J. Eric Oliver and Thomas J. Wood, "Conspiracy Theories, Magical Thinking, and the Paranoid Style(s) of Mass Opinion" (University of Chicago Working Paper Series, 2012).

74. Imhoff and Bruder, "Speaking (Un-)Truth to Power: Conspiracy Mentality as a Generalised Political Attitude."

75. Wood, Douglas, and Sutton, "Dead and Alive: Beliefs in Contradictory Conspiracy Theories."

76. Atkinson and Uscinski, "Why Do People Believe in Conspiracy Theories? The Role of Informational Cues and Predispositions."

77. Karen M. Douglas and Robbie M. Sutton, "Does It Take One to Know One? Endorsement of Conspiracy Theories is Influenced by Personal Willingness to Conspire," *British Journal of Social Psychology* 50, no. 3 (2011); Imhoff and Bruder, "Speaking (Un-)Truth to Power: Conspiracy Mentality as a Generalised Political Attitude."

78. See discussion in Atkinson and Uscinski, "Why Do People Believe in Conspiracy Theories? The Role of Informational Cues and Predispositions"; see also Angus Campbell et al., *The American Voter, Unabridged Edition* (Chicago: The University of Chicago Press, 1960); David O. Sears, "The Persistence of Early Political Predispositions: The Roles of Attitude Object and Life Stage," *Review of Personality and Social Psychology* 4, no. 1 (1983); David O. Sears and S. Levy, "Childhood and Adult Political Development," in *The Oxford Handbook of Political Psychology*, ed. David O Sears, L. Huddy, and R. Jervis (Oxford: Oxford University Press, 2003).

79. David Easton and Robert D. Hess, "The Child's Political World," *Midwest Journal of Political Science* 6, no. 3 (1962).

80. Jack Zeljko Bratich, "Trust No One (On the Internet): The CIA-Crack-Contra Conspiracy Theory and Professional Journalism," *Television & New Media* 5, no. 2 (2004); Tracy, "An Open Letter to the *South Florida Sun-Sentinel.*"

81. Chip Berlet, "Collectivists, Communists, Labor Bosses, and Treason: The Tea Parties as Right-Wing Populist Counter-Subversion Panic," *Critical Sociology* 38, no. 4 (2012); Turkay Nefes, "The History of the Social Constructions of Donmes (Converts)," *Journal of Historical Sociology* 25, no. 3 (2012); Türkay Salim Nefes, "Political Parties' Perceptions and Uses of Anti-Semitic Conspiracy Theories in Turkey," *The Sociological Review* 61, no. 2 (2013); Sharon Parsons et al., "A Test of the Grapevine: An Empirical Examination of the Conspiracy Theories Among African Americans," *Sociological Spectrum* 19, no. 2 (1999); Anita M. Waters, "Conspiracy Theories as Ethnosociologies: Explanations and Intention in African American Political Culture" *Journal of Black Studies* 28, no. 1 (1997); Matt A. Barreto et al., "The Tea Party in the Age of Obama: Mainstream Conservatism or Out-Group Anxiety?" *Political Power and Social Theory* 22, no. 1 (2012); Christopher S. Parker and Matt A. Barreto, *Change They Can't Believe in: The Tea Party and Reactionary Politics in America* (Princeton University Press, 2013).

82. Donald R. Kinder and Cindy D. Kam, *Us Against Them: Ethnocentric Foundations of American Opinion* (Chicago: University of Chicago Press, 2009); Henri Tajfel, *Human Groups and Social Categories* (New York: Cambridge University Press, 1981); Muzafer Sherif et al., *Intergroup Conflict and Cooperation: The Robbers Cave Experiment* (Norman, OK: University of Oklahoma Book Exchange, 1961).

83. Marlone Henderson, "Psychological Distance and Group Judgments: The Effect of Physical Distance on Beliefs about Common Goals," *Personality and Social Psychology Bulletin* 35, no. 10 (2009).

84. E.g., Mays, Coles, and Cochran, "Is There a Legacy of the U.S. Public Health Syphilis Study at Tuskegee in HIV/AIDS-Related Beliefs Among Heterosexual African Americans and Latinos?"; William Paul Simmons and Sharon Parsons, "Beliefs

in Conspiracy Theories Among African Americans: A Comparison of Elites and Masses," *Social Science Quarterly* 86, no. 3 (2005); Waters, "Conspiracy Theories as Ethnosociologies: Explanations and Intention in African American Political Culture."

85. Hannah Darwin, Nick Neave, and Joni Holmes, "Belief in Conspiracy Theories. The Role of Paranormal Belief, Paranoid Ideation and Schizotypy," *Personality and Individual Differences* 50, no. 8 (2011): 1292; see also S. B. Thomas and S. C. Quinn, "The Tuskegee Syphilis Study, 1932 to 1972: Implications for HIV Education and AIDS Risk Education Programs in the Black Community," *American Journal of Public Health* 81, no. 11 (1991); James M. Avery, "The Sources and Consequences of Political Mistrust Among African Americans," *American Politics Research* 34, no. 5 (2006); Mays, Coles, and Cochran, "Is There a Legacy of the U.S. Public Health Syphilis Study at Tuskegee in HIV/AIDS-Related Beliefs Among Heterosexual African Americans and Latinos?"; Simmons and Parsons, "Beliefs in Conspiracy Theories Among African Americans: A Comparison of Elites and Masses"; Waters, "Conspiracy Theories as Ethnosociologies: Explanations and Intention in African American Political Culture."

86. Nicholas Difonzo, Prashant Bordia, and Ralph L. Rosnow, "Reining in Rumors," *Organizational Dynamics* 23 (1994); Louis Farrakhan and Henry Louis Gates, Jr., "Farrakhan Speaks," *Transition*, no. 70 (1996); Goertzel, "Belief in Conspiracy Theories"; Waters, "Conspiracy Theories as Ethnosociologies: Explanations and Intention in African American Political Culture."

87. Spike Lee, "Spike Lee on Real Time with Bill Maher" (HBO, 2007).

88. For example, see Eric Posner, *Law and Social Norms* (Cambridge, MA: Harvard University Press, 2002); Jamil and Rousseau, "Challenging the 'Official' Story of 9/11: Community Narratives and Conspiracy Theories"; Barreto et al., "The Tea Party in the Age of Obama: Mainstream Conservatism or Out-Group Anxiety?"

89. Darryl Fears, "Black Opinion on Simpson Shifts," *Washington Post* (2007).

90. E.g., Charles L. Briggs, "Theorizing Modernity Conspiratorially: Science, Scale, and the Political Economy of Public Discourse in Explanations of a Cholera Epidemic," *American Ethnologist* 31, no. 2 (2004).

91. Stefan Stieger et al., "Girl in the Cellar: A Repeated Cross-sectional Investigation of Belief in Conspiracy Theories About the Kidnapping of Natascha Kampusch," *Frontiers in Psychology* 4 (2013).

CHAPTER 2

1. Richard Hofstadter, *The Paranoid Style of American Politics and Other Essays* (New York: Knopf, 1965), p. 36.

2. Kathryn S. Olmsted, *Real Enemies: Conspiracy Theories and American Democracy, World War I to 9/11* (New York: Oxford University Press, 2008).

3. Eduard Grebe and Nicoli Nattrass, "AIDS Conspiracy Beliefs and Unsafe Sex in Cape Town," *AIDS and Behavior* 16, no. 3 (2012); Nicoli Nattrass, "Understanding the Origins and Prevalence of AIDS Conspiracy Beliefs in the United States and South Africa," *Sociology of Health & Illness* 35, no. 1 (2013); S. B. Thomas and S. C. Quinn, "The Tuskegee Syphilis Study, 1932 to 1972: Implications for HIV Education

and AIDS Risk Education Programs in the Black Community," *American Journal of Public Health* 81, no. 11 (1991); cf. April Clark et al., "Conspiracy Beliefs about HIV Infection are Common But Not Associated with Delayed Diagnosis or Adherence to Care," *AIDS Patient Care and STDs* 22, no. 9 (2008); Catrinel Craciun and Adriana Baban, "'Who Will Take the Blame?': Understanding the Reasons Why Romanian Mothers Decline HPV Vaccination for Their Daughters," *Vaccine* 30, no. 48 (2012); Anna Kata, "A Postmodern Pandora's Box: Anti-vaccination Misinformation on the Internet," *Vaccine* 28, no. 7 (2010); Neil Z. Miller, "Vaccine Science vs. Science Fiction: Make Informed Decisions," Report prepared for VacTruth.com and ThinkTwice.com (2013).

4. Robert B. Reich, "American Bile," *New York Times*, September 21, 2013.
5. Michael Ross, "Glenn Beck Alleges 'Concentrated Effort Now to Label Me a Conspiracy Theorist?,'" *Examiner.com* (2013); "Glenn Beck claims Obama behind conspiracy to depict him as a conspiracy theorist," *Examiner.com* (2013). For the source material behind Beck's complaint, see Cass R. Sunstein and Adrian Vermeule, "Conspiracy Theories: Causes and Cures*," *Journal of Political Philosophy* 17, no. 2 (2009).
6. Stephen Webster, "Glenn Beck sees media conspiracy to label him a 'conspiracy theorist,'" *The Raw Story* (2013). Parent suspects that Beck may have been too dignified to mention the indignity that the alleged errand boy dispatched to discredit him lacked a fancy title. Perhaps when Beck's conspiracy theories improve, his character assassins will have better business cards.
7. Alex Seitz-Wald, "Sandy Hook truther won't quit," *Salon.com* (2013).
8. See Susan Rothstein, "Right-wing conspiracy theories do a number on us," *The Boston Globe* (2012). Also, Leon Neyfakh, "Revealed! Obama's secret agenda," *The Boston Globe* (2012).
9. Rothstein, "Right-wing conspiracy theories do a number on us."
10. See Sigmund Freud, *The Standard Edition of the Complete Psychological Works of Sigmund Freud* (Oxford, UK: Macmillan, 1964).
11. "Brendan Nyhan still isn't credible (Obama, 'Birthers,' 'science,' CNN)," *24ahead.com* (2011).
12. Adam Berinsky, "The Birthers are (Still) Back," *YouGov: What the World Thinks* (2012).
13. "10th Anniversary 9/11 Truth Hit Piece Roundup," *911 Truth News* (2011). The unknown professors in question are the present authors.
14. Joseph E. Uscinski, "Why Are Conspiracy Theories Popular? There's More to It Than Paranoia," *EUROPP: European Politics and Policy* (2013).
15. Stephan Lewandowsky et al., "Recursive Fury: Conspiracist Ideation in the Blogosphere in Response to Research on Conspiracist Ideation," *Frontiers in Psychology* 4 (2013)
16. Stephan Lewandowsky, Klaus Oberauer, and Gilles Gignac, "NASA Faked the Moon Landing—Therefore (Climate) Science Is a Hoax: An Anatomy of the Motivated Rejection of Science," *Psychological Science* 5 (2013).
17. Stephan Lewandowsky et al., "Recursive Fury: Conspiracist Ideation in the Blogosphere in Response to Research on Conspiracist Ideation," *Frontiers in Psychology* 4 (2013): 10. In this study, Parent is Uscinski's stooge (or the other way around).

18. For example, see online discussions by conspiracy theorists in: Michael James Wood and Karen M. Douglas, "'What about Building 7?' A Social Psychological Study of Online Discussion of 9/11 Conspiracy Theories," *Frontiers in Psychology* 4 (2013).

19. Peter M. Hall, "The Quasi-Theory of Communication and the Management of Dissent," *Social Problems* 18, no. 1 (1970): 21.

20. David Coady, *Conspiracy Theories: The Philosophical Debate* (Burlington, VT: Ashgate, 2006), p. 4.

21. Gina Husting and Martin Orr, "Dangerous Machinery: 'Conspiracy Theorist' as a Transpersonal Strategy of Exclusion," *Symbolic Interaction* 30, no. 2 (2007): 147.

22. Kevin Barrett, "New studies: 'Conspiracy theorists' sane; government dupes crazy, hostile," *PressTV* (2013).

23. Lance deHaven-Smith, "When Political Crimes Are Inside Jobs: Detecting State Crimes Against Democracy," *Administrative Theory & Praxis* 28, no. 3 (2006); Laurie A. Manwell, "In Denial of Democracy: Social Psychological Implications for Public Discourse on State Crimes Against Democracy Post-9/11," *American Behavioral Scientist* 53, no. 6 (2010).

24. Charles Pigden, "Popper Revisited, or What is Wrong with Conspiracy Theories?" *Philosophy of the Social Sciences* 25, no. 1 (1995): 4.

25. Coady, *Conspiracy Theories: The Philosophical Debate*, p. 4. Readers should note that this claim was made in 2006, during the Bush administration and at a time when the Truther theory was at an apex. It is unlikely that he would make such a claim after 2009 (regarding the United States, anyway). Once Obama came to office, it was the right who was accused of being prone to conspiracy theories. Our results in Chapter 6 will speak to this.

26. Matthew Atkinson and Joseph E. Uscinski, "Why Do People Believe in Conspiracy Theories? The Role of Informational Cues and Predispositions" (2013) Available at SSRN: http://ssrn.com/abstract=2268782 or http://dx.doi.org/10.2139/ssrn.2268782. For many people, what counts as quality evidence is fantastically elastic. Other studies show that viewing fictional comedies or dodgy documentaries affects the propensity to see conspiracies. Kenneth Mulligan and Philip Habel, "The Implications of Fictional Media for Political Beliefs," *American Politics Research* 41, no. 1 (2013). John A. Banas and Gregory Miller, "Inducing Resistance to Conspiracy Theory Propaganda: Testing Inoculation and Metainoculation Strategies," *Human Communication Research* 39, no. 2 (2013).

27. Brian Keeley, "Of Conspiracy Theories," *Journal of Philosophy* 96, no. 3 (1999).

28. E.g., Adam Berinsky, "Rumors, Truths, and Reality: A Study of Political Misinformation," in http://web.mit.edu/berinsky/www/files/rumor.pdf (MIT2012); Brendan Nyhan, "Why the 'Death Panel' Myth Wouldn't Die: Misinformation in the Health Care Reform Debate," *The Forum* 8, no. 1 (2010).

29. deHaven-Smith, "When Political Crimes Are Inside Jobs: Detecting State Crimes Against Democracy."

30. Pigden, "Popper Revisited, or What is Wrong with Conspiracy Theories?," 5.

31. Sir Karl R. Popper, *Conjectures and Refutations* (London: Routledge Kegan Paul, 1972), pp. 123–125.

32. Donald G. McNeil, Jr., "Panel Hears Grim Details of Venereal Disease Tests," *New York Times*, August 30, 2011.

33. Olmsted, *Real Enemies: Conspiracy Theories and American Democracy, World War I to 9/11*, p. 2.

34. John J. Mearsheimer, *Why Leaders Lie: The Truth about Lying in International Politics* (New York: Oxford University Press, 2011), pp. 49, 58.

35. Keeley, "Of Conspiracy Theories," p. 116; David Aaronovitch, *Voodoo Histories: The Role of Conspiracy Theory in Shaping Modern History* (New York: Riverhead Books, 2010), pp. 5–6; David Coady, "Conspiracy Theories and Official Stories," *International Journal of Applied Philosophy* 17 (2003): 199.

36. CBS, "CBS Poll: JFK Conspiracy Lives," *CBSNews.com*, February 11, 2009.

37. Neil Levy, "Radically Socialized Knowledge and Conspiracy Theories," *Episteme* 4, no. 2 (2007): 188.

38. Cf. Pete Mandik, "Shit Happens," *Episteme* 4, no. 2 (2007): 206.

39. Levy, "Radically Socialized Knowledge and Conspiracy Theories," p. 181; see discussion in Pigden, "Popper Revisited, or What is Wrong with Conspiracy Theories?"

40. See discussion in Coady, "Conspiracy Theories and Official Stories."

41. *Conspiracy Theories: The Philosophical Debate*, p. 2; Jesse Walker, *The United States of Paranoia: A Conspiracy Theory* (USA: Harper, 2013).

42. But more importantly, because our work is concerned with *beliefs* in conspiracy theories, rather than in conspiracy theories as an abstract concept, the primary difference between malevolent conspiracy theories and benevolent conspiracy theories is in why people would hold those views. If one believed that groups were conspiring for the common good, then that is wishful thinking. The conspiracy theorist in that case would be hoping for the outcome. In contrast, believing that groups are conspiring to do widespread harm is a very different kind of thinking. Believers would not want the alleged conspiracy to come to fruition. Even if the conspiracy theorist engaged in wishful thinking to believe that the alleged culprit was sufficiently twisted and conniving enough to engage in these nefarious activities, this is a very different kind of wishful thinking than that which takes place with benevolent conspiracy theories. As readers will notice, much of the heat from conspiracy theories relates to clashing visions of the good. Antagonists tend to exaggerate the aims of their opponents—for example, kneejerk reactions that any centralization of the state is socialism or any decentralization of the state is putting profits before people—but both sides have significant differences in what they deem as good.

43. CBS, "CBS Poll: JFK Conspiracy Lives"; CNN, "Poll U.S. Hiding Knowledge of Aliens," *CNN.com* (1997), http://articles.cnn.com/1997-06-15/us/9706_15_ufo.poll_1_ufo-aliens-crash-site?_s=PM:US.

44. http://www.lennonmurdertruth.com/introduction.asp.

45. Those who innovate and improve conspiracy theories are interesting, but they represent but a tiny population. Our concern is with broadly held beliefs.

46. For purposes of clarity, we will use a slightly different definition in Chapter 4.

47. Coady, *Conspiracy Theories: The Philosophical Debate*, p. 170.

48. Steve Clarke, "Conspiracy Theories and Conspiracy Theorizing," *Philosophy of the Social Sciences* 32, no. 2 (2002).

49. For discarding more, see Keeley, "Of Conspiracy Theories"; Popper, *Conjectures and Refutations*; for discarding less, see Coady, *Conspiracy Theories: The Philosophical Debate*; Pigden, "Popper Revisited, or What is Wrong with Conspiracy Theories?"

50. Mandik, "Shit Happens," p. 205.

51. Coady, *Conspiracy Theories: The Philosophical Debate*.

52. Steve Clarke, "Conspiracy Theories and the Internet: Controlled Demolition and Arrested Development," *Episteme* 4, no. 2 (2007): 174.

53. Nassim Taleb, *Fooled by Randomness: The Hidden Role of Chance in Life and in the Markets*, 2nd updated ed. (New York: Random House, 2008).

54. More likely, people favor the explanation that comports best with their predispositions, be they conspiratorial, political, or otherwise.

55. Given this, it should come as no surprise that scholars have not found much evidence showing that people turn to conspiracy theories because they offer simple explanations. John W. McHoskey, "Case Closed? On the John F. Kennedy Assassination: Biased Assimilation of Evidence and Attitude Polarization," *Basic and Applied Social Psychology* 17, no. 3 (1995); Marina Abalakina-Paap et al., "Beliefs in Conspiracies," *Political Psychology* 20, no. 3 (1999).

56. Keeley, "Of Conspiracy Theories," p. 122.

57. Ibid.

58. E.g., Clark McCauley and Susan Jacques, "The Popularity of Conapiracy Theories of Presidential Assassination: A Bayesian Analysis," *Journal of Personality and Social Psychology* 37, no. 5 (1979).

59. Keeley, "Of Conspiracy Theories," p. 121.

60. Maarten Boudry and Johan Braeckman, "Immunizing Strategies and Epistemic Mechanisms," *Philosophia* 39 (2011): 146.

61. cf. Noam Chomsky, "9-11: Institutional Analysis vs. Conspiracy Theory," *Z Communications* (2006).

62. Nicholas Difonzo, Prashant Bordia, and Ralph L. Rosnow, "Reigning in Rumors," *Organizational Dynamics* 23 (1994).

63. Ibid.

64. Popper, *Conjectures and Refutations*, p. 125.

65. Richard A. Posner, "Instrumental and Noninstrumental Theories of Tort Law," *Indiana Law Journal* 88 (2013).

66. Preston R. Bost and Stephen G. Prunier, "Rationality in Conspiracy Beliefs: The Role of Perceived Motive," unpublished paper (2013).

67. Popper, *Conjectures and Refutations*.

68. Nicholas Schmidle, "Getting Bin Laden: What Happened that Night in Abbottabad," *New Yorker*, August 8, 2011; see also Mark Bowden, *Black Hawk Down: A Story of Modern War* (New York: Atlantic Monthly Press, 1999).

69. Steve Clarke, "Conspiracy Theories and Conspiracy Theorizing." Clarke later changed his mind about fundamental attribution error; see Steve Clarke, "Appealing to the Fundamental Attribution Error: Was it All a Big Mistake?" in *Conspiracy Theories: The Philosophical Debate*, ed. David Coady (London: Ashgate Pub Co., 2006).

70. Steve Clarke, "Conspiracy Theories and Conspiracy Theorizing," p. 146.

71. Pigden, "Popper Revisited, or What is Wrong with Conspiracy Theories?"

72. Keeley, "Of Conspiracy Theories," p. 126.
73. http://www.youtube.com/watch?v=m7SPm-HFYLo.
74. F. Gregory Gause III, *The International Relations of the Persian Gulf* (New York: Cambridge University Press, 2010), pp. 233–240.
75. James T. Richardson and Massimo Introvigne, "'Brainwashing' Theories in European Parlimentary and Administrative Reports on 'Cults' and 'Sects,'" *Journal for the Scientific Study of Religion* 40, no. 2 (2001).
76. Levy, "Radically Socialized Knowledge and Conspiracy Theories," p. 182.
77. Alan B. Krueger and David Laitin, "Faulty Terror Report Card," *Washington Post*, May 17, 2002.
78. Ted Goertzel, "Conspiracy Theories in Science," *EMBO reports* 11, no. 7 (2010); Lewandowsky, Oberauer, and Gignac, "NASA Faked the Moon Landing—Therefore (Climate) Science Is a Hoax: An Anatomy of the Motivated Rejection of Science."
79. Dylan Avery, *Loose Change 9/11: An American Coup* (Microcinema International, 2009).
80. Miller, "Vaccine Science vs. Science Fiction."
81. Ibid.
82. See also Craig Allen Smith, "The Hofstadter Hypothesis Revisited: The Nature of Evidence in Politically 'Paranoid' Discourse," *Southern Journal of Communication* 42, no. 3 (1977). Evidence is often employed similarly by both those espousing and denying a conspiracy.
83. L. Rosenblitz and F. Keil, "The Misunderstood LImits of Folk Science: An Illusions of Explanatory Depth," *Cognitive Science* 26, no. 5 (2002).
84. R. A. Wilson, *Boundaries of the Mind: The Individual in the Fragile Sciences* (Cambridge: Cambridge University Press, 2004).
85. Jeffrey Kimball, "The Influence of Ideology on Interpretive Disagreement: A Report on a Survey of Diplomatic, Military and Peace Historians on the Causes of 20th Century U.S. Wars," *The History Teacher* 17, May (1984); Robert Jervis, "Roundtable on Politics and Scholarship," *H-Diplo/ISSF* 1, no. 2 (2010); M. Mahoney, "Publication Prejudices: An Experimental Study of Confirmatory Bias in the Peer Review System," *Cognitive Therapy and Research* 2, June (1977).
86. Quoted in David H. Freedman, "Are Engineered Foods Evil?," *Scientific American* 309, no. 3 (2013); see also Lawrence Solomon, "The Deniers, Fully Revised: The World-Renowned Scientists Who Stood Up Against Global Warming Hysteria, Political Persecution and Fraud," *Minneapolis: Richard Vigilante Books*(2010).
87. Keeley, "Of Conspiracy Theories," p. 118.
88. http://www.youtube.com/watch?v=m7SPm-HFYLo.
89. Joel Buenting and Jason Taylor, "Conspiracy Theories and Fortuitous Data," *Philosophy of the Social Sciences* 40, no. 4 (2010).
90. Charles S. Taber and Milton Lodge, "Motivated Skepticism in the Evaluation of Political Beliefs," *American Journal of Political Science* 50, no. 3 (2006).
91. We note, however, that people do update opinions and ideologies at both the individual and macro-levels. See Morris P. Fiorina, *Retrospective Voting in American National Elections* (New Haven: Yale University Press, 1981); Michael MacKuen, Robert S. Erikson, and James Stimson, "Macropartisanship," *The American Political Science Review* 83, no. 4 (1989). But stability is more the norm. See also Angus

Campbell et al., *The American Voter, Unabridged Edition* (Chicago: The University of Chicago Press, 1960).

CHAPTER 3

1. Zbigniew Brzezinski, "Quotation of the Day," *New York Times*, January 18, 1981.
2. Proper batteries of questions have been used in the past to access underlying conspiratorial thinking. Herbert McClosky and Dennis Chong, "Similarities and Differences between Left-Wing and Right-Wing Radicals," *British Journal of Political Science* 15, no. 3 (1985); Robert Brotherton, Christopher C. French, and Alan D. Pickering, "Measuring Belief in Conspiracy Theories: The Generic Conspiracist Beliefs Scale," *Frontiers in Psychology* 4, Article 279 (2013); Martin Bruder et al., "Measuring Individual Differences in Generic Beliefs in Conspiracy Theories Across Cultures: The Conspiracy Mentality Questionnaire (CMQ)," *Frontiers in Psychology* 4 (2013); Roland Imhoff and Martin Bruder, "Speaking (Un-)Truth to Power: Conspiracy Mentality as a Generalised Political Attitude," *European Journal of Personality* (2013).
3. We weight the data in our analyses to approximate national demographics as closely as possible. Online appendix available at Joeuscinski.com.
4. We closely examined response rates and found little evidence that non-response was systematic.
5. Benjamin I. Page, *Who Deliberates? Mass Media in Modern Democracy* (Chicago: University of Chicago Press, 1996); Andrew Perrin and Stephen Vaisey, "Parallel Public Spheres: Distance and Discourse in Letters to the Editor," *American Journal of Sociology* 114, no. 3 (2008).
6. Lee Sigelman and Barbara J. Walkosz, "Letters to the Editor as a Public Opinion Thermometer: The Martin Luther King Holiday Vote in Arizona," *Social Science Quarterly* 73 (1992).
7. David B. Hill, "Letter Opinion on ERA: A Test of the Newspaper Bias Hypothesis," *Public Opinion Quarterly* 45 (1981).
8. William A. Gamson, *Talking Politics* (Cambridge, MA: Cambridge University Press, 1992).
9. A randomized counting process was used within each month to choose letters. Some years in the database, especially in the 1800s, did not contain 1,000 letters, but we sought to approximate that number as closely as possible. Also, some of the letters were unreadable and could not be coded. There is no reason to suspect the exclusion of these letters would bias the results in any way. In addition, we oversampled some years, but because of our mode of analysis, this does not affect our results.
10. The end result was a mean of 866 letters, a median of 845 letters, and a range of 347 to 2,477 letters per year.
11. This tack comes at the price of ignoring talk on the fringe; however, since our goal is to examine topics that are resonating in the broader population, examining smaller outlets makes little sense. Examining many outlets of all sizes might provide more depth and breadth, but it is prohibitively expensive and in some cases impossible due to a lack of availability.
12. Tim Groseclose, *Left Turn: How Liberal Media Bias Distorts the American Mind* (New York: St. Martin's Press, 2011).

13. Joseph E. Uscinski, *The People's News: Media, Politics, and the Demands of Capitalism* (New York: New York University Press, 2014).

14. See online appendix.

15. See online appendix.

16. The principal investigators did not perform any of the coding, and coders were unaware of the hypotheses tested in this study. Coders underwent intense training and had to achieve a high level of agreement with a series of training samples (these samples included a higher proportion of letters containing conspiracies than the actual data, both to give the coders more experience with such letters and to provide a better test of reliability). The Krippendorff's alpha coefficient for the tests among trained coders ranged between .8 and 1.0; this is considered adequate by conventional standards. Because coder fatigue would likely be an issue given the size of the actual sample and the fact that coders had to manually read the entirety of the letters, coders worked short shifts and were provided frequent breaks. Coders were periodically retrained and retested. To be sure that the coding of the actual data was reliable, we performed periodic tests, recoding portions of the sample using different coders. Coder agreement between conspiracy theory letters and non-conspiracy theory letters in these tests was consistently above 99 percent. Krippendorff's alpha in these tests met conventional standards. Disagreements were settled by a third coder. This high level of agreement was expected given that most letters in the sample clearly did not meet the criteria that would indicate discussion of a conspiracy theory.

17. Letters proffering a conspiracy theory are self-explanatory, but letters discounting a conspiracy theory have to recite the alleged plot but argue that the accusations were false. We analyze letters proffering and discounting conspiracy theories together because the letters discounting conspiracy theories, while not indicating that the letter writers adhere to the theory, indicate that the conspiracy theory is resonating in the population widely enough to merit writing and publishing a letter to discount it. Also, combining letters discounting and proffering conspiracy theories acts as a further check on editorial bias. Hypothetically, if the *Times* editorial staff were to show a left-leaning bias, we would expect them to favor letters that discounted conspiratorial allegations made at actors on the left as opposed to letters alleging conspiratorial actions by actors on the left (and vice versa). Media coverage of the recent Birther conspiracy theory bears this out. Pew analysis of cable news coverage shows that MSNBC (the liberal outlet) gave as much attention as either CNN (the moderate outlet) or Fox News (the conservative outlet) to the recent Birther conspiracy theory. Julie Moos, "Factchecking Obama: Birther Controversy was 4% of Newshole, Not 'Dominant' Story," *Poynter.* http://www.poynter.org/latest-news/top-stories/129708/factchecking-obama-birther-controversy-was-3-4-of-newshole-economy-was-39/, April 27 (2011). The vast majority of this attention was to deny the conspiracy. On this logic, and should editorial ideological bias manifest, we would then expect the *New York Times* to publish fewer letters proffering the Birther conspiracy, for example, and more denying it.

18. For the first element, a group could refer to any entity, from a collection of countries, a single country, an institution, a party, a religious sect, a trade union, interest

group, to a small band of unaffiliated collaborators. Some letters name a single conspirator but make clear that that person was in concert with others to orchestrate the plot. The groups could be out of power or in power; they could be a large majority or a minor fringe; they could be political, economic, social, or religious in nature.

For the second element, acting in secret, the alleged actions of the villain had to take place outside of normal institutional channels. To provide a few examples, if a group openly advertised that it advocated and was willing to take part in the forceful overthrow of the U.S. government, this would not qualify because our coding excludes harms done in broad daylight. Likewise, if a writer contended that Mormons were supporting the election of Republican candidates, this would not be viewed as a conspiracy either because such actions are part of normal democratic processes. However, if a letter contended that Mormons were orchestrating the stealthy stuffing of ballot boxes, then this would indicate that they were acting in secret and outside of normal channels.

For the third element, the letter had to indicate that the group was attempting to alter institutions, usurp power, hide truth, or gain some other form of utility for themselves. This might involve instituting a communist regime, illegally achieving election, concealing vital information from the public, or gaining illicit riches. For instance, the theory that NASA faked the moon landing fits this criterion because the allegation assumes that high-level government officials are hiding this fact (and other important facts about outer space) from the people.

For the fourth element, the letter writer had to claim that, if carried out, the plot would come at the expense of the common good. Judgments regarding harm were left solely to letter writers. This might involve swindling the unsuspecting out of large sums of money, brainwashing naïve citizens, unleashing baleful legislation, or enslaving the country under an unscrupulous regime. Benevolent plots and private wrongs were excluded. So if one contended that secret forces were curing cancer, these would not fit our definition of a conspiracy theory.

19. The number of total elite letters averaged 74 per year, representing 8.5 percent of the total letters. Non-elite letters averaged 792 letters per year.

20. Before beginning the sampling and coding process, we performed a series of simple word searches in the *New York Times Historical Database*. Letters containing terms such as "conspiracy" yielded less than 1 percent of the letters in the database.

21. In each letter, we identified the alleged villains and made a distinction between villains and pawns—pawns being basically puppets while villains are the puppet-masters.

22. Two coders, each unaware of the hypotheses being tested, coded each of the villains into the eight categories. Most of the letters were explicit enough to make the categorization fairly easy. They agreed on 794 out of the 836. The majority of the 42 disagreements appeared to stem from the antiquity of the villain; however, research into the context of the letter or research into the named villain led to near-unanimous agreement. Remaining disagreements were settled by a third coder who was also unaware of the hypotheses being tested.

23. McClosky and Chong, "Similarities and Differences between Left-Wing and Right-Wing Radicals."

24. We make the distinction between left and communist based first on how the actor, rather than the action, is described: if the actor is on the left but wants to institute communist/socialist policies, then that person is coded as left. If the person(s) is a communist or socialist first and foremost, or is only described as an actor having communist intentions, then that person(s) is coded as communist. These distinctions are sometimes subtle given that fears of communist plots have historically been used to attack liberal causes; see Elmer Eric Schattschneider, *The Semisovereign People: A Realist's View of Democracy in America* (Orlando, FL: Harcourt Brace Jovanovich, Inc., 1960), p. 71.

25. Were the FBI conspiring at the behest of President George W. Bush for partisan aims, then this would be coded as an actor on the right. Were the FBI conspiring for its own ends, without partisan aims, and not at the behest of another partisan actor, then this would be coded as government.

26. Given that many of the conspiracies in our data center on communist plots, we should be clear about how we differentiate foreign communist actors from communist actors. If domestic communist groups were working within this country to brainwash schoolchildren, this would be coded as communist. However, if groups in Latin America were plotting with the Soviet Union, to do harm in Latin America or to the United States from abroad, then this would be foreign.

27. Christopher A. Cooper, H. Gibbs Knotts, and Mashe Haspel, "The Content of Political Participation: Letters to the Editor and the People Who Write Them," *PS: Political Science and Politics* 42 (2009).

28. Emmett H. Buell, "Eccentrics or Gladiators? People Who Write about Politics in Letters-to-the-Editor," *Social Science Quarterly* 56 (1975); Thomas J. Volgy et al., "Some of My Best Friends Are Letter Writers: Eccentrics and Gladiators Revisited," *Social Science Quarterly* 58, no. 2 (1977).

29. Sidney Verba et al., "Public Opinion and the War in Vietnam," *American Political Science Review* 61(1967): 330.

30. Hill, "Letter Opinion on ERA: A Test of the Newspaper Bias Hypothesis"; Sigelman and Walkosz, "Letters to the Editor as a Public Opinion Thermometer: The Martin Luther King Holiday Vote in Arizona."

31. Thomas Feyer, "To the Reader," *New York Times Book Review*, September 14, 2003. See also Karin Wahl-Jorgenson, "A 'Letigimate Beef' or 'Raw Meat'? Civility, Multiculturalism, and Letters to the Editor," *Communication Review* 7 (2004).

32. Perrin and Vaisey, "Parallel Public Spheres: Distance and Discourse in Letters to the Editor," 787. But to err on the safe side, we take steps to account for relevant news content in our later analyses and find significant divergences between these two parts of newspapers.

33. Daniel M. Butler and Emily Schofield, "Were Newspapers More Interested in Pro-Obama Letters to the Editor in 2008? Evidence From a Field Experiment," *American Politics Research* 38, no. 2 (2010); H. Schuyler Foster and Carl J. Friedrich, "Letters to the Editor as a Means of Measuring the Effectiveness of Propaganda," *The American Political Science Review* 31, no. 1 (1937); see also Paula Cozort Renfro, "Bias in Selection of Letters to the Editor," *Journalism Quarterly* 56 (1979).

34. Hill, "Letter Opinion on ERA: A Test of the Newspaper Bias Hypothesis," 384. Not being ones to take matters on faith, we performed statistical models that controlled for the *Times'* changing editorship, ownership, circulation, and amount of local competition. The outcome accords with previous literature: these variables, which should pick up any potential biases, detect little and are inconsequential to our results (see online appendices).

35. E.g., Carol Morello, "Conspiracy Theories Flourish on the Internet," *Washington Post* (2004); Jill Edy and Erin Baird, "The Persistence of Rumor Communities: Public Resistance to Official Debunking in the Internet Age" (paper presented at the APSA 2012 Annual Meeting Paper); Anna Kata, "A Postmodern Pandora's Box: Anti-vaccination Misinformation on the Internet," *Vaccine* 28, no. 7 (2010); Darrin M. McMahon, "Conspiracies so vast: Conspiracy theory was born in the Age of Enlightenment and has metastasized in the age of the internet. Why won't it go away?" *The Boston Globe*, Feb. 1, 2004.

36. Steve Clarke, "Conspiracy Theories and the Internet: Controlled Demolition and Arrested Development," *Episteme* 4, no. 02 (2007); see also Jack Zeljko Bratich, "Trust No One (On the Internet): The CIA-Crack-Contra Conspiracy Theory and Professional Journalism," *Television & New Media* 5, no. 2 (2004).

37. The principal investigators did not perform any of the coding. Coders underwent intense training and had to achieve a high level of agreement with a series of training samples. Coders read the title, short blurb provided by Google, and relevant portions of the article identified by word searches. Positive stories were those that supported the veracity of a conspiracy theory; neutral stories either took no position or argued that the theory could be true or false; and negative stories argued the conspiracy theory was either false or its adherents were deficient in some way.

38. To be sure that the coding of the actual data was reliable, different coders recoded portions of the sample. Coder agreement on tone (positive, neutral, and negative) was consistently above 95 percent. Krippendorff's alpha in these tests met conventional standards. Disagreements were settled by a third coder.

39. Stefan Stieger et al., "Girl in the Cellar: A Repeated Cross-sectional Investigation of Belief in Conspiracy Theories About the Kidnapping of Natascha Kampusch," *Frontiers in Psychology* 4 (2013).

CHAPTER 4

1. John Updike, *Problems and Other Stories* (New York: Knopf, 1979).

2. Roland Imhoff and Martin Bruder, "Speaking (Un-)Truth to Power: Conspiracy Mentality as a Generalised Political Attitude," *European Journal of Personality* (2013); Martin Bruder et al., "Measuring Individual Differences in Generic Beliefs in Conspiracy Theories Across Cultures: The Conspiracy Mentality Questionnaire (CMQ)," *Frontiers in Psychology* 4 (2013); Robert Brotherton, Christopher C. French, and Alan D. Pickering, "Measuring Belief in Conspiracy Theories: The Generic Conspiracist Beliefs Scale," *Frontiers in Psychology* 4, Article 279 (2013).

3. Angus Campbell et al., *The American Voter Unabridged Edition* (Chicago: The University of Chicago Press, 1960).

4. Ted Marzilli, "Cain's Candidacy Splits Pizza Scores," *YouGov: BrandIndex* (2011). A similar phenomenon happened during the recent trial of George Zimmerman. See Rebecca Leber, "Poll Reveals Wide Racial, Partisan Divide On George Zimmerman Trial," *Think Progress* (2013).

5. Tucker, Josh "The Effects of Partisanship: Ben Bernanke as a Natural Experiment?" MonkeyCage.org April 13, 2009 http://themonkeycage.org/2009/04/13/the_effects_of_partisanship_be/

6. John Zaller, *The Nature and Origins of Mass Opinion.* Cambridge Studies in Public Opinion and Political Psychology (Cambridge, UK: Cambridge University Press, 1992); Philip E. Converse, "The Nature of Belief Systems in Mass Publics (1964)," *Critical Review* 18, nos. 1–3 (2006).

7. Herbert McClosky and Dennis Chong, "Similarities and Differences between Left-Wing and Right-Wing Radicals," *British Journal of Political Science* 15, no. 3 (1985); Brotherton, French, and Pickering, "Measuring Belief in Conspiracy Theories: The Generic Conspiracist Beliefs Scale"; Bruder et al., "Assessing Conspiracy Mentality Across Cultures"; Imhoff and Bruder, "Speaking (Un-)Truth to Power: Conspiracy Mentality as a Generalised Political Attitude."

8. This summary measure was produced using factor analysis. Factor loadings in parentheses: "Much of our lives are being controlled by plots hatched in secret places"(.836), "Even though we live in a democracy, a few people will always run things anyway" (.818), "The people who really 'run' the country are not known to the voters" (.865). Online appendix available at Joeuscinski.com.

9. Excluding non-respondents, this provided 1,161 respondents in our sample. We performed several tests to see if non-response was systematic; we did not find evidence to suggest such. For this reason, and to make our analyses as transparent as possible (and not computationally impute responses for conspiracy theorists), we simply exclude non-respondents.

10. Conspiratorial predispositions are a statistically significant predictor of trust when accounting for demographics, such as income, education, and party identification. Regression model provided in online appendix.

11. Conspiratorial predispositions are a statistically significant predictor of responses to this question when accounting for demographics, such as income, education, and party identification. Regression model provided in online appendix.

12. Conspiratorial predispositions are a statistically significant predictor of the number of groups thought to be working in secret against the rest of us when accounting for demographics, such as income, education, and party identification. Regression model provided in online appendix.

13. E.g., Aaron M. McCright and Riley E. Dunlap, "Cool Dudes: The Denial of Climate Change among Conservative White Males in the United States," *Global Environmental Change* 21, no. 4 (2011).

14. Sarah Hepola, "Whoopi Goldberg: Was the moon landing a hoax? 'The View' co-host celebrates the 40th anniversary of Apollo 11 by spreading wacky conspiracy theories," *Salon.com* (2009); Bob Owens, "Ex 'The View' co-host entertains Zimmerman case conspiracy theories," *Bob-Owens.com* (2012); "Rosie O'Donnell 9/11 Conspiracy Comments: *Popular Mechanics* Responds," *Popular Mechanics* (2009);

Rachel Lincoln Sarnoff, "Jenny McCarthy's Got the Wrong View on Vaccinations," *Huffington Post* (2013).

15. Education and family income are also significant predictors—they are both negatively correlated with conspiratorial thinking—but race remains significant when other factors are controlled for. See online appendix. This is one area where the temporal context of the poll may matter greatly. While more polling is needed, we suggest that our measure of conspiratorial dispositions for African Americans may be a slight underestimation given that blacks have lived under a black president for four years.

16. We suspect this is a product of changing socialization and environment as opposed to a life-cycle effect because other races show the opposite effect.

17. When we examined the strength of conspiratorial predispositions across the ages of our respondents, there is over time variation, but it does not have a linear or easily explainable relationship with age. Therefore, we suggest that generational analysis is most appropriate here. Of course, more studies need to track this over time to better disentangle generational and life-cycle effects.

18. Karl Mannheim, "The Problem of Generations," in *Essays on the Sociology of Knowledge* (London: Routledge & Keegan, 1952); William Strauss and Neil Howe, *Generations: The History of America's Future, 1584 to 2069* (New York: Perennial, 1991); Stephen C. Craig and Stephen Earl Bennett, eds., *After the Boom: The Politics. of Generation X* (New York: Rowman & Littlefield, 1997); Michael X. DelliCarpini, "Age and History: Generations and Sociopolitical Change," in *Political Learning in Adulthood: A Sourcebook of Theory and Research*, ed. Roberta S. Sigel (Chicago: University of Chicago Press, 1989); William R. Klecka, "Applying Political Generations to the Study of Political Behavior: A Cohort Analysis."

19. The effect is more pronounced for whites, where we expect more generational dynamism in response to societal events given their unthreatened majority status.

20. Craig and Bennett, *After the Boom: The Politics of Generation X*; Neil Howe and William Strauss, *Millennials Rising: The Next Great Generation* (USA: Vintage, 2000); Diana Owen, "Mixed Signals: Generation X's Attitudes toward the Political System," in *After the Boom: The Politics of Generation X*, ed. Stephen C. Craig and Spephen Earl Bennett (New York: Rowman & Littlefield Publishers, Inc., 1997).

21. Margaret Levi and Laura Stoker, "Political Trust and Trustworthiness," *Annual Review of Political Science* 3, no. 1 (2000): 478.

22. Benjamin I. Page and Gordon Scott Fulcher, *Navigating Public Opinion: Polls, Policy, and the Future of American Democracy: Polls, Policy, and the Future of American Democracy* (New York: Oxford University Press, 2002), p. 159.

23. In a study that correlates the two, the authors must disclose personal details relevant to the analysis. This study was written by two unmarried, 30-something, overeducated white males. Uscinski advises the local College Republican and Libertarian groups and Parent interned for Democratic politicians, but neither identifies with either major party or votes consistently for one.

24. Zaller, *The Nature and Origins of Mass Opinion*; Campbell et al., *The American Voter, Unabridged Edition*; Philip Converse, "Belief Systems in Mass Publics," in *Ideology*

and Its Discontents, ed. David E. Apter (New York: The Free Press of Glencoe, 1964); Joseph E. Uscinski and Ryden W. Butler, "The Problems of Fact-Checking," *Critical Review* 25, no. 2 (2013).

25. Paul Krugman, "Who's Crazy Now?" *New York Times* (2006); "The Wonk Gap," *New York Times* (2013).

26. "Crazy Consipracy Theorists," *New York Times* (2008). For like examples, see Jonathan Chait, *The Big Con: The True Story of How Washington Got Hoodwinked and Hijacked by Crackpot Economics* (Boston: Houghton Mifflin Company, 2007), p. 242.

27. "Celebrity 9/11 Conspiracy Club Still Growing," *Washington Times* (2008).

28. Please be aware that those identifying as conservative and very conservative have slightly fewer people falling into the high category than either those identifying as liberal or very liberal.

29. Chait, *The Big Con: The True Story of How Washington Got Hoodwinked and Hijacked by Crackpot Economics*, p. 242. Chris Matthews, MSNBC, 4:00pm, March 29, 2013.

30. Brendan Nyhan, "9/11 and Birther Misperceptions Compared," *Brendan-nyhan.com/blog* (2009).

31. We do not mean to imply that all conspiratorial beliefs held by the right or left are equally held by the other side. We compare the Birther and Truther beliefs because they are contemporarily prominent and often compared.

32. Chait, *The Big Con: The True Story of How Washington Got Hoodwinked and Hijacked by Crackpot Economics*, p. 242.

33. Dan Cassino and Krista Jenkins, "Conspiracy Theories Prosper: 25% of Americans are 'Truthers,'" press release (2013).

34. Dara Kam and John Lantigua, "Former Florida GOP leaders say voter suppression was reason they pushed new election law," *Palm Beach Post* (2012); Ari Berman, "The GOP War on Voting," *Rolling Stone* (2011).

35. Chris Mooney, "The More Republicans Know About Politics, the More They Believe Conspiracy Theories," *Mother Jones* (2013); Kim Messick, "The Tea Party's paranoid aesthetic," *Salon.com* (2013); Matt A. Barreto et al., "The Tea Party in the Age of Obama: Mainstream Conservatism or Out-Group Anxiety?" *Political Power and Social Theory* 22, no. 1 (2012).

36. Dana R. Carney et al., "The Secret Lives of Liberals and Conservatives: Personality Profiles, Interaction Styles, and the Things They Leave Behind," *Political Psychology* 29, no. 6 (2008).

37. Stanley Rothman, S. Robert Lichter, and Neil Nevitte, "Politics and Professional Advancement Among College Faculty," *The Forum* 3, no. 1 (2005); Melisa Gao, "Professors Fund Liberal Candidates," *The Daily Princetonian*, September 13, 2004; Howard Kurtz, "College Faculties a Most Liberal Lot, Study Finds," *Washington Post*, March 29, 2005; S. Robert Lichter, Stanley Rothman, and Linda Lichter, *The Media Elite: America's New Power-brokers* (Bethesda, MD: Adler & Alder, 1986); Bernard Goldberg, *Bias: A CBS Insider Exposes How the Media Distort the News* (Washington D.C.: Renergy, 2002); *A Slobbering Love Affair: The True (And Pathetic) Story of the Torrid Romance Between Barack Obama and the Mainstream Media* (New York: Regnery Publishing, 2009).

38. Joseph E. Uscinski and Arthur Simon, "Partisanship as a Source of Presidential Rankings," *White House Studies* 11, no. 1 (2011); Stanley Rothman and S. Robert Lichter, "Elite Ideology and Risk Perception in Nuclear Energy Policy," *American Political Science Review* 81, no. 2 (1987); Uscinski and Butler, "The Problems of Fact-Checking"; M. Mahoney, "Publication Prejudices: An Experimental Study of Confirmatory Bias in the Peer Review System," *Cognitive Therapy and Research* 2, June (1977); Robert Jervis, "Roundtable on Politics and Scholarship," *H-Diplo/ISSF* 1, no. 2 (2010); Jeffrey Kimball, "The Influence of Ideology on Interpretive Disagreement: A Report on a Survey of Diplomatic, Military and Peace Historians on the Causes of 20th Century U.S. Wars," *The History Teacher* 17, May (1984).

39. Geoff Peterson and J. Mark Wrighton, "Expressions of Distrust: Third-Party Voting and Cynicism in Government," *Political Behavior* 20, no. 1 (1998).

40. Conspiratorial predispositions are a statistically significant predictor of attitudes toward Iraq when accounting for party identification. Regression model provided in online appendix.

41. Michael Barone, "Dems Sour on Obama's 'Good War' in Afghanistan," *The Washington Examiner* (2010).

42. Conspiratorial predispositions are a statistically significant predictor of attitudes toward Afghanistan when accounting for party identification. Regression model provided in online appendix.

43. Conspiratorial predispositions are a statistically significant predictor of both registration and voter turnout when controlling for education and income. Regression model provided in online appendix.

44. Conspiratorial predispositions are a statistically significant predictor of participation when accounting for education and income. Regression model provided in online appendix.

45. Rachel Maddow, MSNBC, 9:00 pm, August 9, 2013.

46. Jamie Bartlett and Carl Miller, *The Power of Unreason: Conspiracy Theories, Extremism and Counter-Terrorism.* (London: Demos, 2010).

47. Conspiratorial predispositions are a statistically significant predictor of attitudes toward violence when controlling for education and income. Regression model provided in online appendix.

48. Conspiratorial predispositions are a statistically significant predictor of attitudes toward violence when controlling for education and income. Regression model provided in online appendix. When we isolate the extremities for this question, it is those with lower conspiratorial predispositions who are more likely, slightly, to agree that violence is acceptable to stop politically extreme groups from doing harm, 22 to 18 percent. It is likely that those on the extremity of conspiratorial beliefs are self-preserving in this question. They are likely to consider their own views politically extreme in some way.

49. Karen M. Douglas and Robbie M. Sutton, "Does It Take One to Know One? Endorsement of Conspiracy Theories is Influenced by Personal Willingness to Conspire," *British Journal of Social Psychology* 50, no. 3 (2011).

50. Conspiratorial predispositions are a statistically significant predictor of attitudes toward gun restrictions when controlling for party affiliation. Regression model provided in online appendix.

51. Our data suggest that moving from low to medium conspiratorial predispositions, or from medium to high, is significantly associated with discussing important matters with one-half less friend. Regression model provided in appendix.

52. Conspiratorial predispositions are a statistically significant predictor of income and inventing when controlling for education and income. Regression model provided in online appendix.

CHAPTER 5

1. Walter A. McDougall, *Freedom Just Around the Corner: A New American History, 1585–1828* (New York: Harper Collins, 2004), p. 106.

2. David Aaronovitch, *Voodoo Histories: The Role of Conspiracy Theory in Shaping Modern History* (New York: Riverhead Books, 2010), p. 15; Annie Jacobsen, "The United States of conspiracy: Why, more and more, Americans cling to crazy theories," *NYDailyNews.com*, August 7, 2011, http://articles.nydailynews.com/2011-08-07/news/29878465_1_conspiracy-theories-bavarian-illuminati-nefarious-business; Andrew Rosenthal, "No Comment Necessary: Conspiracy Nation," *New York Times* (2013); Joseph E. Uscinski, *The People's News: Media, Politics, and the Demands of Capitalism* (New York: New York University Press, 2014). In his perceptive review, *New York Times* columnist Ross Douthat doubts that: "If anything, Aaronovitch's book suggests that the paranoid style's direct power over Western politics has declined precipitously over the last 50 years." See Ross Douthat, "Nuts and Dolts," *New York Times Book Review* (2010).

3. Darrin M. McMahon, "Conspiracies so vast: Conspiracy theory was born in the Age of Enlightenment and has metastasized in the age of the internet. Why won't it go away?" *Boston Globe*, February 1, 2004.

4. Lou Cannon, "Gary Sick's Lingering Charges," *Washington Post* (1991); Kenn Thomas, "Clinton Era Conspiracies! Was Gennifer Flowers on the Grassy Knoll? Probably Not, but Here Are Some Other Bizarre Theories for a New Political Age," *Washington Post*, January 16, 1994. Charles Krauthammer, columnist for the *Post*, agreed with his employer in the first instance, but as far as we can tell, not in the second. See Charles Krauthammer, "A Rash of Conspiracy Theories," *Washington Post*, July 5, 1991.

5. Georgie Anne Geyer, "The Rewriting of History to Fit Our Age of Conspiracy," *Los Angeles Times* (1977).

6. "The Warren Commission Report," *New York Times* (1964).

7. Jonathan Kay, *Among the Truthers: A Journey through America's Growing Conspiracist Underground* (New York: Harper Collins Publishers 2011), p. xiii.

8. Gordon B. Arnold, *Conspiracy Theory in Film, Television, and Politics* (Westport, CT: Praeger, 2008), p. 9; Robert Alan Goldberg, *Enemies Within: The Culture of Conspiracy in Modern America* (New Haven: Yale University Press, 2001), p. xii; Daniel Pipes, *Conspiracy: How the Paranoid Style Flourishes and Where It Comes From* (New York: Touchstone, 1997), p. xii.

9. Brion David Davis, "Foreward," in *Conspiracy Theories in American History vol. 1*, ed. Peter Knight (Santa Barbara, CA: ABC CLIO, 2003).

10. Paul K. MacDonald, "'Retribution Must Succeed Rebellion': The Colonial Origins of Counterinsurgency Failure," *International Organization* 67, no. 2 (2013); Joseph

Parent, "Tomorrow's Disintegration: Security and Unity in an Era of Entropy" (Oslo: Norwegian Nobel Institute, 2012); David M. Edelstein, "Managing Uncertainty: Beliefs about Intentions and Rise of Great Powers," *Security Studies* 12, no. 1 (2002).

11. Adam Smith, *The Theory of Moral Sentiments* (Indianapolis: Liberty Fund, 1982), pp. 181–185; Frank Knight, *The Ethics of Competition* (New Brunswick, NJ: Transaction Publishers, 1997), pp. 15–27; 58–67.

12. Katherine Levine Einstein and David M. Glick, "Scandals, Conspiracies and the Vicious Cycle of Cynicism" (2013).

13. Ernst B. Haas, "The Study of Regional Integration: Reflections of the Joy and Anguish of Pretheorizing," *International Organization* 24, no. 4 (1970).

14. Martin J. Sklar, *The Corporate Reconstruction of American Capitalism, 1890–1916: The Market, the Law, and Politics* (Cambridge, UK: Cambridge University Press, 1988).

15. Cathie Jo Martin and Duane Swank, "The Political Origins of Coordinated Capitalism: Business Organizations, Party Systems, and State Structure in the Age of Innocence," *The American Political Science Review* 102, no. 2 (2008); Lewis L. Gould, *Presidency of William McKinley* (Lawrence, KS: University Press of Kansas, 1981).

16. Marc Trachtenberg, *A Constructed Peace: The Making of European Settlement, 1945–1963* (Princeton, NJ: Princeton University Press, 1999); James McAllister, *No Exit: America and the German Problem, 1943–1954* (Ithaca, NY: Cornell University Press, 2002); Fred Kaplan, *The Wizards of Armageddon* (Stanford, CA: Stanford University Press, 1983).

17. We constructed a series of control variables to test for potential biases stemming from the *Times*. We tracked changes in the *New York Times* ownership, editorship, circulation, and local competition. These variables provided little explanatory power, and therefore we excluded them from the shown model. Models that include these are available at Joeuscinski.com. Note that the way we discuss our method may open us to the *post hoc ergo propter hoc* fallacy. Because we gathered our hypotheses from qualitative researchers, all of our hypotheses have effectively weathered plausibility probes and been checked for anticipatory effects.

18. Aliyah Shahid and Corky Siemaszko, "President Obama Takes on Preacher Terry Jones and Controverisal Plan for Sept. 11 Koran Burn," *New York Daily News* (2010).

19. James T. LaPlant, "No Winning This Argument," *New York Times* (2011).

20. Peter Gourevitch, *Politics in Hard Times: Comparative Responses to International Economic Crises* (Ithaca, NY: Cornell University Press, 1986), pp. 143–147; Charles P. Kindleberger, *The World in Depression: 1929–1939*, Revised and Enlarged Edn. (Berkeley: University of California Press, 1986); Gary Jacobson, "Barack Obama and the American Public: The First 18 Months," presented at Annual Meeting of the American Political Science Association, Washington, D.C., 2010.

21. Sharon Parsons et al., "A Test of the Grapevine: An Empirical Examination of the Conspiracy Theories Among African Americans," *Sociological Spectrum* 19, no. 2 (1999); Ted Goertzel, "Belief in Conspiracy Theories," *Political Psychology* 15 (1994).

22. For years prior to the national income tax, there is little way to calculate income inequality since personal incomes were not reported. However, we attempted to estimate the GINI coefficient for these years based upon accounts of economic historians.

23. Leslie Kaufman and Kate Zernike, "Activists Fight Green Projects, Seeing U.N. Plot," *New York Times* (2012).

24. Richard Hofstadter, *Anti-Intellectualism in American Life* (New York: Vintage, 1963), p. 6; Gordon S. Wood, "Conspiracy and the Paranoid Style: Causality and Deceit in the Eighteenth Century," *William and Mary Quarterly* 39, no. 3 (1982): 407–420; Peter Knight, "Introduction: A Nation of Conspiracy Theorists," in *Conspiracy Nation: The Politics of Paranoia in Postwar America*, ed. Peter Knight (New York: New York University Press, 2002), p. 7; William Gribbin, "Antimasonry, Religious Radicalism, and the Paraniod Style of the 1820s," *History Teacher* 7, no. 2 (1974): 241–244; William M. Hogue, "The Religious Conspiracy Theory of the American Revolution: Anglican Motive," *Church History* 45, no. 3 (1976): 291.

25. Mark Fenster, *Conspiracy Theories: Secrecy and Power in American Culture* (Minneapolis: University of Minnesota Press, 1999), pp. viii, xiv; Timothy Melley, *Empire of Conspiracy: The Culture of Paranoia in Postwar America* (Ithaca: Cornell University Press, 2000); Kathryn S. Olmsted, *Real Enemies: Conspiracy Theories and American Democracy, World War I to 9/11* (New York: Oxford University Press, 2008), pp. 4, 8–9.

26. Emily Erikson and Joseph Parent, "Central Authority and Order," *Sociological Theory* 25, no. 3 (2007).

27. Michael Tesler and David O. Sears, *Obama's Race: The 2008 Election and the Dream of a Post-Racial America*, Chicago Studies in American Politics (Chicago: University of Chicago Press, 2010), p. 153.

28. Timothy Tackett, "Conspiracy Obsession in a Time of Revolution: French Elites and the Origins of the Terror, 1789–1792," *American Historical Review* 105, no. 3 (2000): 42; Richard Hofstadter, *The Paranoid Style in American Politics, and Other Essays* (Cambridge: Harvard University Press, 1964), pp. 32, 39; ibid., p. 7; David Brion Davis, *The Slave Power Conspiracy and the Paranoid Style* (Baton Rouge: Louisiana State University Press, 1969), pp. 25–26; Wood, "Conspiracy and the Paranoid Style: Causality and Deceit in the Eighteenth Century," pp. 404–405, 411, 430; Seymour Martin Lipset and Earl Raab, *The Politics of Unreason: Right-Wing Extremism in America 1790–1977* (Chicago: University of Chicago Press, 1978), pp. 460, 488; Aaronovitch, *Voodoo Histories: The Role of Conspiracy Theory in Shaping Modern History*, p. 355; Amos Hofman, "Opinion, Illusion, and the Illusion of Opinion: Barruel's Theory of Conspiracy," *Eighteenth-Century Studies* 27, no. 1 (1993): 33; Matt A. Barreto et al., "The Tea Party in the Age of Obama: Mainstream Conservatism or Out-Group Anxiety?" *Political Power and Social Theory* 22, no. 1 (2012); Christopher S. Parker and Matt A. Barreto, *Change They Can't Believe in: The Tea Party and Reactionary Politics in America* (Princeton: Princeton University Press, 2013).

29. Fenster, *Conspiracy Theories: Secrecy and Power in American Culture*; Anita M. Waters, "Conspiracy Theories as Ethnosociologies: Explanations and Intention in African American Political Culture," *Journal of Black Studies* 28, no. 1 (1997); Jeff Woods, *Black Struggle, Red Scare: Segregation and Anti-Communism in the South, 1948–1968* (Baton Rouge: Louisiana State University Press, 2004).

30. Staff, "Ten Classic Conspiracy Theories," *New Zealand Herald* (2009).

31. Alan Riding, "Sept. 11 as Right-Wing U.S. Plot: Conspiracy Theory Sells in France," *New York Times* (2002).

32. Ted Thornhill, "James Holmes Case: The Conspiracy Theories Surrounding The Aurora Shooting," *The Huffington Post United Kingdom* (2012).

33. Hofstadter, *Anti-Intellectualism in American Life; The Paranoid Style in American Politics, and Other Essays.*

34. Cass R. Sunstein and Adrian Vermeule, "Conspiracy Theories: Causes and Cures*," *Journal of Political Philosophy* 17, no. 2 (2009).

35. Alexa.com.

36. See arguments by Steve Clarke, "Conspiracy Theories and the Internet: Controlled Demolition and Arrested Development," *Episteme* 4, no. 02 (2007).

37. Some argue that conspiratorial rhetoric simply migrated to the Web away from newspaper letters to the editor. We discussed the faulty logic of this argument in Chapter 3.

38. Machael Barkun, *A Culture of Conspiracy: Apocalyptic Visions in Contemporary America* (Berkeley: University of California Press, 2006), p. 33.

39. Susan Jacoby, *The Age of American Unreason* (New York: Vintage, 2008); Arnold, *Conspiracy Theory in Film, Television, and Politics.*

40. Lisa D. Butler, Cheryl Koopman, and Philip G. Zimbardo, "The Psychological Impact of Viewing the Film *JFK*: Emotions, Beliefs, and Political Behavioral Intentions," *Political Psychology* 16, no. 2 (1995); Robert Markley, "Alien Assassinations: The X-Files and the Paranoid Structure of History," *Camera Obscura* 14, no. 1–2, 40–1 (1997); Kenneth Mulligan and Philip Habel, "The Implications of Fictional Media for Political Beliefs," *American Politics Research* 41, no. 1 (2013); John A. Banas and Gregory Miller, "Inducing Resistance to Conspiracy Theory Propaganda: Testing Inoculation and Metainoculation Strategies," *Human Communication Research* 39, no. 2 (2013).

41. Uscinski, *The People's News: Media, Politics, and the Demands of Capitalism.*

42. For discussion, see Thomas C. Reeves, "Movie Reviews— *JFK* directed by Oliver Stone," *Journal of American History* 79, no. 3 (1992).

43. The term "conspiracy theory" gained traction in the 1930s, so we also employed alternative timeframes for testing and confirmed our results.

44. Brendan Simms, *Europe: The Struggle for Supremacy from 1453 to the Present* (New York: Basic Books, 2013), p. 189.

45. E.g., Joseph M. Parent, "Publius's Guile and the Paranoid Style," *Public Integrity* 12, no. 3 (2010).

46. Eamonn Callan, "Rejoinder: Pluralism and Moral Polarization," *Canadian Journal of Education/Revue canadienne de l'éducation* 20, no. 3 (1995): 315.

47. Keith T. Poole and Howard Rosenthal, "Patterns of Congressional Voting," *American Journal of Political Science* 35, no. 1 (1991); Nolan McCarty, Keith T. Poole, and Howard Rosenthal, *Polarized America: The Dance of Ideology and Unequal Riches* (Cambridge: MIT Press, 2006); Keith T. Poole and Howard Rosenthal, "The Polarization of American Politics," *Journal of Politics* 46, no. 4 (1984); *Ideology and Congress* (New Brunswick, NJ: Transaction Publishers, 2007).

48. Keith T. Poole and Howard Rosenthal, *Congress: A Political-Economic History of Roll Call Voting* (New York: Oxford University Press, 2000). Elite polarization and public

polarization may be related, so our measure may be tracing elite sentiment, public sentiment, or both. Because there is no correlation, this concern is moot.

49. "The Rachel Maddow Show," *MSNBC*, June 20, 2012.

50. Anderson Cooper, "Muslim Conspiracy Theory; Mitt Romney's Overseas Trip; Fight for Syrian City of Aleppo," *CNN* (2012).

51. Einstein and Glick, "Scandals, Conspiracies and the Vicious Cycle of Cynicism."

52. No doubt conspiracy theories pass through interpersonal communication as well, but because we are interested in examining conspiratorial beliefs at the mass level, it is appropriate to focus on wholesale sources of information and the broader marketplace of ideas.

CHAPTER 6

1. George F. Kennan, *At a Century's Ending: Reflections 1982–1995* (New York: W.W. Norton, 1997), p. 97.

2. John Mueller, *War, Presidents, and Public Opinion* (Lanham, MD: University Press of America, 1985), pp. 53, 58; Georg Simmel, *Conflict and the Web of Group-Affiliations*, trans. Kurt Wolff (New York: Free Press, 1964); Arthur A. Stein, "Conflict and Cohesion: A Review of the Literature," *Journal of Conflict Resolution* 20, no. 1 (1976); Kenneth N. Waltz, *Theory of International Relations* (New York: McGraw Hill, 1979).

3. This means that the most important, albeit highly crude, determinant of threats is gross domestic product (GDP), but many other factors contribute, including military expenditure, research and development investment, per capita GDP, ideology, regime type, and contributions from allies. Then there is a geographical component, which focuses on how distance dulls threats, water and mountains inhibit attack, and technology mediates how force can be used in different environments.

4. Stephen M. Walt, *The Origin of Alliances* (Ithaca: Cornell University Press, 1990); Waltz, *Theory of International Relations*; John J. Mearsheimer, *The Tragedy of Great Power Politics* (New York: W.W. Norton & Company, 2003).

5. Paul Bedard, "NRA Boss: Obama's Gone in 2012," *US News and World Report*, June 27, 2011.

6. Peter Robinson and John Crewdson, "NRA Raises $200 Million as Gun Lobby Toasters Burn Logo on Bread," *Bloomberg* (2011).

7. Ralph L. Rosnow, "Psychology of Rumor Reconsidered," *Psychological Bulletin* 87, no. 3 (1980); Ralph L. Rosnow, James L. Esposito, and Leo Gibney, "Factors Influencing Rumor Spreading: Replication and Extension," *Language & Communication* 8, no. 1 (1988); Ralph L. Rosnow, John H. Yost, and James L. Esposito, "Belief in Rumor and Likelihood of Rumor Transmission," *Language & Communication* 6, no. 3 (1986).

8. Herbert McClosky and Dennis Chong, "Similarities and Differences between Left-Wing and Right-Wing Radicals," *British Journal of Political Science* 15, no. 3 (1985); Sharon Parsons et al., "A Test of the Grapevine: An Empirical Examination of the Conspiracy Theories Among African Americans," *Sociological Spectrum* 19, no. 2 (1999).

9. David Laitin, *Identity in Formation: The Russian-Speaking Populations in the New Abroad* (Ithaca, NY: Cornell University Press, 1998); Daniel Posner, *Institutions and Ethnic Politics in Africa* (Cambridge: Cambridge University Press, 2005).

10. Please note that a letter does not need to specifically name the person in power, or the country(s) that the United States has declared war against. For domestic actors, letters need only accuse an actor within the group or within the associated group. On the foreign front, if the United States were to declare war against Germany, then we would expect an increase in letters accusing all foreign actors of conspiracy, and not just Germany (though we would expect specific accusations against Germany in this case to rise as well).

11. John Mueller, "Is There Still a Terrorist Threat: The Myth of the Omnipresent Enemy," *Foreign Affairs* 85, no. 5 (2006); *Overblown: How Politicians and the Terrorism Industry Inflate National Security Threats, and Why We Believe Them* (New York: Free Press, 2009); *Policy and Opinion in the Gulf War* (Chicago: University Press of Chicago, 1994). While we did not expect non-great power wars or militarized disputes to increase conspiracy theories leveled at foreign actors, to be inclusive we tested these anyway. A dummy measuring U.S. major combat operations and the Militarized Interstate Dispute (MID) dataset's highest hostility level were not robust predictors of foreign conspiracy theorizing.

12. Cathie Jo Martin and Duane Swank, "The Political Origins of Coordinated Capitalism: Business Organizations, Party Systems, and State Structure in the Age of Innocence," *American Political Science Review* 102, no. 2 (2008).

13. We constructed a long series of control variables, which we analyze and report in the appendix. First, we collected variables tracking changes in the *New York Times* ownership, editorship, circulation, and local competition. We examined these to test for potential biases stemming from the *New York Times*. We also gathered variables tracking television use and the prevalence of the Internet. We employed these to account for the changing overall media market and the availability of information. In addition, we included economic variables measuring unemployment and economic growth as well as political variables measuring election years and realignment to test the effects of the macro-polity on conspiracy talk. The results of these tests are shown and explained in the appendix. In short, we found that the control variables provided little explanatory power and did not affect the main results of this study. As such, the results reported in the chapter rely on parsimonious comparisons.

14. Katherine Levine Einstein and David M Glick, "Scandals, Conspiracies and the Vicious Cycle of Cynicism" (2013).

15. So far, we have presented and tested specific expectations regarding the balance of power within the executive and legislative branches of government. What about the balance of power on the Supreme Court? For several reasons, we expected the court to have a minor effect on conspiracy talk. One reason is that the court is the least powerful branch and is badly positioned to allocate resources. Another reason is that the court is viewed less as a political institution and more as a long-term legal institution, above the fray of partisan advantage and current policies.

Nevertheless, we checked our perspective against the evidence. Unlike the presidency and Congress, where party control is straightforward and easy to measure, the party affiliation/ideology of the court is less so. So, to do this, we used a numerical score that tracked the ideology of the median justice on the court. These highly technical scores were available from 1937 forward. Correlation coefficients between the ideology of the median Supreme Court justice and the percentage of right, left, capitalist, and communist conspiracy theories each year indicated a minor but correctly signed effect.

The expected relationships showed up as expected, but weakly. All four correlations were in the expected direction, ranging between $-.25$ and $.13$. For example, the correlation between the court median and the percentage of left conspiracies each year was $-.25$, indicating that as the court became more liberal, there was a slightly higher percentage of letters accusing the left of conspiring. This was also true with right conspiracy letters: as the median justice of the court became more conservative, letters contained slightly more conspiracy talk accusing the right of conspiring (a coefficient of $.11$).

16. Dina Shapiro, "The Risk of Disease Stigma: Threat and Support for Coercive Public Heath Policy," in *APSA Pre-Conference on Political Communication* of Risk (Seattle, Washington, 2011), p. 9.

17. "The Empire's Thermonuclear War," *LaRouche Political Action Committee Newsletter* (2012).

18. Lyndon LaRouche, "Remarks from Lyndon LaRouche: WW3 Showdown, or Global Policy for Growth," *LaRouche Political Action Committee Newsletter*, September 9, 2013.

19. Stossel, *Fox News*, June 6, 2013, 9:00 pm.

20. All posts taken from "MillionsTtSSPpAgainstTtSSPpMonsantoTtSSPpbyTtSSP-pOrganicConsumers.org" Facebook page, https://www.facebook.com/millions-against, dated 8/13–8/14, 2013.

21. Naomi Wolf, "The Shocking Truth about the Crackdown on Occupy," *TheGuardian.com* (2011).

22. Quoted on the *Charlie Rose Show*, November 2005.

23. Facebook, Libertarian Party, September 29, 2013. https://www.facebook.com/libertarians.

24. Stossel, *Fox News*, June 28, 2013: 9:00 pm.

25. Daryl Johnson, *Right-Wing Resurgence: How a Domestic Terrorist Threat is Being Ignored* (New York: Rowman & Littlefield, 2013).

26. Niccolò Machiavelli, *Discourses on Livy*, trans. Harvey Mansfield and Nathan Tarcov (Chicago: University of Chicago Press, 1996), pp. 155, 218–235 [II.13, III.6].

CHAPTER 7

1. Quoted in G. B. Trudeau, *In Search of Cigarette Holder Man* (Kansas City: Andrews and McMeel, 1994), p. 5.

2. Richard Hofstadter, *The Paranoid Style in American Politics, and Other Essays* (Cambridge: Harvard University Press, 1964), p. 39.

3. Gordon B. Arnold, *Conspiracy Theory in Film, Television, and Politics* (Westport, CT: Praeger, 2008).

4. Olga Orda, "The Romantic View of Nature and the Conspiracy Theory in Environmental Documentaries" (Calgary: University of Calgary, 2012).

5. Ugo Corte and Bob Edwards, "White Power music and the mobilization of racist social movements," *Music and Arts in Action* 1, no. 1 (2008). See also the music of Akon, the Black Crowes, Bone Thugs-N-Harmony, Buffalo Springfield, J. Cole, the Dead Milkmen, Steve Earle, Eminem, Lupe Fiasco, Jay-Z, Lil Wayne, Mos Def and Immortal Technique, Onyx, Paramore, Rockwell, and Kanye West.

6. Matthew Atkinson and Joseph E. Uscinski, "Why Do People Believe in Conspiracy Theories? The Role of Informational Cues and Predispositions" (2013).

7. John Zaller, *The Nature and Origins of Mass Opinion.* Cambridge Studies in Public Opinion and Political Psychology (Cambridge, UK: Cambridge University Press, 1992); Atkinson and Uscinski, "Why Do People Believe in Conspiracy Theories? The Role of Informational Cues and Predispositions"; Adam Berinsky, "Poll Shows False Obama Beliefs a Function of Partisanship," *Huffington Post*, http://www.huffingtonpost.com/adam-berinsky/poll-shows-false-obama-be_b_714503.html.

8. Take also two contemporary conspiracy theorists: Donald Trump and Jesse Ventura. Trump appears convinced that President Obama was either born in another country or has something to hide on his college records. Ventura hosts a show, *Conspiracy Theory with Jesse Ventura*, in which he uncovers the truth behind government cover-ups and malfeasance. Both men are financially successful and have been mentioned as possible presidential contenders. Ventura was elected Governor of Minnesota. Gregarious and flamboyant, yes; mentally impaired, no.

9. The truly sick suffer from delusions but seldom from conspiratorial beliefs. See comments by Ken Duckworth, medical director of the National Alliance of Mental Illness. More importantly, we object to the psychopathological explanation on grounds that there is no clear causal link between psychopathology and conspiracy theories. If one asserted that conspiracy theorists were insane, would that imply that believing in conspiracy theories leads people to become pathological, or would it conversely imply that mental pathologies lead people into believing in conspiracy theories? We have not seen any evidence to suggest a relationship in either direction. http://abcnews.go.com/Health/MindMoodNews/story?id=6443988&page=2#.T15zG_VmmW8.

10. Jean-Jacques Rousseau, *The Basic Political Writings*, trans. Donald A. Cress (Indianapolis, IN: Hackett, 1987), Book III, chap. 6, p. 183.

11. David Icke, *Children of the Matrix: How an Interdimensional Race has Controlled the World for Thousands of Years—and Still Does* (Wildwood, MO: Bridge of Love Publications USA, 2001).

12. http://www.davidicke.com/headlines/85612-important-update-about-our-peoples-voice-campaign.

13. Cass R. Sunstein and Adrian Vermeule, "Conspiracy Theories: Causes and Cures*," *Journal of Political Philosophy* 17, no. 2 (2009); David Ray Griffin, *Cognitive Infiltration: An Obama Appointee's Plan to Undermine the 9/11 Conspiracy Theory* (USA: Olive Branch Press, 2010).

14. Brendan Nyhan, "Backsliding on the 'Death Panels' Myth," *Columbia Journalism Review* (2013).
15. For example, the left derided the right for its death panel conspiracy theories. But the left could have seen these conspiracy theories as an indication from a large portion of the country that the bill was not all that good and perhaps represented an overreach of federal power.
16. Felix Gilbert, *Machiavelli and Guicciardini: Politics and History in Sixteenth Century Florence* (New York: Norton, 1984), pp. 34–41; Hans Baron, *The Crisis of the Early Italian Renaissance* (Princeton: Princeton University Press, 1966).
17. Chaim D. Kaufman, "Threat Inflation and the Failure of the Marketplace of Ideas: The Selling of the Iraq War," *International Security* 29, no. 1 (2004); Jack Snyder, Robert Y. Shapiro, and Yaeli Bloch-Elkon, "Ree Hand Abroad, Divide and Rule at Home," *World Politics* 61, no. 1 (2009).
18. John Mueller, *Overblown: How Politicians and the Terrorism Industry Inflate National Security Threats, and Why We Believe Them* (New York: Free Press, 2009).
19. Niccolò Machiavelli, *Il Principe* (Milan: Oscar Mondadori, 1994), p. 42. Translated from original by Joseph M. Parent.

REFERENCES

"10th Anniversary 9/11 Truth Hit Piece Roundup." *911 Truth News*. Published electronically September 12, 2011.

Aaronovitch, David. *Voodoo Histories: The Role of Conspiracy Theory in Shaping Modern History*. New York: Riverhead Books, 2010.

Abalakina-Paap, Marina, Walter G. Stephan, Traci Craig, and W. Larry Gregory. "Beliefs in Conspiracies." *Political Psychology* 20, no. 3 (1999): 637–647.

Allport, G. W., and L. J. Postman. *The Psychology of Rumor*. New York: Holt, Rinehart & Winston, 1947.

Anthony, S. "Anxiety and Rumor." *Journal of Personality and Social Psychology* 89 (1973): 91–98.

Arnold, Gordon B. *Conspiracy Theory in Film, Television, and Politics*. Westport, CT: Praeger, 2008.

Atkinson, Matthew, and Joseph E. Uscinski. "Why Do People Believe in Conspiracy Theories? The Role of Informational Cues and Predispositions." (2013). Available at SSRN: http://ssrn.com/abstract=2268782 or http://dx.doi.org/10.2139/ssrn.2268782.

Avery, Dylan. *Loose Change 9/11: An American Coup*. Microcinema International, 2009.

Avery, James M. "The Sources and Consequences of Political Mistrust among African Americans." *American Politics Research* 34, no. 5 (2006): 653–682.

Bailyn, Bernard. *The Ideological Origins of the American Revolution*. Cambridge: Harvard University Press, 1992.

Banas, John A., and Gregory Miller. "Inducing Resistance to Conspiracy Theory Propaganda: Testing Inoculation and Metainoculation Strategies." *Human Communication Research* 39, no. 2 (2013): 184–207.

Barkun, Michael. *A Culture of Conspiracy: Apocalyptic Visions in Contemporary America*. Berkeley: University of California Press, 2006.

Baron, Hans. *The Crisis of the Early Italian Renaissance*. Princeton: Princeton University Press, 1966.

Barone, Michael. "Dems Sour on Obama's 'Good War' in Afghanistan. *Washington Examiner*. Published electronically 2010.

Barreto, Matt A., Betsy L. Cooper, Benjamin Gonzalez, Christopher S. Parker, and Christopher Towler. "The Tea Party in the Age of Obama: Mainstream Conservatism or Out-Group Anxiety?" *Political Power and Social Theory* 22, no. 1 (2012): 105–136.

Barrett, Kevin. "New Studies: 'Conspiracy Theorists' Sane; Government Dupes Crazy, Hostile." *PressTV*. Published electronically July 12, 2013.

Bartlett, Jamie, and Carl Miller. "The Power of Unreason: Conspiracy Theories, Extremism and Counter-Terrorism." *London: Demos* (2010) http://www.demos.co.uk/files/Conspiracy_theories_paper.pdf?1282913891.

Bedard, Paul. "NRA Boss: Obama's Gone in 2012." *US News and World Report*, June 27, 2011.

Berinsky, Adam. "The Birthers Are Back." In *YouGov: What the World Thinks*. Published electronically February 3, 2012.

Berinsky, Adam. "The Birthers Are (Still) Back." In *YouGov: What the World Thinks*. Published electronically July 11, 2012.

Berinsky, Adam. "Poll Shows False Obama Beliefs a Function of Partisanship." *Huffington Post*, http://www.huffingtonpost.com/adam-berinsky/poll-shows-false-obama-be_b_714503.html.

Berinsky, Adam. "Rumors, Truths, and Reality: A Study of Political Misinformation." In http://web.mit.edu/berinsky/www/files/rumor.pdf. MIT, 2012.

Berinsky, Adam. "Telling the Truth About Believing the Lies?" Presented to American Political Science Association, Chicago, IL, 2013.

Berlet, Chip. "Collectivists, Communists, Labor Bosses, and Treason: The Tea Parties as Right-Wing Populist Counter-Subversion Panic." *Critical Sociology* 38, no. 4 (2012): 565–587.

Berman, Ari. "The GOP War on Voting." *Rolling Stone*. Published electronically August 30, 2011.

Betts, Stephen. "Local Residents Claim Regional Road Planning Is International Plot." *Waldo Village Soup* (2010) viewed July 15, 2013; http://waldo.villagesoup.com/p/local-residents-claim-regional-road-planning-is-international-plot/366006.

Bock, Alan W. "Ambush at Ruby Ridge." *Reason Magazine* (1993) viewed July 15, 2013 Reason.com, http://reason.com/archives/1993/10/01/ambush-at-ruby-ridge.

Bost, Preston R., and Stephen G. Prunier. "Rationality in Conspiracy Beliefs: The Role of Perceived Motive." Unpublished paper (2013).

Boudry, Maarten, and Johan Braeckman. "Immunizing Strategies and Epistemic Mechanisms." *Philosophia* 39 (2011): 145–161.

Bowden, Mark. *Black Hawk Down: A Story of Modern War*. New York: Atlantic Monthly Press, 1999.

Bratich, Jack Zeljko. "Trust No One (on the Internet): The CIA-Crack-Contra Conspiracy Theory and Professional Journalism." *Television & New Media* 5, no. 2 (May 1, 2004): 109–139.

"Brendan Nyhan Still Isn't Credible (Obama, "Birthers", "Science", CNN)." *24ahead.com*. Published electronically April 28, 2011.

Briggs, Charles L. "Theorizing Modernity Conspiratorially: Science, Scale, and the Political Economy of Public Discourse in Explanations of a Cholera Epidemic." *American Ethnologist* 31, no. 2 (2004): 164–187.

Brotherton, Robert, Christopher C. French, and Alan D. Pickering. "Measuring Belief in Conspiracy Theories: The Generic Conspiracist Beliefs Scale." *Frontiers in Psychology* 4, Article 279 (2013): 1–15.

Bruder, Martin, Peter Haffke, Nick Neave, Nina Nouripanah, and Roland Imhoff. "Measuring Individual Differences in Generic Beliefs in Conspiracy Theories across Cultures: The Conspiracy Mentality Questionnaire (CMQ)." *Frontiers in Psychology* 4 (April 30, 2013): 1–15.

Brzezinski, Zbigniew. "Quotation of the Day." *New York Times*, January 18, 1981.

Buell, Emmett H. "Eccentrics or Gladiators? People Who Write About Politics in Letters-to-the-Editor." *Social Science Quarterly* 56 (1975): 440–449.

Buenting, Joel, and Jason Taylor. "Conspiracy Theories and Fortuitous Data." *Philosophy of the Social Sciences* 40, no. 4 (2010): 567–578.

Butler, Lisa D., Cheryl Koopman, and Philip G. Zimbardo. "The Psychological Impact of Viewing the Film *JFK*: Emotions, Beliefs, and Political Behavioral Intentions." *Political Psychology* 16, no. 2 (1995): 237–257.

Butler, Daniel M., and Emily Schofield. "Were Newspapers More Interested in Pro-Obama Letters to the Editor in 2008? Evidence from a Field Experiment." *American Politics Research* 38, no. 2 (2010): 356–371.

Callan, Eamonn. "Rejoinder: Pluralism and Moral Polarization." *Canadian Journal of Education/Revue canadienne de l'éducation* 20, no. 3 (1995): 315–332.

Campbell, Angus, Philip Converse, Warren Miller, and Donald E. Stokes. *The American Voter, Unabridged Edition.* Chicago: The University of Chicago Press, 1960.

Cannon, Lou. "Gary Sick's Lingering Charges." *Washington Post*, 1991.

Caplan, Bryan. *The Myth of the Rational Voter: Why Democracies Choose Bad Policies.* Princeton: Princeton University Press, 2007.

Carney, Dana R., John T. Jost, Samuel D. Gosling, and Jeff Potter. "The Secret Lives of Liberals and Conservatives: Personality Profiles, Interaction Styles, and the Things They Leave Behind." *Political Psychology* 29, no. 6 (2008): 807–840.

Cassino, Dan, and Krista Jenkins. "Conspiracy Theories Prosper: 25% of Americans Are 'Truthers.'" press release (2013).

CBS. "CBS Poll: JFK Conspiracy Lives." *CBSNews.com*, February 11, 2009 (viewed July 25, 2011).

"Celebrity 9/11 Conspiracy Club Still Growing." *Washington Times*. Published electronically March 6, 2008.

Chait, Jonathan. *The Big Con: The True Story of How Washington Got Hoodwinked and Hijacked by Crackpot Economics.* Boston: Houghton Mifflin Company, 2007.

Chomsky, Noam. "9-11: Institutional Analysis vs. Conspiracy Theory." *Z Communications*. Published electronically October 6, 2006.

Clark, April, Jennifer K. Mayben, Christine Hartman, Michael A. Kallen, and Thomas P Giordano. "Conspiracy Beliefs About HIV Infection Are Common but Not Associated with Delayed Diagnosis or Adherence to Care." *AIDS Patient Care and STDs* 22, no. 9 (2008): 753–759.

Clarke, Steve. "Appealing to the Fundamental Attribution Error: Was It All a Big Mistake?" In *Conspiracy Theories: The Philosophical Debate*, edited by David Coady. London: Ashgate Pub Co, 2006.

Clarke, Steve. "Conspiracy Theories and Conspiracy Theorizing." *Philosophy of the Social Sciences* 32, no. 2 (2002): 131–150.

Clarke, Steve. "Conspiracy Theories and the Internet: Controlled Demolition and Arrested Development." *Episteme* 4, no. 02 (2007): 167–180.

CNN. "Poll U.S. Hiding Knowledge of Aliens." *CNN.com*. Published electronically June 15, 1997. http://articles.cnn.com/1997-06-15/us/9706_15_ufo.poll_1_ufo-aliens-crash-site?_s=PM:US.

Coady, David. "Conspiracy Theories and Official Stories." *International Journal of Applied Philosophy* 17 (2003): 197–209.

Coady, David. *Conspiracy Theories: The Philosophical Debate*. Burlington, VT: Ashgate, 2006.

"Conspiracy Theories: Separating Fact from Fiction." *Time.com*. Published electronically July 20, 2009.

Converse, Philip. "Belief Systems in Mass Publics." In *Ideology and Its Discontents*, edited by David E. Apter. New York: The Free Press of Glencoe, 1964.

Converse, Philip E. "The Nature of Belief Systems in Mass Publics (1964)." *Critical Review* 18, no. 1–3 (2006): 1–74.

Cooper, Anderson. "Muslim Conspiracy Theory; Mitt Romney's Overseas Trip; Fight for Syrian City of Aleppo." *CNN*, 2012.

Cooper, Christopher A., H. Gibbs Knotts, and Mashe Haspel. "The Content of Political Participation: Letters to the Editor and the People Who Write Them." *PS: Political Science and Politics* 42 (2009): 131–137.

Corte, Ugo, and Bob Edwards. "White Power Music and the Mobilization of Racist Social Movements." *Music and Arts in Action* 1, no. 1 (2008): 4–20.

Craciun, Catrinel, and Adriana Baban. ""Who Will Take the Blame?": Understanding the Reasons Why Romanian Mothers Decline HPV Vaccination for Their Daughters." *Vaccine* 30, no. 48 (2012): 6789–6793.

Craig, Stephen C., and Stephen Earl Bennett, eds. *After the Boom: The Politics of Generation X*. New York: Rowman & Littlefield, 1997.

Darwin, Hannah, Nick Neave, and Joni Holmes. "Belief in Conspiracy Theories. The Role of Paranormal Belief, Paranoid Ideation and Schizotypy." *Personality and Individual Differences* 50, no. 8 (2011): 1289–1293.

Davis, Brion David. "Foreword." In *Conspiracy Theories in American History Vol. 1*, edited by Peter Knight, pp. ix–x. Santa Barbara, CA: ABC CLIO, 2003.

Davis, David Brion. *Inhuman Bondage: The Rise and Fall of Slavery in the New World*. New York: Oxford University Press, 2006.

Davis, David Brion. *The Slave Power Conspiracy and the Paranoid Style*. Baton Rouge: Louisiana State University Press, 1969.

deHaven-Smith, Lance. "When Political Crimes Are inside Jobs: Detecting State Crimes against Democracy." *Administrative Theory & Praxis* 28, no. 3 (2006): 330–355.

Dehghanpisheh, Babak. "Conspiracy Theories with a Bite: Shark Attacks in Egypt Prompt Charges of Outsider Sabotage of Tourism." *Newsweek*. Published electronically December 8, 2010.

DelliCarpini, Michael X. "Age and History: Generations and Sociopolitical Change." In *Political Learning in Adulthood: A Sourcebook of Theory and Research*, edited by Roberta S. Sigel. Chicago: University of Chicago Press, 1989.

"Democrats and Republicans Differ on Conspiracy Theory Beliefs." *Public Policy Polling*. Published electronically April 2, 2013.

DiFonzo, Nicholas, and Prashant Bordia. *Rumor Psychology: Social and Organizational Approaches*. Washington, DC: American Psychological Association, 2007.

Difonzo, Nicholas, Prashant Bordia, and Ralph L. Rosnow. "Reigning in Rumors." *Organizational Dynamics* 23 (1994): 47–62.

Douglas, Karen M., and Robbie M. Sutton. "Does It Take One to Know One? Endorsement of Conspiracy Theories Is Influenced by Personal Willingness to Conspire." *British Journal of Social Psychology* 50, no. 3 (2011): 544–552.

Douthat, Ross. "Nuts and Dolts." *New York Times Book Review*, 2010.

Easton, David, and Robert D Hess. "The Child's Political World." *Midwest Journal of Political Science* 6, no. 3 (1962): 229–246.

Edelstein, David M., "Managing Uncertainty: Beliefs about Intentions and Rise of Great Powers," Security Studies 12, no. 1 (2002).

Edy, Jill, and Erin Baird. "The Persistence of Rumor Communities: Public Resistance to Official Debunking in the Internet Age." Paper presented at the APSA 2012 Annual Meeting.

Einstein, Katherine Levine, and David M. Glick. "Scandals, Conspiracies and the Vicious Cycle of Cynicism." Unpublished paper (2013).

"The Empire's Thermonuclear War." *LaRouche Political Action Committee Newsletter*. Published electronically March 4, 2012.

Erikson, Emily, and Joseph Parent. "Central Authority and Order." *Sociological Theory* 25, no. 3 (2007): 245–267.

Erikson, Robert S., and Kent L. Tedin. *American Public Opinion: Its Origins, Content, and Impact*. 7th ed. New York: Pearson Longman, 2005.

Farrakhan, Louis, and Henry Louis Gates, Jr. "Farrakhan Speaks." *Transition*, no. 70 (1996): 140–167.

Fears, Darryl. "Black Opinion on Simpson Shifts." *Washington Post*. Published electronically September 27, 2007.

Fenster, Mark. *Conspiracy Theories: Secrecy and Power in American Culture*. Minneapolis: University of Minnesota Press, 1999.

Feyer, Thomas. "To the Reader." *New York Times Book Review*, September 14, 2003.

Fiorina, Morris P. *Retrospective Voting in American National Elections*. New Haven: Yale University Press, 1981.

Freedman, David H. "Are Engineered Foods Evil?" *Scientific American* 309, no. 3 (2013): 85.

Freud, Sigmund. *The Standard Edition of the Complete Psychological Works of Sigmund Freud*. Oxford, UK: Macmillan, 1964.

Fulcher, Benjamin I. Page, and Gordon Scott. *Navigating Public Opinion: Polls, Policy, and the Future of American Democracy: Polls, Policy, and the Future of American Democracy*. New York: Oxford University Press, 2002.

Gamson, William A. *Talking Politics*. Cambridge, MA: Cambridge University Press, 1992.

Gao, Melisa. "Professors Fund Liberal Candidates." *The Daily Princetonian*, September 13, 2004.

Gause III, George. *The International Relations of the Persian Gulf*. New York: Cambridge University Press, 2010.

Geyer, Georgie Anne. "The Rewriting of History to Fit Our Age of Conspiracy." *Los Angeles Times*, 1977.

Gilbert, Felix. *Machiavelli and Guicciardini: Politics and History in Sixteenth-Century Florence*. New York: Norton, 1984.

Gilens, Martin. "Political Ignorance and Collective Policy Preferences." *American Political Science Review* 95, no. 2 (2001): 379–396.

Goertzel, Ted. "Belief in Conspiracy Theories." *Political Psychology* 15 (1994): 733–744.

Goertzel, Ted. "The Conspiracy Meme." *Skeptical Inquirer* (2013).

Goertzel, Ted. "Conspiracy Theories in Science." *EMBO Reports* 11, no. 7 (2010): 493–499.

Goldberg, Bernard. *Bias: A CBS Insider Exposes How the Media Distort the News*. Washington, DC: Renergy, 2002.

Goldberg, Bernard. *A Slobbering Love Affair: The True (and Pathetic) Story of the Torrid Romance between Barack Obama and the Mainstream Media*. New York: Regnery Publishing, 2009.

Goldberg, Robert Alan. *Enemies Within: The Culture of Conspiracy in Modern America*. New Haven: Yale University Press, 2001.

Goldman, Adam, Eric Tucker, and Matt Apuzzo. "Tamerlan Tsarnaev, Influenced by Mysterious Muslim Radical, Turned Towards Fundamentalism." *Huffington Post*. Published electronically April 23, 2013.

Gould, Lewis L. *Presidency of William McKinley*. Lawrence: University Press of Kansas, 1981.

Gourevitch, Peter. *Politics in Hard Times: Comparative Responses to International Economic Crises*. Ithaca, NY: Cornell University Press, 1986.

Grebe, Eduard, and Nicoli Nattrass. "AIDS Conspiracy Beliefs and Unsafe Sex in Cape Town." *AIDS and Behavior* 16, no. 3 (2012): 761–773.

Gribbin, William. "Antimasonry, Religious Radicalism, and the Paranoid Style of the 1820s." *History Teacher* 7, no. 2 (1974): 239–254.

Griffin, David Ray. *Cognitive Infiltration: An Obama Appointee's Plan to Undermine the 9/11 Conspiracy Theory*. USA: Olive Branch Press, 2010.

Groseclose, Tim. *Left Turn: How Liberal Media Bias Distorts the American Mind*. New York: St. Martin's Press, 2011.

Haas, Ernst B. "The Study of Regional Integration: Reflections of the Joy and Anguish of Pretheorizing." *International Organization* 24, no. 4 (1970): 607–646.

Hall, Peter M. "The Quasi-Theory of Communication and the Management of Dissent." *Social Problems* 18, no. 1 (1970): 18–27.

Hamm, Mark S. *Apocalypse in Oklahoma: Waco and Ruby Ridge Revenged*. Boston: Northeastern University Press, 1997.

Hargrove, Thomas. "Third of Americans Suspect 9/11 Government Conspiracy." *Scripps News*, August 1, 2006.

Hartman, Todd K., and Adam J. Newmark. "Motivated Reasoning, Political Sophistication, and Associations between President Obama and Islam." *PS: Political Science and Politics* 45, no. 3 (2012): 449–455.

Heins, Volker. "Critical Theory and the Traps of Conspiracy Thinking." *Philosophy & Social Criticism* 33, no. 7 (2007): 787–801.

Hellinger, Daniel. "Paranoia, Conspiracy, and Hegemony in American Politics." In *Transparency and Conspiracy: Ethnographies of Suspicion in the New World Order*, edited by Harry G. West and Todd Sanders. Durham: Duke University Press, 2003.

Henderson, Marlone. "Psychological Distance and Group Judgments: The Effect of Physical Distance on Beliefs About Common Goals." *Personality and Social Psychology Bulletin* 35, no. 10 (2009): 1330–1341.

Hepola, Sarah. "Whoopi Goldberg: Was the Moon Landing a Hoax? 'The View' Co-Host Celebrates the 40th Anniversary of Apollo 11 by Spreading Wacky Conspiracy Theories." *Salon.com*. Published electronically July 20, 2009.

Hill, David B. "Letter Opinion on Era: A Test of the Newspaper Bias Hypothesis." *Public Opinion Quarterly* 45 (1981): 384–392.

Hofman, Amos. "Opinion, Illusion, and the Illusion of Opinion: Barruel's Theory of Conspiracy." *Eighteenth-Century Studies* 27, no. 1 (1993): 27–60.

Hofstadter, Richard. *Anti-Intellectualism in American Life*. New York: Vintage, 1963.

Hofstadter, Richard. *The Paranoid Style in American Politics, and Other Essays*. Cambridge: Harvard University Press, 1964.

Hofstadter, Richard. *The Paranoid Style of American Politics and Other Essays*. New York: Knopf, 1965.

Hogue, William M. "The Religious Conspiracy Theory of the American Revolution: Anglican Motive." *Church History* 45, no. 3 (1976): 277–292.

Howe, Neil, and William Strauss. *Millennials Rising: The Next Great Generation*. USA: Vintage, 2000.

Husting, Gina, and Martin Orr. "Dangerous Machinery: "Conspiracy Theorist" as a Transpersonal Strategy of Exclusion." *Symbolic Interaction* 30, no. 2 (2007): 127–150.

Icke, David. *Children of the Matrix: How an Interdimensional Race Has Controlled the World for Thousands of Years—and Still Does*. Wildwood, MO: Bridge of Love Publications USA, 2001.

Imhoff, Roland, and Martin Bruder. "Speaking (Un-)Truth to Power: Conspiracy Mentality as a Generalised Political Attitude." *European Journal of Personality* (2013): 25–43.

Jacobsen, Annie. "The United States of Conspiracy: Why, More and More, Americans Cling to Crazy Theories." *NYDailyNews.com*, August 7, 2011. http://articles.nydailynews.com/2011-08-07/news/29878465_1_conspiracy-theories-bavarian-illuminati-nefarious-business.

Jacobson, Gary. "Barack Obama and the American Public: The First 18 Months." Presented to Annual Meeting of the American Political Science Association, Washington, DC, 2010.

Jacoby, Susan. *The Age of American Unreason*. New York: Vintage, 2008.

Jamil, Uzma, and Cécile Rousseau. "Challenging the 'Official' Story of 9/11: Community Narratives and Conspiracy Theories." *Ethnicities* 11, no. 2 (2011): 245–261.

Jervis, Robert. "Roundtable on Politics and Scholarship." *H-Diplo/ISSF* 1, no. 2 (2010).

Johnson, Daryl. *Right-Wing Resurgence: How a Domestic Terrorist Threat Is Being Ignored*. New York: Rowman & Littlefield, 2013.

Jonsson, Patrik. "Blackbirds Fall from Sky, Fish Die Off: What's a Conspiracy Theorist to Think?" *Christian Science Monitor*. Published electronically January 3, 2011.

Kam, Dara, and John Lantigua. "Former Florida GOP Leaders Say Voter Suppression Was Reason They Pushed New Election Law." *Palm Beach Post*. Published electronically November 25, 2012.

Kaplan, Fred. *The Wizards of Armageddon*. Stanford: Stanford University Press, 1983.

Kata, Anna. "A Postmodern Pandora's Box: Anti-Vaccination Misinformation on the Internet." *Vaccine* 28, no. 7 (2010): 1709–1716.

Kaufman, Chaim D. "Threat Inflation and the Failure of the Marketplace of Ideas: The Selling of the Iraq War." *International Security* 29, no. 1 (2004): 5–48.

Kaufman, Chaim D., and Robert A. Pape. "Explaining Costly International Moral Action: Britain's Sixty-Year Campaign against the Atlantic Slave Trade." *International Organization* 53, Autumn (1999): 631–668.

Kaufman, Leslie, and Kate Zernike. "Activists Fight Green Projects, Seeing U.N. Plot." *New York Times*. Published electronically February 3, 2012.

Kay, Jonathan. *Among the Truthers: A Journey through America's Growing Conspiracist Underground*. New York: Harper Collins Publishers, 2011.

Kay, Aaron E., Jennifer A. Whitson, Danielle Gaucher, and Adam D. Galinsky. "Conspensatory Control: Achieving Order through the Mind, Our Institutions, and the Heavens." *Current Directions in Psychological Science* 18, no. 5 (2009): 264–268.

Keeley, Brian. "Of Conspiracy Theories." *Journal of Philosophy* 96, no. 3 (1999): 109–126.

Kennan, George F. *At a Century's Ending: Reflections 1982–1995*. New York: W.W. Norton, 1997.

Kimball, Jeffrey. "The Influence of Ideology on Interpretive Disagreement: A Report on a Survey of Diplomatic, Military and Peace Historians on the Causes of 20th Century U.S. Wars." *The History Teacher* 17, May (1984): 356–384.

Kinder, Donald R., and Cindy D. Kam. *Us against Them: Ethnocentric Foundations of American Opinion*. Chicago: University of Chicago Press, 2009.

Kindleberger, Charles P. *The World in Depression: 1929–1939*, Revised and enlarged ed. Berkeley: University of California Press, 1986.

Klecka, William R. "Applying Political Generations to the Study of Political Behavior: A Cohort Analysis." *Public Opinion Quarterly* 35(3), 358–373

Knight, Frank. *The Ethics of Competition*. New Brunswick, NJ: Transaction Publishers, 1997.

Knight, Peter. "Introduction: A Nation of Conspiracy Theorists." In *Conspiracy Nation: The Politics of Paranoia in Postwar America*, edited by Peter Knight. New York: New York University Press, 2002.

Knight, Peter. "Outrageous Conspiracy Theories: Popular and Official Responses to 9/11 in Germany and the United States." *New German Critique* 35, no. 1 (2008): 165–193.

Krauthammer, Charles. "A Rash of Conspiracy Theories." *Washington Post*, July 5, 1991.

Krueger, Alan B., and David Laitin. "Faulty Terror Report Card." *Washington Post*, May 17, 2002.

Krugman, Paul. "Crazy Conspiracy Theorists." *New York Times*. Published electronically December 22, 2008.

Krugman, Paul. "Who's Crazy Now?" *New York Times*. Published electronically May 8, 2006.

Krugman, Paul. "The Wonk Gap." *New York Times*. Published electronically September 8, 2013.

Kuklinski, James H., Paul J. Quirk, Jennifer Jerit, David Schwieder, and Robert F. Rich. "Misinformation and the Currency of Democratic Citizenship." *Journal of Politics* 62, no. 3 (2000): 790–816.

Kurtz, Howard. "College Faculties a Most Liberal Lot, Study Finds." *Washington Post* March 29, 2005, p. C01.

Laitin, David. *Identity in Formation: The Russian-Speaking Populations in the New Abroad*. Ithaca: Cornell University Press, 1998.

LaPlant, James T. "No Winning This Argument." *New York Times*. Published electronically April 22, 2011.

LaRouche, Lyndon. "Remarks from Lyndon Larouche: WW3 Showdown, or Global Policy for Growth." *LaRouche Political Action Committee Newsletter*. Published electronically September 9, 2013.

Lee, Spike. "Spike Lee on Real Time with Bill Maher." HBO, 2007.

Levi, Margaret, and Laura Stoker. "Political Trust and Trustworthiness." *Annual Review of Political Science* 3, no. 1 (2000): 475–507.

Levy, Neil. "Radically Socialized Knowledge and Conspiracy Theories." *Episteme* 4, no. 02 (2007): 181–192.

Lewandowsky, Stephan, John Cook, Klaus Oberauer, and Michael Marriott. "Recursive Fury: Conspiracist Ideation in the Blogosphere in Response to Research on Conspiracist Ideation." *Frontiers in Psychology* vol. 4 article 73 (2013): 1–15.

Lewandowsky, Stephan, Klaus Oberauer, and Gilles Gignac. "Nasa Faked the Moon Landing—Therefore (Climate) Science Is a Hoax: An Anatomy of the Motivated Rejection of Science." *Psychological Science* 5 (2013): 622–633.

Lichter, S. Robert, Stanley Rothman, and Linda Lichter. *The Media Elite: America's New Power-Brokers*. Bethesda, MD: Adler & Alder, 1986.

Lipset, Seymour Martin, and Earl Raab. *The Politics of Unreason: Right-Wing Extremism in America 1790–1977*. Chicago: University of Chicago Press, 1978.

Lodge, Milton, and Charles S Taber. *The Rationalizing Voter*. New York: Cambridge University Press, 2013.

MacDonald, Paul K. "Is Imperial Rule Obsolete? Assessing the Barriers to Overseas Adventurism." *Security Studies* 18, no. 1 (2009): 79–114.

MacDonald, Paul K. "'Retribution Must Succeed Rebellion': The Colonial Origins of Counterinsurgency Failure." *International Organization* 67, no. 2 (2013): 253–286.

Machiavelli, Niccolò. *Discourses on Livy*. Translated by Harvey Mansfield and Nathan Tarcov. Chicago: University of Chicago Press, 1996.

Machiavelli, Niccolò. *Il Principe*. Milan: Oscar Mondadori, 1994.

Machiavelli, Niccolò. *The Prince*. Translated by Harvey C. Mansfield. Chicago: University of Chicago Press, 1998.

MacKuen, Michael, Robert S. Erikson, and James Stimson. "Macropartisanship." *American Political Science Review* 83, no. 4 (1989): 1125–1142.

Mahoney, M. "Publication Prejudices: An Experimental Study of Confirmatory Bias in the Peer Review System." *Cognitive Therapy and Research* 2, June (1977): 161–175.

Maier, Pauline. *American Scripture: Making the Declaration of Independence*. New York: Vintage Books, 1998.

Mandik, Pete. "Shit Happens." *Episteme* 4, no. 2 (2007): 205–218.

Mannheim, Karl. "The Problem of Generations." In *Essays on the Sociology of Knowledge*. London: Routledge & Keegan, 1952.

Manwell, Laurie A. "In Denial of Democracy: Social Psychological Implications for Public Discourse on State Crimes against Democracy Post-9/11." *American Behavioral Scientist* 53, no. 6 (2010): 848–884.

Markley, Robert. "Alien Assassinations: The *X-Files* and the Paranoid Structure of History." *Camera Obscura* 14, no. 1–2, 40–1 (1997): 75–102.

Martin, Cathie Jo, and Duane Swank. "The Political Origins of Coordinated Capitalism: Business Organizations, Party Systems, and State Structure in the Age of Innocence." *American Political Science Review* 102, no. 2 (2008): 181–198.

Marzilli, Ted. "Cain's Candidacy Splits Pizza Scores." *YouGov: BrandIndex*. Published electronically November 15, 2011.

Mays, Vickie M., Courtney N. Coles, and Susan D. Cochran. "Is There a Legacy of the U.S. Public Health Syphilis Study at Tuskegee in HIV/AIDS-Related Beliefs among Heterosexual African Americans and Latinos?" *Ethics & Behavior* 22, no. 6 (2012): 461–471.

McAllister, James. *No Exit: America and the German Problem, 1943–1954*. Ithaca: Cornell University Press, 2002.

McCarty, Nolan, Keith T. Poole, and Howard Rosenthal. *Polarized America: The Dance of Ideology and Unequal Riches*. Cambridge: MIT Press, 2006.

McCauley, Clark, and Susan Jacques. "The Popularity of Conspiracy Theories of Presidential Assassination: A Bayesian Analysis." *Journal of Personality and Social Psychology* 37, no. 5 (1979): 637–644.

McClosky, Herbert, and Dennis Chong. "Similarities and Differences between Left-Wing and Right-Wing Radicals." *British Journal of Political Science* 15, no. 3 (1985): 329–363.

McCright, Aaron M., and Riley E. Dunlap. "Cool Dudes: The Denial of Climate Change among Conservative White Males in the United States." *Global Environmental Change* 21, no. 4 (2011): 1163–1172.

McDougall, Walter A. *Freedom Just around the Corner: A New American History, 1585–1828*. New York: Harper Collins, 2004.

McHoskey, John W. "Case Closed? On the John F. Kennedy Assassination: Biased Assimilation of Evidence and Attitude Polarization." *Basic and Applied Social Psychology* 17, no. 3 (1995): 395–409

McMahon, Darrin M. "Conspiracies So Vast: Conspiracy Theory Was Born in the Age of Enlightenment and Has Metastasized in the Age of the Internet. Why Won't It Go Away?" *Boston Globe*, February 1, 2004.

McNeil, Donald G., Jr. "Panel Hears Grim Details of Venereal Disease Tests." *New York Times*, August 30, 2011.

Mearsheimer, John J. *The Tragedy of Great Power Politics*. New York: W.W. Norton & Company, 2003.

Mearsheimer, John J. *Why Leaders Lie: The Truth About Lying in International Politics.* New York: Oxford University Press, 2011.

Melley, Timothy. *Empire of Conspiracy: The Culture of Paranoia in Postwar America.* Ithaca: Cornell University Press, 2000.

Messick, Kim. "The Tea Party's Paranoid Aesthetic." *Salon.com.* Published electronically August 10, 2013.

Middlekauff, Robert. *The Glorious Cause: The American Revolution, 1763–1789.* New York: Oxford University Press, 2005.

Miller, Neil Z. "Vaccine Science Vs. Science Fiction: Make Informed Decisions," Report prepared for VacTruth.com and ThinkTwice.com" (2013).

Mooney, Chris. "The More Republicans Know About Politics, the More They Believe Conspiracy Theories." *Mother Jones.* Published electronically January 24, 2013.

Moos, Julie. "Factchecking Obama: Birther Controversy Was 4% of Newshole, Not 'Dominant' Story." *Poynter.* http://www.poynter.org/latest-news/top-stories/129708/ factchecking-obama-birther-controversy-was-3-4-of-newshole-economy-was-39/, April 27, 2011.

Morello, Carol. "Conspiracy Theories Flourish on the Internet." *Washington Post.* Published electronically October 7, 2004.

Mueller, John. "Is There Still a Terrorist Threat: The Myth of the Omnipresent Enemy." *Foreign Affairs* 85, no. 5 (2006): 2–8.

Mueller, John. *Overblown: How Politicians and the Terrorism Industry Inflate National Security Threats, and Why We Believe Them.* New York: Free Press, 2009.

Mueller, John. *Policy and Opinion in the Gulf War.* Chicago: University Press of Chicago, 1994.

Mueller, John. *War, Presidents, and Public Opinion.* Lanham, MD: University Press of America, 1985.

Mulligan, Kenneth, and Philip Habel. "The Implications of Fictional Media for Political Beliefs." *American Politics Research* 41, no. 1 (2013): 122–146.

Murphy, Dan. "Fort Hood Shooting: Was Nidal Malik Hasan Inspired by Militant Clerics?" *Christian Science Monitor.* November 10, 2009 Viewed July 25, 2013) http:// www.csmonitor.com/World/Global-News/2009/1110/fort-hood-shooting-was-nidal-malik-hasan-inspired-by-militant-cleric

Nacos, Brigitte L., Yaeli Bloch-Elkon, and Robert Y. Shapiro. *Selling Fear: Counterterrorism, the Media, and Public Opinion.* Chicago Studies in American Politics. Chicago: University of Chicago Press, 2011.

Nattrass, Nicoli. "How Bad Ideas Gain Social Traction." *The Lancet* 380, no. 9839 (2012): 332–333.

Nattrass, Nicoli. "Understanding the Origins and Prevalence of AIDS Conspiracy Beliefs in the United States and South Africa." *Sociology of Health & Illness* 35, no. 1 (2013): 113–129.

Nefes, Turkay. "The History of the Social Constructions of Donmes (Converts)." *Journal of Historical Sociology* 25, no. 3 (2012): 413–439.

Nefes, Türkay Salim. "Political Parties' Perceptions and Uses of Anti-Semitic Conspiracy Theories in Turkey." *Sociological Review* 61, no. 2 (2013): 247–264.

Newheiser, Anna-Kaisa, Miguel Farias, and Nicole Tausch. "The Functional Nature of Conspiracy Beliefs: Examining the Underpinnings of Belief in the *Da Vinci Code* Conspiracy." *Personality and Individual Differences* 51, no. 8 (2011): 1007–1011.

Neyfakh, Leon. "Revealed! Obama's Secret Agenda." *Boston Globe*. Published electronically July 22, 2013.

Nyhan, Brendan. "9/11 and Birther Misperceptions Compared." *Brendan-nyhan.com/blog* (2009).

Nyhan, Brendan. "Backsliding on the 'Death Panels' Myth." *Columbia Journalism Review*. Published electronically May 10, 2013.

Nyhan, Brendan. "Why Conspiracy Theories Die Hard." *CNN.com* (2011). http://www.cnn.com/2011/OPINION/04/28/nyhan.birther.truth/index.html.

Nyhan, Brendan. "Why the 'Death Panel' Myth Wouldn't Die: Misinformation in the Health Care Reform Debate." *The Forum* 8, no. 1 (2010): Article 5.

Nyhan, Brendan, Eric McGhee, John Sides, Seth Masket, and Steven Greene. "One Vote out of Step? The Effects of Salient Roll Call Votes in the 2010 Election." *American Politics Research* 40 no. 5 (2012): 844–879.

Nyhan, Brendan, and Jason Reifler. "The Effects of Semantics and Social Desirability in Correcting the Obama Muslim Myth" Unpublished manuscript (2009).

Nyhan, Brendan, and Jason Reifler. "Opening the Political Mind: The Effects of Self–Affirmation and Graphical Information on Factual Misperceptions" *Unpublished manuscript, Dartmouth College, Hanover, NH* (2011).

Nyhan, Brendan, and Jason Reifler. "When Corrections Fail: The Persistence of Political Misperceptions." *Political Behavior* 32, no. 2 (2010): 303–330.

Nyhan, Brendan, Jason Reifler, and Peter A Ubel. "The Hazards of Correcting Myths About Health Care Reform." *Medical Care* 51, no. 2 (2013): 127–132.

Oliver, J. Eric, and Thomas J. Wood. "Conspiracy Theories, Magical Thinking, and the Paranoid Style(s) of Mass Opinion." University of Chicago Working Paper Series, 2012.

Olmsted, Kathryn S. *Real Enemies: Conspiracy Theories and American Democracy, World War I to 9/11*. New York: Oxford University Press, 2008.

Orda, Olga. "The Romantic View of Nature and the Conspiracy Theory in Environmental Documentaries." University of Calgary, Communication & Culture Department, 2012.

O'Reilly, Bill. "Who Is Running Sandra Fluke?" *The O'Reilly Factor*. Published electronically March 8, 2012.

Owen, Diana. "Mixed Signals: Generation X's Attitudes toward the Political System." In *After the Boom: The Politics of Generation X*, edited by Stephen C. Craig and Spephen Earl Bennett, pp. 85–106. New York: Rowman & Littlefield Publishers, Inc., 1997.

Owens, Bob. "Ex 'The View' Co-Host Entertains Zimmerman Case Conspiracy Theories." *Bob-Owens.com*. Published electronically May 19, 2012.

Page, Benjamin I. *Who Deliberates? Mass Media in Modern Democracy*. Chicago: University of Chicago Press, 1996.

Palin, Sarah. "Statement on the Current Health Care Debate." *Facebook*. Published electronically August 7, 2009.

Parent, Joseph M. "Publius's Guile and the Paranoid Style." *Public Integrity* 12, no. 3 (2010): 221–239.

Parent, Joseph. "Tomorrow's Disintegration: Security and Unity in an Era of Entropy." Oslo: Norwegian Nobel Institute, 2012.

Parker, Christopher S, and Matt A Barreto. *Change They Can't Believe In: The Tea Party and Reactionary Politics in America.* Princeton, NJ: Princeton University Press, 2013.

Parsons, Sharon, WIlliam Simmons, Frankie Shinhoster, and John Kilburn. "A Test of the Grapevine: An Empirical Examination of the Conspiracy Theories among African Americans." *Sociological Spectrum* 19, no. 2 (1999): 201–222.

Perrin, Andrew, and Stephen Vaisey. "Parallel Public Spheres: Distance and Discourse in Letters to the Editor." *American Journal of Sociology* 114, no. 3 (2008): 781–810.

Peterson, Geoff, and J. Mark Wrighton. "Expressions of Distrust: Third-Party Voting and Cynicism in Government." *Political Behavior* 20, no. 1 (1998): 17–34.

Pigden, Charles. "Popper Revisited, or What Is Wrong with Conspiracy Theories?." *Philosophy of the Social Sciences* 25, no. 1 (1995): 3–34.

Pipes, Daniel. *Conspiracy: How the Paranoid Style Flourishes and Where It Comes From.* New York: Touchstone, 1997.

Plait, Phil. "Antivaccine Megachurch Linked to Texas Measles Outbreak." *Slate.com.* Published electronically August 26, 2013.

Poole, Keith T, and Howard Rosenthal. *Congress: A Political-Economic History of Roll Call Voting.* New York: Oxford University Press, 2000.

Poole, Keith T., and Howard Rosenthal. *Ideology and Congress.* New Brunswick, NJ: Transaction Publishers, 2007.

Poole, Keith T., and Howard Rosenthal. "Patterns of Congressional Voting." *American Journal of Political Science* 35, no. 1 (1991): 228–278.

Poole, Keith T., and Howard Rosenthal. "The Polarization of American Politics." *Journal of Politics* 46, no. 4 (1984): 1061–1079.

Popper, Sir Karl R. *Conjectures and Refutations.* London: Routledge Kegan Paul, 1972.

Posner, Daniel. *Institutions and Ethnic Politics in Africa.* Cambridge: Cambridge University Press, 2005.

Posner, Eric. *Law and Social Norms.* Cambridge: Harvard University Press, 2002.

Posner, Richard A. "Instrumental and Noninstrumental Theories of Tort Law." *Indiana Law Journal* 88 (2013): 474.

Rattner, Steven. "Beyond Obamacare." *New York Times.* Published electronically September 16, 2012.

Reeves, Thomas C. "Movie Reviews—*JFK* Directed by Oliver Stone." *Journal of American History* 79, no. 3 (1992): 1262.

Reich, Robert B. "American Bile." *New York Times.* Published electronically September 21, 2013.

Remnick, David. "The Culprits." *The New Yorker.* Published electronically April 29, 2013.

Renfro, Paula Cozort. "Bias in Selection of Letters to the Editor." *Journalism Quarterly* 56 (1979): 822–826.

Richardson, James T., and Massimo Introvigne. "'Brainwashing' Theories in European Parlimentary and Administrative Reports on 'Cults' and 'Sects.'" *Journal for the Scientific Study of Religion* 40, no. 2 (2001): 143–168.

Riding, Alan. "Sept. 11 as Right-Wing U.S. Plot: Conspiracy Theory Sells in France." *New York Times*. Published electronically June 22, 2002.

Robinson, Peter, and John Crewdson. "NRA Raises $200 Million as Gun Lobby Toasters Burn Logo on Bread." *Bloomberg*. Published electronically December 29, 2011.

Rosenblitz, L., and F. Keil. "The Misunderstood Limits of Folk Science: An Illusions of Explanatory Depth." *Cognitive Science* 26, no. 5 (2002): 521–562.

Rosenthal, Andrew. "No Comment Necessary: Conspiracy Nation." *New York Times*. Published electronically January 17, 2013.

"Rosie O'Donnell 9/11 Conspiracy Comments: *Popular Mechanics* Responds." *Popular Mechanics*. Published electronically October 1, 2009.

Rosnow, Ralph L. "Psychology of Rumor Reconsidered." *Psychological Bulletin* 87, no. 3 (1980): 578–591.

Rosnow, Ralph L., James L. Esposito, and Leo Gibney. "Factors Influencing Rumor Spreading: Replication and Extension." *Language & Communication* 8, no. 1 (1988): 29–42.

Rosnow, Ralph L., John H. Yost, and James L. Esposito. "Belief in Rumor and Likelihood of Rumor Transmission." *Language & Communication* 6, no. 3 (1986): 189–194.

Ross, Michael. "Glenn Beck Alleges 'Concentrated Effort Now to Label Me a Conspiracy Theorist?'" *Examiner.com*. Published electronically May 28, 2013.

Ross, Michael. "Glenn Beck Claims Obama Behind Conspiracy to Depict Him as a Conspiracy Theorist." *Examiner.com*. Published electronically June 5, 2013.

Rothman, Stanley, and S. Robert Lichter. "Elite Ideology and Risk Perception in Nuclear Energy Policy." *American Political Science Review* 81, no. 2 (1987): 383–404.

Rothman, Stanley, S. Robert Lichter, and Neil Nevitte. "Politics and Professional Advancement among College Faculty." *The Forum* 3, no. 1 (2005): 1–26.

Rothstein, Susan. "Right-Wing Conspiracy Theories Do a Number on Us." *Boston Globe*. Published electronically July 29, 2012.

Rousseau, Jean-Jacques. *The Basic Political Writings*. Translated by Donald A. Cress. Indianapolis: Hackett, 1987.

Sarnoff, Rachel Lincoln. "Jenny McCarthy's Got the Wrong View on Vaccinations." *Huffington Post*. Published electronically July 17, 2013.

Schattschneider, Elmer Eric. *The Semisovereign People: A Realist's View of Democracy in America*. Orlando: Harcourt Brace Jovanovich, Inc., 1960.

Schmidle, Nicholas. "Getting Bin Laden: What Happened That Night in Abbottabad." *New Yorker*, August 8, 2011.

Schuyler, Foster H., and Carl J. Friedrich. "Letters to the Editor as a Means of Measuring the Effectiveness of Propaganda." *The American Political Science Review* 31, no. 1 (1937): 71–79.

Sears, David O. "The Persistence of Early Political Predispositions: The Roles of Attitude Object and Life Stage." *Review of Personality and Social Psychology* 4, no. 1 (1983): 79–116.

Sears, David O., and S. Levy. "Childhood and Adult Political Development." In *The Oxford Handbook of Political Psychology*, edited by David O. Sears, L. Huddy, and R. Jervis, Oxford: Oxford University Press, 2003. pp. 60–109.

Seitz-Wald, Alex. "Sandy Hook Truther Won't Quit." *Salon.com*. Published electronically January 18, 2013.

Shahid, Aliyah, and Corky Siemaszko. "President Obama Takes on Preacher Terry Jones and Controverisal Plan for Sept. 11 Koran Burn." *New York Daily News*. Published electronically September 10, 2010.

Shapiro, Dina. "The Risk of Disease Stigma: Threat and Support for Coercive Public Heath Policy." In *APSA Pre-Conference on Political Communication of Risk*. Seattle, WA, 2011.

Sherif, Muzafer, O. J. Harvey, B. Jack White, William R. Hood, and Carolyn W. Sherif. *Intergroup Conflict and Cooperation: The Robbers Cave Experiment*. Norman: University of Oklahoma Book Exchange, 1961.

Sigelman, Lee, and Barbara J. Walkosz. "Letters to the Editor as a Public Opinion Thermometer: The Martin Luther King Holiday Vote in Arizona." *Social Science Quarterly* 73 (1992): 938–946.

Simmel, Georg. *Conflict and the Web of Group-Affiliations*. Translated by Kurt Wolff. New York: Free Press, 1964.

Simmons, William Paul, and Sharon Parsons. "Beliefs in Conspiracy Theories among African Americans: A Comparison of Elites and Masses." *Social Science Quarterly* 86, no. 3 (2005): 582–598.

Simms, Brendan. *Europe: The Struggle for Supremacy from 1453 to the Present*. New York: Basic Books, 2013.

Sklar, Martin J. *The Corporate Reconstruction of American Capitalism, 1890–1916: The Market, the Law, and Politics*. Cambridge: Cambridge University Press, 1988.

Smith, Craig Allen. "The Hofstadter Hypothesis Revisited: The Nature of Evidence in Politically "Paranoid" Discourse." *Southern Journal of Communication* 42, no. 3 (1977): 274–289.

Smith, Adam. *The Theory of Moral Sentiments*. Indianapolis: Liberty Fund, 1982.

Snyder, Jack, Robert Y. Shapiro, and Yaeli Bloch-Elkon. "Free Hand Abroad, Divide and Rule at Home." *World Politics* 61, no. 1 (2009): 155–187.

Solomon, Lawrence. *The Deniers, Fully Revised: The World-Renowned Scientists Who Stood up against Global Warming Hysteria, Political Persecution and Fraud*. Minneapolis: Richard Vigilante (2010).

Staff. "Ten Classic Conspiracy Theories." *New Zealand Herald*. Published electronically September 4, 2009.

Stein, Arthur A. "Conflict and Cohesion: A Review of the Literature." *Journal of Conflict Resolution* 20 no. 1 (1976): 143–172.

Stieger, Stefan, Nora Gumhalter, Ulrich S Tran, Martin Voracek, and Viren Swami. "Girl in the Cellar: A Repeated Cross-Sectional Investigation of Belief in Conspiracy Theories About the Kidnapping of Natascha Kampusch." *Frontiers in Psychology* 4 (2013): 1–8.

Strauss, William, and Neil Howe. *Generations: The History of America's Future, 1584 to 2069*. New York: Perennial, 1991.

Sullivan, Daniel, Mark J. Landau, and Zachary K. Rothschild. "An Existential Function of Enemyship: Evidence That People Attribute Influence to Personal and Political Enemies to Compensate for Threats to Control." *Journal of Personality and Social Psychology* 98, no. 3 (2010): 434–449.

Sunstein, Cass, and Adrian Vermeule. "Conspiracy Theories." *Social Science Research Network* (2008). Harvard Public Law Working Paper No. 08-03; University of Chicago, Public Law Working Paper No. 199; U of Chicago Law & Economics, Olin Working Paper No. 387. Available at SSRN: http://ssrn.com/abstract=1084585 or http://dx.doi.org/10.2139/ssrn.1084585

Sunstein, Cass R., and Adrian Vermeule. "Conspiracy Theories: Causes and Cures*." *Journal of Political Philosophy* 17, no. 2 (2009): 202–227.

Swami, Viren, Jakob Pietschnig, Ulrich S. Tran, Ingo W. Nader, Stefan Stieger, and Martin Voracek. "Lunar Lies: The Impact of Informational Framing and Individual Differences in Shaping Conspiracist Beliefs About the Moon Landings." *Applied Cognitive Psychology* 27, no. 1 (2013): 71–80.

Taber, Charles S., and Milton Lodge. "Motivated Skepticism in the Evaluation of Political Beliefs." *American Journal of Political Science* 50, no. 3 (2006): 755–769.

Tackett, Timothy. "Conspiracy Obsession in a Time of Revolution: French Elites and the Origins of the Terror, 1789–1792." *American Historical Review* 105, no. 3 (2000): 691–713.

Tajfel, Henri. *Human Groups and Social Categories*. New York: Cambridge University Press, 1981.

Taleb, Nassim. *Fooled by Randomness: The Hidden Role of Chance in Life and in the Markets*. 2nd updated ed. New York: Random House, 2008.

Tesler, Michael, and David O. Sears. *Obama's Race: The 2008 Election and the Dream of a Post-Racial America*. Chicago Studies in American Politics. Chicago: University of Chicago Press, 2010.

Thomas, Kenn. "Clinton Era Conspiracies! Was Gennifer Flowers on the Grassy Knoll? Probably Not, but Here Are Some Other Bizarre Theories for a New Political Age." *Washington Post*, January 16, 1994.

Thomas, S. B., and S. C. Quinn. "The Tuskegee Syphilis Study, 1932 to 1972: Implications for HIV Education and AIDS Risk Education Programs in the Black Community." *American Journal of Public Health* 81, no. 11 (1991): 1498–1505.

Thomson, Robert, Naoya Ito, Hinako Suda, Fangyu Lin, Yafei Liu, Ryo Hayasaka, Ryuzo Isochi, and Zian Wang. "Trusting Tweets: The Fukushima Disaster and Information Source Credibility on Twitter." Paper presented at the Proceedings of the 9th International Conference on Information Systems for Crisis Response and Management, 2012.

Thornhill, Ted. "James Holmes Case: The Conspiracy Theories Surrounding the Aurora Shooting." *Huffington Post United Kingdom*. Published electronically July 24, 2012.

Trachtenberg, Marc. *A Constructed Peace: The Making of European Settlement, 1945–1963*. Princeton: Princeton University Press, 1999.

Tracy, James. "An Open Letter to the South Florida Sun–Sentinel." *memoryholeblog.com* (2013).

Trudeau, G. B. *In Search of Cigarette Holder Man*. Kansas City: Andrews and McMeel, 1994.

Tucker, Josh "The Effects of Partisanship: Ben Bernanke as a Natural Experiment?" MonkeyCage.org April 13, 2009 http://themonkeycage.org/2009/04/13/the_effects_of_partisanship_be/

Updike, John. *Problems and Other Stories*. New York: Knopf, 1979.

Uscinski, Joseph E. *The People's News: Media, Politics, and the Demands of Capitalism*. New York: New York University Press, 2014.

Uscinski, Joseph E. "Why Are Conspiracy Theories Popular? There's More to It Than Paranoia." *EUROPP: European Politics and Policy*. Published electronically June 26, 2013.

Uscinski, Joseph E., and Ryden W. Butler. "The Problems of Fact-Checking." *Critical Review* 25, no. 2 (2013).

Uscinski, Joseph E., and Arthur Simon. "Partisanship as a Source of Presidential Rankings." *White House Studies* 11, no. 1 (2011): 1–14.

Verba, Sidney, Richard A. Brody, Edwin B. Parker, Norman H. Nie, Nelson W. Polsby, Paul Ekman, and Gordon S. Black. "Public Opinion and the War in Vietnam." *American Political Science Review* 61 (1967): 317–333.

Volgy, Thomas J., Margaret Krigbaum, Mary Kay Langan, and Vicky Mosher. "Some of My Best Friends Are Letter Writers: Eccentrics and Gladiators Revisited." *Social Science Quarterly* 58, no. 2 (1977): 321–327.

Vollers, Maryanne. *Lone Wolf: Eric Rudolph: Murder, Myth, and the Pursuit of an American Outlaw*. New York: HarperCollins, 2006.

Wahl-Jorgenson, Karin. "A 'Letigimate Beef' or 'Raw Meat'? Civility, Multiculturalism, and Letters to the Editor." *Communication Review* 7 (2004): 89–105.

Walker, Jesse. *The United States of Paranoia: A Conspiracy Theory*. USA: Harper, 2013.

Walt, Stephen M. *The Origin of Alliances*. Ithaca: Cornell University Press, 1990.

Waltz, Kenneth N. *Theory of International Relations*. New York: McGraw Hill, 1979.

"The Warren Commission Report." *New York Times*, 1964.

Waters, Anita M. "Conspiracy Theories as Ethnosociologies: Explanations and Intention in African American Political Culture ." *Journal of Black Studies* 28, no. 1 (1997): 112–125.

Webster, Stephen. "Glenn Beck Sees Media Conspiracy to Label Him a 'Conspiracy Theorist'." *The Raw Story*. Published electronically May 29, 2013.

Wedel, Janine. *Shadow Elite: How the World's New Power Brokers Undermine Democracy, Government, and the Free Market*. New York: Basic Books, 2009.

Whitson, Jennifer A., and Adam D. Galinsky. "Lacking Control Increases Illusory Pattern Perception." *Science* 322, no. 3 (2008): 115–117.

Whittemore, Andrew. "Finding Sustainability in Conservative Contexts: Topics for Conversation between American Conservative Élites, Planners and the Conservative Base." *Urban Studies* 50 no. 12 (2013): 2460–2477.

Whitty, Christopher J. M., Monty Jones, Alan Tollervey, and Tim Wheeler. "Biotechnology: Africa and Asia Need a Rational Debate on Gm Crops." *Nature* 497, no. 7447 (2013): 31–33.

Wilson, R. A. *Boundaries of the Mind: The Individual in the Fragile Sciences.* Cambridge: Cambridge University Press, 2004.

Wolf, Naomi. "The Shocking Truth About the Crackdown on Occupy." *TheGuardian. com.* Published electronically November 25, 2011.

Wood, Gordon S. "Conspiracy and the Paranoid Style: Causality and Deceit in the Eighteenth Century." *William and Mary Quarterly* 39, no. 3 (1982): 402–441.

Wood, Gordon S. *The Creation of the American Republic, 1776–1787.* Chapel Hill: University of North Carolina Press, 1998.

Wood, Michael James, and Karen M. Douglas. ""What About Building 7?" a Social Psychological Study of Online Discussion of 9/11 Conspiracy Theories." *Frontiers in Psychology* 4 (2013).

Wood, Michael J., Karen M. Douglas, and Robbie M. Sutton. "Dead and Alive: Beliefs in Contradictory Conspiracy Theories." *Social Psychological and Personality Science* (January 25, 2012).Woods, Jeff. *Black Struggle, Red Scare: Segregation and Anti-Communism in the South, 1948–1968.* Baton Rouge: Louisiana State University Press, 2004.

Zaller, John. *The Nature and Origins of Mass Opinion* Cambridge Studies in Public Opinion and Political Psychology. Cambridge, UK: Cambridge University Press, 1992.

INDEX

Note: Letter 'n' followed by the locators refer to notes, *fig* and *tab* refer to figures and tables.

Printed in the USA/Agawam, MA
August 5, 2014

594572.046